D0424947

WILLIAM GASTON

CAROLINIAN

JUSTICE GASTON

COURTESY OF MRS. GEO. VAUX,
BRYN MAWR, PA.

# William Gaston

## CAROLINIAN

*J. Herman Schauinger*



THE BRUCE PUBLISHING COMPANY
*Milwaukee*

To Mother
and
To Dad
who was so like
Gaston

# Foreword

WHEN Thomas Ruffin, Jr., son of the chief justice of North Carolina, wrote his father, "Judge Gaston has run a long course of glory and goodness and he died but to be buried in the memories of his countrymen," his was but one of many such expressions throughout the state and nation. Negroes as well as those of his own race were deeply moved. In the capital of the nation the news oppressed all who had known him. The state's representative wrote home that "the sensation, which the news of his death produced here, went to show how high was his reputation for talents and for virtue even in the most distant parts of the country." All who knew him were always powerfully impressed by his virtues, his talent, his integrity, and his vast learning. That regard has continued to this present day. All who have been fortunate enough to have studied his life in some detail have been inspired. Those who have aided me in writing this biography know something of all this, and I wish to acknowledge my indebtedness and deep gratitude to them.

My sister, Helen Schauinger, will never be repaid for the aid she has given me. The long hours of patient reading, the many suggestions for improvement of style and form which were offered by my wife, Margaret Jones Schauinger, makes my acknowledgment to her not the mere perfunctionary and usual husbandly gesture. To Miss Mary G. Hawks, great-granddaughter of Gaston through his daughter, Hannah, I shall always feel under obligation for allowing me the complete use of the Gaston manuscripts, for many suggestions, for the portraits of the Gaston family, and finally for permission to begin the work. I am indebted also to Gaston's great-great-granddaughters, Mrs. J. William Cromwell of Stamford, Connecticut, and Mrs. George Vaux of Bryn Mawr, Pennsylvania, who graciously supplied me with copies of the original paintings in their possession. To Dr. R. D. W. Connor, former archivist of the United States, whose permission was also extended for the use of the manuscripts under his care I am highly grateful. Dr. J. G. de Rouhlac Hamilton, and Mrs. Lyman Cotten, of the University of North Carolina Library and Archives, gave me the gracious aid and kind consideration they are so famous for among scholars of Southern history. Mr. Hopkins of Philadelphia kindly gave me permission to use the Gaston letters in his possession.

I wish especially to thank those who have read this entire manuscript, or parts of it, and made many suggestions for its improvement. Particularly am I indebted to my former professor and friend, Dr. Bernard Mayo, of the University of Virginia, under whose inspiration and direction, at Georgetown University, I began this study. Dr. Albert R. Newsome, University of North Carolina, read one of the first drafts and so also suffered its beginnings.

Others who have greatly aided me are: Dr. Tibor Kerekes, Georgetown University; Dr. Powrie V. Doctor, Gaullaudet College; Dr. Richard J. Purcell, Catholic University of America; Dr. C. C. Crittenden, North Carolina Historical Commission; Judge William Dudine, formerly of the Appellate Court of Indiana; Thomas McAvoy, C.S.C., University of Notre Dame; Wilfrid Parsons, S.J., Georgetown University; Dr. Marshall Smelser, University of Notre Dame, and Dr. Robert Fogerty, College of St. Thomas, who read the entire final manuscript and made many valuable suggestions.

J. Herman Schauinger

College of St. Thomas
St. Paul, Minnesota
January 6, 1949

# Contents

# WILLIAM GASTON

CAROLINIAN

*I was baptized an American in the blood of a martyred father.* — WILLIAM GASTON

## CHAPTER ONE

# Youth and Education

AMERICANS of the generation between the Revolutionary War and the Civil War lived with the Websters, the Calhouns, the Clays, the Marshalls, and the Jacksons in what has been described as America's Silver Age. Judge William Gaston of North Carolina, partly through his own wishes, partly through his conservative Federalism in a period of rampant Republicanism, and in some degree through his religious faith, never reached the same pinnacle of fame as these contemporaries. Yet, by them and by most of the great of his time he was respected for his talent, loved for his character, admired for his integrity and spotless purity of soul. Daniel Webster and John Marshall, Bishop John England and Bishop Simon Bruté were numbered among his closest friends. Henry Clay feared his wit as one of the leaders of the opposition against the War Hawks of 1812, while John C. Calhoun, in a breathless moment in the House of Representatives dodged a duel with the fiery Carolinian.

A southern Federalist in the days of Jefferson was an oddity, but combine him in the same person with an outstanding southern Catholic and then note how even old, experienced John Quincy Adams' eyebrows twitched. And finally, this was a rare man indeed, a real southern statesman who long after the conspiracy of silence had sealed the southern conscience regarding its peculiar social institution dared to warn young southerners that slavery alone was hindering the progress of that region. Not only was the warning issued, but his bold speech was heard by the dignitaries of the state, praised by all, quoted extensively, and even reprinted by a learned society of the state university. Almost any other person would have been ridden out of the state on a rail, for Garrison's *Liberator* was already in the land. His decisions on the bench of the supreme court of North Carolina proclaimed even more vividly his philosophy. To this slaveholder the Negro was a man with human failings and passions, and with the soul and mind and every other attribute that made a man. Not only did the slave have human rights, but the freed Negro, as a citizen, had civil rights. The Negroes of his home town remembered all he had done for their race and knew why they were wearing black arm bands when he passed from their midst. While warning the South concerning the evils of slavery, and holding up to the scorn of the nation, at Princeton, the evils of American Nativism, he also attempted to check within his own beloved "old North State" the scourge of religious intolerance. His words on this could be used today without any change. Finding romance with three young wives, he managed to live a full life in sixty-six years, with a career of courage and satisfaction, of learning and deeds.

Whence came this anomaly of Catholicism and Federalism into the life of a quick-tempered southerner of Huguenot ancestry, who was from one of the most anti-Catholic and the most Republican states of the Union? Born in New Bern, North Carolina, on September 19, 1778, William Joseph, the second son of Dr. Alexander Gaston and Margaret Sharpe not only came into the world at the most exciting period of his nation's history, but was also fortunate in having as parents two remarkable personalities. Dr. Gaston had come to New Bern sometime before May 1, 1764.[1] The Gastons of America trace their family back to Jean Gaston, a French Huguenot, born around 1600. At the age of forty Jean left France for Scotland because of the religious conflicts then raging in France. In Scotland some twenty-five years later his three sons, John, William, and Alexander, also became involved in religious difficulties, so they with their wives fled to Ireland.

To William here, in Ballymena, County Antrim, Alexander was born.[2] One of his older brothers, Hugh Gaston, became an eminent Presbyterian minister, author of a religious book called *Gaston's Concordat.* Alexander received his medical degree from the University of Edinburgh, and then joined the royal British navy as a surgeon. He was with the fleet in 1762 when Havana was taken by the British, an episode of the Seven Years' War between England and France. An epidemic dysentery broke out and created havoc among the troops, and because of his devoted attention to the men Dr. Gaston was also stricken. The exhausting heat further broke his health, so he resigned his commission in the navy and decided to seek new health in the American colonies. He finally settled at New Bern where he was quickly accepted as a physician and member of the existing society. In the ten years that intervened between his arrival here and the outbreak of the Revolution Gaston became one of the most respectable citizens of the town. During this time he managed to acquire considerable land, including a plantation along Brice's Creek about eight miles from New Bern. In all, he purchased almost two thousand acres of land, most of it bordering on Brice's Creek, which ran into the Trent River about two miles from town. For all this he paid not quite a thousand pounds. He also had property in town.[3]

A short time before the war Margaret Sharpe arrived from England on a visit to her two brothers, Joseph and Girarde, merchants of New Bern. Probably through them she met the enthusiastic, likable physician, whose wife she became in May, 1775, although she had had no thought of remaining in this country. She had been born in Cumberland County, England, in 1755 of a devout Roman Catholic family and was sent to a convent in Calais, France, for her education. There she learned the principles of her religion, which were to influence her throughout life. The couple's three children were all born in the midst of war. The first son did not live, and Jane, their daughter, was two years younger than William. In a comparatively brief time both grew to love their adopted country and especially the old colonial town, their children's birthplace.

New Bern in the colonial period and for some time afterward was known as New Berne. It was named after Berne, Switzerland, the native city of the man who had been chiefly instrumental in founding it, Baron Christopher De Graffenreid. With others, the Baron, in 1707, contracted with the proprietors of the Carolinas for ten thousand acres of land on or between the Cape Fear and the Neuse Rivers. In 1710 the first settlers located on the strip of land between the Neuse River and the Chattawka, or, as it is now known, Trent River. Within a couple years the Tuscarora Indians attacked the settlements all along the Neuse and Pamlico Rivers, and all but wiped out New Bern. In disgust the Swiss sold out to Colonel Thomas Pollock, one of the most prominent men of the province.

Many of the remaining settlers then left for the comparative comforts of South Carolina, but the natural advantages of the town as a trading center attracted people from the surrounding country. De Graffenreid had plotted New Berne with two main streets, one starting at the Neuse River to run toward the forest, while the other was at right angles, intersecting the narrow piece of land between the Trent and Neuse. A church was to be placed at this intersection so as to be in the center of the town. Christ Church, New Bern's oldest, is now there. He planned for two other streets to follow the banks of the rivers. All streets were to be very broad, while lots were to be of three acres in size. Although the savage raid of the Tuscaroras in 1711 interrupted this planning, the town was actually laid out in that way. The two large rivers met to flow into Pamlico Sound, and so on to the ocean about thirty-five miles away. In a few years New Bern was considered the largest town in the province. Edenton, on Albemarle Sound, seventy miles northeast of New Bern; Wilmington on the Cape Fear River, one hundred miles south; Fayetteville, one hundred miles west, revolutionary capital, were next in importance. These coast towns were almost the only ones in the province. Certainly they were the most important. By the time of the Revolution New Berne had a population of six hundred,[4] and was then the capital of the province. Here Governor William Tyron at a cost of five thousand pounds built his palace, one of the most pretentious buildings then in America.

With the coming of the Revolution, the liberty-loving physician became deeply involved in the patriot cause. When the Committee of Safety of New Berne was formed he was a member, and, on March 4, 1775, he, together with Richard Cogdell, Abner Nash, and others, signed a memorial to remind the citizens of the regulations of the Continental Congress, pleading with them to remain firm in the cause of liberty and to implore assistance from God for the success of Congress.[5] In his report to the home government, Governor Josiah Martin branded it an atrocious falsehood and a rebellious document, and at the same time sent in the names of the signers that they might be listed as traitors.[6] However, as the Tories were in a minority in the capital, the patriots made it so unpleasant for this last royal governor of North Carolina that he was forced to seek refuge elsewhere. On June 23, 1775, after his flight, the Committee of Safety in person went to the palace to claim the six pieces of artillery as rebel spoils.[7]

On September 9 Gaston was appointed to the Provincial Council for New Berne. The Committee of Safety was kept busy from the very beginning of the next year. It not only seized ships and their cargoes, but also confiscated supplies from stubborn Tories. The next month Richard Cogdell was given orders to put down a Tory insurrection within the state, while militia was to be raised for the protection of New Berne.[8] On the Committee there served Cogdell, John Easton, William Thompson, William Tisdale, Richard Ellis, William Brown, and Dr. Alexander Gaston. Several others who had been appointed to it never appeared.

In March of 1777 Dr. Gaston was appointed by the Council a justice for Craven County, and in May he and James Davis were made judges for the District of New Berne.[9] Late that month several of the judges met at Gaston's home, and as they sat on the piazza a disorderly crowd led by a William Davis appeared before them. Davis had had some trouble with a Frenchman which was not settled to his satisfaction, so after abusing the justices, he threatened to raise a mob to drive every Frenchman out of town.[10] Davis did not get his way, although the town was in an uproar for a time. Such were the times.

Dr. Gaston, by his activities on the Committee of Safety, had attracted the notice and aroused the ire of the Tories of the district, so it is no wonder that he received their attention when the tables were turned. Furthermore he had served at intervals in the North Carolina state line. Generally this was in the capacity of a surgeon, but in the spring of 1776 he was captain of a volunteer corps and marched at its head to Wilmington when the movements of Sir Henry Clinton threatened that town.

With the shifting of the war from the North to the South late in 1778, the British were soon in North Carolina. Wilmington was one of the towns in which they stationed troops, and in August of 1781 Major Craig decided to bring some British forces to New Berne. When the report of this movement reached town Dr. Gaston retired to his plantation on Brice Creek. The alarm died away so he returned to town. On Sunday, August 19, as he was eating breakfast a startled neighbor hurried to his house to report that the British were not far away. Although he did not believe this, at the urging of his friends, he hurried to the wharf to row across the river to his plantation, while Mrs. Gaston remained at home with the babies. A band of Tories, led by one particularly obnoxious to the rebels, Captain John Cox, had come ahead of the regular troops and completely surprised the town. Meeting no resistance, they galloped directly to the wharf. The doctor was still within range so the soldiers began to shoot, but in their eagerness left him untouched. At the first fire the Negro boy rowing the boat dived overboard, while Mrs. Gaston hearing them and anxious about the fate of her husband hurried to the scene. As their home was on Craven Street, between Pollock and Front, it was but a very short distance. When she arrived her husband was trying to row away, so she begged the Tory to let him go. Damning his followers for being such poor shots and disregarding the tearful pleas of the wife, Cox leveled his gun, aimed deliberately, and with the report of his rifle Dr. Gaston fell across the oars of the boat, which then aimlessly drifted downstream.[11] His widow recovered the body, despite the efforts of the Tories who tried to prevent her, and after the burial faced the future of supporting herself and two infant children. His affairs had been left in confusion; William McClure, a nephew, was the only one remaining to settle them, as Mrs. Gaston's brothers had died some time before her husband's death.[12] In 1784, in recognition of her husband's services, the state granted her a tract of land, and although at times she had difficulty meeting financial obligations it did not prevent her obtaining from the state assembly permission to free a slave. Her reason for this action was not revealed.

Margaret Gaston never ceased to mourn her husband, wearing black until her death in 1811. At the time of her husband's death she was twenty-six, described as a woman of calm, gray eyes, beautiful features, and stately carriage. She had very strict ideas as to the conduct of the young. It is said that her daughter was not allowed to look into a mirror, nor to let her shoulders touch the back of a chair in her mother's presence. Margaret was a nurse to the indigent sailors landing at New Berne whenever they needed such care. Although she became a rebel and an exile from her native land, she was English enough conscientiously to have her tea every afternoon at four o'clock.[13] Bishop John England once said that "her piety, her intelligence, and her attachment to the principles and practices of her religion, under circumstances peculiarly trying, have been worthy of the best days of Christianity."[14]

William Gaston often asserted that he owed everything to his mother. With a fine hand she molded his character during youth. Her beauty was reflected in her son, but he had inherited from his father a wild temper, which she helped him to control as much as possible. Concerning Mrs. Gaston's efforts Bishop England stated:

> After the recovery of the town and the success of the heroes of freedom, she was enabled to remain with her little charges, in the place of her former residence where she was almost the only member of the Roman Catholic Church; yet she had been so well instructed in its tenets that she never wavered for a moment, and as soon as the minds of her children were capable of receiving the divine word she was careful to implant it.

She was also determined that her son should have every worldly advantage possible. Therefore, when she learned that a Catholic college would be opened in Maryland, at Georgetown on the Potomac River, she immediately decided to send him there. So, in the spring of 1791, at the age of twelve, William Gaston left New Bern for college in the company of John Devereux, an old friend of the family. As the college was not yet opened when they arrived, Devereux took the young boy to Philadelphia, leaving him in the charge of a French Dominican priest, Francis Fleming. At this time Philadelphia was the capital of the United States. Gaston was in this city, dignified at this time by the presence of the government and President Washington for about five months, from June to November. He lodged with a Mrs. Brewer at 74 Lumber Street.

Although Philadelphia's charms were lost on the homesick lad, those of Father Fleming were not. This priest, who at one time had been rector of the Irish College at Lisbon, was one of the many to flee revolutionary France. Arriving in Philadelphia on December 3, 1789, he was made pastor of St. Mary's Church. He was an eloquent preacher and profound scholar. His sermon of March 17, 1790, printed by Mathew Carey, was the first on St. Patrick to be published in the United States. The high regard in which he was held may be seen from the fact that Bishop John Carroll made him vicar-general of the northern district of Maryland. His courage was displayed during the yellow fever plague of 1793 that paralyzed Philadelphia. Those who had the means fled, but Father Fleming remained in the panic-stricken city to care for the sick and dying. In October of 1793, while engaged in this work, he himself took the fever and died.[15]

Under his direction Gaston began to prepare for college. He got up in the morning at six o'clock to attend Mass. After breakfast, he wrote French exercises until eight o'clock, then went to an English school until noon. While waiting for his lunch he read Latin and Greek exercises. Then he returned to the English class until five o'clock. The next hour he spent in Father Fleming's library reading whatever the priest thought proper. Three times a week he went to one of the many French schools that dotted Philadelphia, established by those who had fled revolutionary France. There he studied that language for an hour. By September he was able to tell his mother that he had learned "so much of the French language as to be able to hold a conversation tolerably well."[16]

Soon after William's arrival, Fleming wrote Mrs. Gaston to inform her that he would care for her son until the opening of the college, which he stated was to have occurred the past spring, but which had been delayed because an accident interfered with its completion. However, on November 2, 1791, after a three days' journey by stagecoach, Father Fleming brought the boy to Georgetown. During the latter's stay at Philadelphia his expenses had come to forty-one pounds, but as he had had only thirty the priest paid the remaining amount. Fleming advised the boy's mother to establish a credit in Baltimore with Robert Walsh, who was very willing to serve her. He also told her it would be necessary to pay the fees a half year in advance because the college was in its infancy.[17]

At this time Georgetown was but a little village in Maryland. However, this was the place designed by Bishop Carroll as the site for the new college. Perhaps it was picked, as many others were in those days, because of its very inaccessibility. It was thought that the students would be far from the temptations of the world, could study and meditate in leisure. Known even now as "The Hill-top," it was at that time very advantageously placed. The twelve-year-old boy writing to his mother, said of it:

> . . . A more beautiful situation than this in which the college is, could not be imagined, on a high hill with a view on one side of the river, on the other of the town, quite surrounded with trees, and everything that could make it either beautiful or useful, it stands as if it were made on purpose for the erecting of some such building.[18]

This single, small, two-story building was to be both home and school to him. For five months he had waited in Philadelphia for its opening. When he finally arrived, it was only to find that it was still uncompleted. In December he wrote home that, as the river was frozen over, the delivery of material needed for the college was delayed, and that consequently classes would not begin until after Christmas.[19] The deed for the land had been secured in 1789, so Georgetown College began its career in the same year that the new government of the United States came into existence. Although this was well known to its founder, he could have had no intimation that the government would take over the same place for its capital city. Bishop John Carroll, the first Roman Catholic bishop of the United States, was also the founder of Georgetown, the first Catholic college in this country, and the North Carolinian became its first student.

Desirous of obtaining the best possible faculty, Bishop Carroll spent a great deal of time and went to considerable trouble in selecting a president. He wished one whose prestige and learning would command respect and draw students from every point in the country. Such a man was found in Reverend Robert

Plunkett of England.[20] The other professors were Father Francis Neal, Samuel Browne, and John de Mondesir; Father Neal became the second president. Among the early students were Enoch and Benedict Fenwick; the latter was to attain fame as the bishop of Boston. Philemon Charles Wederstrandt, the second student to be admitted, arrived a month after Gaston, December 20, 1791. Seven years later he became a midshipman of the *Constellation* and within ten years was commander of his own ship, the *Argus*. Some time later he had a flotilla under his command in the Gulf of Mexico.[21]

These few students were soon joined by others, until by June of 1792 there were forty. They lived with the people of the town near the college in order to be as far as possible under the direct supervision of the president and masters. Gaston was the only one to room and board within the college, and this was probably the result of his premature arrival. In the couple of months before classes began he lived with Father Plunkett, who soon became very fond of him, attracted by his personality, manners, and mind. It was evident to the discerning president that here was one with promise of a brilliant future. In writing to the mother concerning her son he stated that he would have objected to his removal from Philadelphia had he known of it in time, as the lad had to stay over two weeks at a tavern after coming to Georgetown. He also told her that "Billy" was the best scholar and most exemplary youth at Georgetown, although "perhaps he is rather deficient in paying that attention to outward gracefulness which is held in too high estimation abroad." And in this respect, so far as clothes were concerned, he was to remain deficient all his life, but this was a common characteristic affected by the southern gentleman. A few months later Father Plunkett was praising him for good management with money, and also remarked that his engaging manners and eminent merits assured their affectionate attention. He told the distant and anxious mother that her son was growing tall and graceful, having gained at least six inches in height since leaving New Bern.[22]

The routine in general was that practiced in most colleges of the time. Gaston arose at six o'clock in the morning and went to bed at half past eight o'clock. On Wednesday and Saturday afternoons the young students were required to take a long walk, while every day three and a half hours were set aside for recreation. Their courses consisted of English, Latin, Greek, French, elocution, arithmetic in all its branches, geography, and "use of the globe." As might be expected from the extreme youth of the students, the same curriculum was not offered as now. The college soon attracted boys from all over the country. The majority were from Virginia and Maryland, two were from Philadelphia, one from New York, and four from the West Indies. Gaston was expecting three more North Carolinians to arrive soon after him, for although the University of North Carolina had been chartered by the first session of the assembly of that state in 1789, its doors were not open until 1795. In September, 1792, Gaston reported that the college had taken so many boys that the building was to be made a hundred and thirty feet longer and a story higher, and this improvement was soon made.

The next month he was writing his mother that it was useless to send a bed to him, and that he did not need blankets as the college furnished all such items. He informed her too that the stockings which she was knitting should be four inches longer than the last. He was even regretting the time that would be lost on a visit home, because of his position at the head of his class.[23] However, in December he caught a severe cold, even though he did "always wear a flannel jacket next his skin under his shirt," and despite the mildness of the winter. In several letters to his mother the president urged her not to be alarmed about his condition, as it was common to the other boys owing to wet shoes and damp weather.[24]

As his health had little improved by April, fearing consumption, Mrs. Gaston determined to bring her son back to the more healthful climate of North Carolina. On April 25, 1793, after an absence of a year and ten months, William left Georgetown in the company of a Mr. Manning who was to see him home. This moved Father Plunkett to say:

> I need not mention the universal regret that his departure has occasioned, the only circumstance that can moderate it is the assurance of his return, grounded on your promise and your son's resolution. God grant stability to the latter, and North America will be pleased with a *bishop* native of New Bern.[25]

This revealed how highly William's talents were thought of even at this early time. It was not the last time such a prediction was to be made. As Father Plunkett had resigned to give place to Father Neal, he hoped to visit the Gastons on his way to Charleston. Father Neal continued to write them, urging the boy's return. He even kept a room vacant, hoping for that event, although the room was needed for the increasing enrollment. In his opinion the loss of the room was negligible if by its vacancy Gaston would again occupy it. However, in December he gave up hope of the lad's return.

Back in North Carolina Gaston rapidly recovered his health. He spent the next year in the New Bern Academy, which was conducted by the Reverend Thomas Irving, a Presbyterian and graduate of Princeton. The school contained twenty-three students, among whom were Isaac Guion, a lifelong friend of Gaston's. These two had things pretty much their own way, as in every recorded event taking place at the academy, the leading part was held by them. Thus began his training in the classics, and there was developed one of his outstanding characteristics, his forensic ability, which so often moved his contemporaries to profound admiration. Concerning this, the author of the latest history of North Carolina states that among the leading orators of the day were John Stanly, a fellow New Bernian, Archibald D. Murphey, William Gaston "whose spontaneity, fluency, and literary ease have scarcely been equalled in the history of the state," and George E. Badger, another native of New Bern, "upon whom, it was said, Gaston's cloak fell at his death."[26]

In April of 1794 the *Gazette* reported that the pupils of the academy were examined by the trustees, a large number of the townspeople being present, and concluded this notice by stating that Mr. Gaston and Mr. Guion "could not be too highly commended for the accuracy and elegancy of their translation of Homer and Horace." The affair ended with a parliamentary debate.[27] When the academy closed in the middle of July it was Gaston who gave the valedictory. His theme, "The Rising Glory of America," was delivered, so the *Gazette* said, with singular eloquence.[28]

His mother had not given up the idea of giving him the best education available in America. She determined to send him away again for that purpose. Irving wished him to go to Princeton and succeeded in winning her to his view, but she sought the advice of Father Neal before making a decision. In May the president of Georgetown told Gaston that he was personally opposed to this project because of the danger to his religious faith. Although at first very anxious in this regard, by July he was admitting there was more danger in Philadelphia than at Princeton, and that he would rather Gaston go to the New Jersey college than to one in the Quaker City. Mrs. Gaston did not wish him to return to Georgetown because of his health; perhaps the fact that this college was not then empowered to grant degrees might also have had some consideration. At any rate, young Will was in Philadelphia by September of 1794, although he did not know what the ultimate choice would be. Bishop Carroll then was consulted, and the two finally decided that Princeton was the better choice. Before entering, Gaston went over to meet Dr. Samuel Smith, the president, who presented him to two young men from North Carolina. These introduced him to several other students, who treated him with such politeness as to amaze the southerner. Even at this early time there existed a feeling among the cultured southerners that all northerners were

Yankees, thinking only of money, living with the sole purpose of acquiring more, and not too particular how this was done; in fine, acting like boors. The young man from New Bern was so surprised that he exclaimed, "I never was more agreeably disappointed in my expectations. For compliance, civility, and good breeding I've scarcely seen their equals. Their behavior, in short, quite charmed me." Irving's letter to the Cliosophic Society, which Gaston was to enter, was given to one who declared it a duty to present him to the most worthy members of the college.[29]

From Philadelphia William kept his mother informed of all these events. One bit of news which he sent her has more than ordinary interest because of the persons involved. Two years before, Rembrandt Peale, whom Gaston stated was the son of the museum keeper there, at the age of fifteen, had been converted to Catholicism. Concerning this Gaston wrote his mother:

> What he suffers from his parents and relations on that point you cannot conceive. On Friday and Saturday they would have nothing but meat . . . and he would be obliged to have no dinner or make out with a piece of bread.[30]

This museum keeper was, of course, none other than one of Philadelphia's foremost citizens, the remarkable Charles Willson Peale. Although he attained distinction as a portrait painter as well as author and naturalist, we also remember him as the painter who named his children after famous artists as Rembrandt, Raphael, Rubens, Titian, and Vandyke. Of the sons who followed his profession Rembrandt became the more famous, painting portraits of many distinguished characters. At seventeen (he was but a few months older than Gaston) he did one of President Washington in three sittings, which Congress later purchased. Young Peale even entered a seminary to study for the priesthood, after finally convincing his father of his sincerity, but soon left that institution because of a girl with whom he fell in love. Because of her influence his friends feared for his

Catholicism, and in this they were justified as he soon gave up this religion.[31]

By this time the girls were also interesting the handsome lad from North Carolina, as in a letter to his sister he speaks jokingly of himself being a magnet that attracted the young ladies. In another letter to a young lady back home he pointed out that she would be required to pay for his writing her "by a great number of tunes upon my return home."

At his entrance to Princeton in November of 1794 the college was under the direction of Dr. Samuel Smith, its seventh president. Founded during colonial times, it was more advanced than Georgetown, with more teachers and a curriculum of higher studies. These included geography, logic, mathematics, natural and moral philosophy, astronomy, belles lettres, and chemistry. The last-named branch was added while Gaston was there. As has always been the case with college students, he had to write home several times for money. Even before his arrival at Princeton he wrote that $210 was not enough in those times, but that a little more would do as he behaved with a frugality he hoped no one could doubt. Here, too, students were required to pay a half year in advance, but not having enough, he was forced to borrow $40 from a French priest and a companion to make up the required $59. Board cost $2.50 a week, while each student was expected to cut his own firewood.[32]

Admitted to the junior class, Gaston was very pleased with his lot and the college in general. During his stay there were about eighty-seven students. Among them was Isaac Guion, with whom he roomed, as well as several others from North Carolina. Noah Webster was there as a tutor. At the end of this year Gaston was one of the students of his class to give an oration at the final exercises. The next year, at the age of eighteen, he was graduated at the head of the class. Among the graduates were Philip Pendleton of Virginia, who became a judge of his state; John Berrien of Georgia, who became President Andrew Jackson's first attorney general; and Frederick Beasley of Maryland, who remained Gaston's lifelong friend. The latter, after his graduation, went to Philadelphia to receive the Sacraments of his Church, and then turned his steps toward home, mother, and sister.

Upon graduation from Princeton his portrait was done by James Peale of Philadelphia, who became a painter through the encouragement and interest of his brother, Charles Willson. This exquisite miniature of William shows the young man attired in a waistcoat and a white, flowing cravat. The oval-shaped face with its delicately tinted cheeks; deep-set blue eyes with eyebrows so perfectly pointed as to seem almost molded or plucked; finely chisled nose; round, deep chin; and a firm, beautifully expressive mouth were framed against a mass of wavy, chestnut, powdered hair falling about and below the ears.

Returning home he found the family in a new home, for which his mother had expended seven hundred pounds. The old home had been burned in a destructive fire which swept through New Bern a short time before his arrival. Had it not been for Devereux, perhaps not even their lives would have been spared. While the new house was being built the Gastons were given two rooms in his home. Mrs. Gaston was somewhat involved in debt, mostly to Devereux, but she expected to discharge this by selling the stock as soon as her son returned from school.

After this second sojourn from his birthplace he might have found it a little changed. New Bern was described at this time by a distinguished traveler as a "trading and growing town, with between seven hundred and a thousand houses, among which were some respectable brick edifices, a new, neat, elegant court house and a famous Masonic building."[33] The fire of 1794 may have caused the building of many of these.

Once here it did not take Gaston long to decide upon his future career. The most notable profession in the country with best chances of advancement, prestige, and earning power was the bar. The national legislature as well as the state assemblies to a large extent consisted of lawyers, and in North Carolina they exerted more influence and power than any other body of men. The great majority of bright young men, with any sort of ambition at all, generally gravitated toward law. Since his talents fitted him well for the bar, Gaston naturally decided to follow that profession. There being few schools of law in the country at that time, those who wished to study law generally did so in the offices of one of their town lawyers, hoping that the lawyer knew enough or at least had books enough to start them toward a knowledge of it. As by the third decade of the next century the state had a very brilliant bar, many of the towns must have had men well qualified for the task. New Bern certainly did, as William Gaston who studied his law under such a man, could testify.

His teacher, Francois Xavier Martin, a French Catholic, settled in New Bern during the Revolution and was employed in a printing office of which he soon became the owner. He published several legal works, among them *Decisions of the Superior Courts of North Carolina* (1797), and *Revisal of the Laws of North Carolina* (1804). Many years later, while a citizen of Louisiana, he compiled his *History of North Carolina* (1829) which, despite certain inaccuracies, preserved many interesting facts. He was the owner and editor of the only newspaper of New Bern, the *Gazette*. An anti-Federalist, an ardent Democrat, he opposed Alexander Hamilton and all his works and became a warm supporter of Thomas Jefferson. In 1809 Martin was appointed by President Madison a federal judge of the Mississippi Territory, and a year later was transferred to the Territory of New Orleans. When it was admitted to the Union as the state of Louisiana, he became the first attorney general, then a judge of the state supreme court, and finally its chief justice. He practically created the jurisprudence of the state, bringing order where chaos had before existed.[34] Remarkable in talent, he was even more so in personality. A short man, with a massive head better fitted for a giant like Jackson, his craggy face, hooked nose, and long, loose, flowing white hair reminds one of Matthew Brady's portrait of the aged Jackson. His clothes were always tacky, his slouch hat seemed ready to crumble into dust, and he was too economical "to afford the luxury of a wife." This poor old man at death was discovered to be worth half a million dollars, at a time when money was valued at some five times the present rate.

Gaston could not have found a more versatile teacher. Under his tutelage Gaston learned his law well enough that on September 22, 1798, having applied to the judges of the superior court, professed a competent knowledge of the law, passed an examination, and found to be of good moral character, he was admitted to the bar.[35] He took the oath of allegiance before the clerk of the County Court of Carteret, paid a tax of ten pounds, and stepped forth from the building, a lawyer, just three days after his twentieth birthday.

Sometime in the year before this event, his sister Jane, at seventeen, had married John Louis Taylor, a lawyer of Fayetteville. Taylor, then twenty-eight years old, was a handsome man, good natured, ingenious, a powerful orator destined to rise rapidly and far in his profession. He was born in London of Irish parents and came to America at the age of twelve. Licensed at the bar in 1788, four years later he entered politics as a Federalist to represent the borough town of Fayetteville in the House of Commons. He served in this capacity several times. There he supported legislation to encourage trade, to prohibit the importation of slaves and to permit their manumission, and to improve the administration of justice. Jane Gaston was his second wife; his first, Julia Rowan, by whom he had a daughter, had died.

In 1798 the General Assembly elected Taylor a judge of the superior court. As there was no supreme court in North Carolina possessing appellate duty only, from 1799 the judges of the superior courts met at Raleigh to determine questions of law and equity not settled on the circuits. In July of 1811 he was elected by these justices the presiding judge and called the chief justice. In 1819, largely through the efforts of Gaston a new supreme court was formed, and Taylor was elected the first chief justice of this new court.[36]

With his elevation to the bench in 1798 he became much too busy to handle his extensive practice, so turned part of it over to his young brother-in-law. Gaston, at an age when most lawyers were acting as little more than glorified debt collectors, was given a full-sized practice that even a more mature man would have found exacting and difficult.

As Taylor, so Gaston became a Federalist in politics, and one looks in vain for an explanation from his own lips as to what led him to this decision. It may well be explained, however, by the circumstances of his environment as well as the political upheaval which upset the entire world. The political philosophy of democracy and liberty which brought on the Revolution, beginning to culminate in the fuller Jeffersonian democracy for the masses, found little response in the commercial town of New Bern. This place where he lived and received his legal training was conservative; Princeton, where he received part of his cultural education was a very hotbed of conservatism; Georgetown, which had done so much to form his character was Roman Catholic and naturally had no sympathy for the extreme ideas of the French Revolution. As a devoted Catholic Gaston hated the policies of the French revolutionists, with whom to a considerable extent the Jeffersonian Republicans had identified themselves.

When the quasi war with France broke out Gaston offered his services to the governor of North Carolina, William R. Davie. The latter accepted them, with the assurance that his name had been placed on the list of officers in a grade which he hoped would be acceptable.[37] However, he was not called upon to serve in the armed forces of the state. This was the closest he came to such a career.

## NOTES FOR CHAPTER ONE

1. *Craven County Deed Book* (N.C.), II. May, 1764. This is the first record of Dr. Gaston's presence in North Carolina that I can find. On May 1, he bought, at the sheriff's sale, a hundred acres of land on the east side of Pamlico Road, it being part of Juniper Swamp, for which he paid two pounds. He must have been here some time before that date.

2. Edward F. McSweeney, *The Gastons,* Boston, 1926.

3. In May of 1764 Alexander bought a hundred acres at a sheriff's sale; also buying a half acre on Craven Street in December for seventy pounds. In 1767 he bought two hundred acres for two hundred seventy-five pounds; in July of 1768 one hundred and sixty-six acres for one hundred and eight pounds; in August of 1768 for one hundred and fifty pounds over three hundred acres. In 1771 he bought four hundred and sixty acres. The next year he bought five hundred and twenty acres on Brice's Creek. In February of 1775 he purchased a plantation for three hundred pounds, as well as a lot in town, but sold both the following month. For the former he got three hundred and ten pounds. See *Deed Books of Craven County,* II, 437; XII–XIII, 189; XV, 296; XV, 333, 337; XIX, 70; XX, 102; XXI, 238, 251.

4. F. X. Martin, *History of North Carolina,* II, 395.

5. *North Carolina Colonial Records,* IX, 1144.

6. "State Papers On File In The Public Rolls Of England Concerning Colonial North Carolina," p. 186. *MS.*, John H. Wheeler Papers, Library of Congress.

7. H. G. Connor, "William Gaston," *Great American Lawyers,* III, 39. Judge Connor states that Cogdell, Nash, Gaston, and others seized the artillery, but Governor Martin, in another report to the government, gleefully says that his servants spiked the guns and so prevented their capture and removal. Martin may have been mistaken, and Judge Connor may have had an authentic account which has escaped my notice. For Martin's account see Wheeler, *loc. cit.*

8. *North Carolina Colonial Records,* X, 414, 456.

9. *Ibid.,* XI, 710; XII, 109.

10. *Ibid.,* XIII, 142, 425, 429.

11. There seems to be no record remaining of the marriage of Alexander and Margaret. Evidently Margaret told her son, William, that the wedding took place sometime in May of 1775. In the Gaston *MSS.* a document by William tells the story of the death of his father. In it he states that the story was told to him many times by his weeping mother. The New Bern *Spectator* of December 19, 1834, takes to task the *National Portrait Gallery of Distinguished Americans* (1834) for stating in the sketch of Gaston that

his father had left Margaret and the children on the wharf instead of at home.

12. *North Carolina Colonial Records,* XVI, 470.

13. Elizabeth F. Ellet, *The Women of the American Revolution,* II, 159–165. Susan Gaston Donaldson gave her this material. However, Mrs. Gaston could not have died in 1809, as Ellet states, for she made her will in March of 1810.

14. *The United States Catholic Miscellany,* II, 11, March 17, 1824.

15. Francis Neal to Gaston, Dec. 11, 1793, Gaston *MSS.* Unless stated otherwise reference to the Gaston *MSS.* denotes the Gaston Collection at the University of North Carolina Library, Chapel Hill, N. C.

16. Gaston to his mother, Aug. 25, 1791; Sept. 16, 1791, Gaston *MSS.*

17. Fleming to Mrs. Gaston, Nov. 7, 1791, Gaston *MSS.*

18. Gaston to his mother, Nov. 5, 1791, Gaston *MSS.* (Very widely quoted.)

19. Gaston to his mother, Dec. 15, 1791, Gaston *MSS.*

20. John G. Shea, *History of Georgetown College,* p. 15.

21. Shea, *loc. cit.*

22. Robert Plunkett to Mrs. Gaston, June 23, 1792; Sept. 19, 1792, Gaston *MSS.*

23. Gaston to his mother, Sept. 24, 1792, Gaston *MSS.*

24. Plunkett to Mrs. Gaston, Dec. 1792; Jan. 21, Feb. 12, March 6, March 30, 1793, Gaston *MSS.*

25. Plunkett to Mrs. Gaston, April 24, 1793, Gaston *MSS.*

26. Guion G. Johnson, *Ante-Bellum North Carolina: A Social History,* p. 813.

27. New Bern *Gazette,* April 5, 1794.

28. *Ibid.*, July 12, 1794.

29. Gaston to his mother, Sept. 12, 1794, Gaston *MSS.*

30. Gaston to his mother, Feb. 8, 1792, Gaston *MSS.*

31. Gaston to his mother, Nov. 24, 1794, Gaston *MSS.*

32. John Maclean, *History of the College of New Jersey,* p. 25.

33. Johnson, *op. cit.*, p. 121.

34. J. de R. Hamilton, "Francois X. Martin," *Dictionary of American Biography,* XII, 335. Quoted hereafter as *D.A.B.* There is no biography of Martin.

35. License, State of North Carolina, Gaston *MSS.*

36. Albert R. Newsome, "John Louis Taylor," *D.A.B.*, XVIII, 334. No biography of Judge Taylor exists.

37. Governor W. R. Davie to Gaston, Aug. 20, 1799, Gaston *MSS.*

*Gaston is destined to fill the first place in his profession in the country.* — LUTHER MARTIN

## CHAPTER TWO

# Young Lawyer and Husband

GASTON is destined to fill the first place in his profession in the country," said Luther Martin of Maryland, after a chance hearing of a case argued by Gaston in New Bern, and the opinion of such a figure commanded respect, for he was recognized during that generation as one of the leaders of the American bar.[1]

Yet, before Gaston really could settle down to law practice, his mind turned to the adventure of romance and marriage. New Bern was not deficient in its quota of winsome maidens, and the handsome young man, tall, curly haired, and witty, did not lack company at the social affairs of the town. In 1800 a former classmate, writing him for a recommendation to a judge for appointment as clerk of court, asked if he had "any new flame or was with the old one." Two years later his friend's sister, Nancy Guion, gave him her glove with instructions to tie it around his head before going to bed; the next day he was to report what dreams it had occasioned. If the young lady hoped this would lead to a romance or a declaration of love she was disappointed, but the very next year wedding bells did peal for Gaston. Taylor had moved back to Fayetteville, and between visits to his sister there and the press of legal business William found the companionship of a young friend of his sister rather delightful. Susan Hay, daughter of John Hay, a lawyer of Fayetteville, and niece of William Barry Grove, one of the most prominent Federalists of North Carolina, was the girl. She was beautiful, lively, and the life of the younger set. Walter Troy, a student of Dr. William Hopper, once exclaimed to his teacher, "Oh, Sir! she is enough to melt the frigidity of a Stoic and excite rapture in the breast of a hermit."[2]

During the summer Gaston visited his sister while Susan was there. He thought this was the most pleasant time of his life, and told his sister that "residing under the same roof with my dear Susan and enjoying her confidence I have had an opportunity of a more intimate acquaintance of her excellencies. To say that I love her more though would not be true." He also told Jane that of all the girls he knew or had ever met Susan seemed most likely to render him happy. Gaston was twenty-five while Susan was only sixteen when they were married at Fayetteville on September 4, 1803.[3]

The marriage seems to have taken place in the bride's home. It was a gala time for the whole town. Grand carriages swept up the drive to bring the older and more dignified such as William B. Grove, the bride's uncle, Mrs. Gaston, and other New Bern residents, as John Stanly. Gigs, behind high-stepping horses brought the younger couples, including Gaston's sister, Jane, and her husband, Judge Taylor. The young blades dashed up with a flourish on horseback. The wedding over, the younger people rolled back the rugs in the large parlor which became a ballroom, and they danced and drank and flirted throughout the night, while the older and more sedate played cards and gossiped in other rooms. Outside the windows could be heard the soft murmur, the songs, and an occasional wild burst of laughter from the Negroes as they too celebrated the occasion.[4]

The couple took a short trip toward the ocean and then returned to New Bern. Gaston settled down to gather the necessary materials for his brief on the important Granville case; smaller cases, such as the collection of debts, took up much of his time; he began even to take in students to study for the bar. The world looked bright for the young couple, but their happiness was of short duration, for just eight months and sixteen days after the wedding, on April 20, 1804, the young bride died. It was a hard blow to Gaston, but the practice of law kept him busy.

He was young, and the companionship of the young ladies was not unwelcome, so it was not surprising that a year and a half later the widower again sought the altar. This time he fell in love with a distant cousin, Hannah McClure, the daughter of General William McClure. Their friends, noticing the deepening intimacy, laughed at her for calling him "cousin." She asked Gaston what should be substituted for this, saying, "what will be pleasing that your Hannah would call you?" It was not long before the term became "husband" for they were married in New Bern on October 6, 1805, by Father Simon Felix Gallagher. The bride was nineteen, the groom twenty-seven.

Hannah McClure was described by one of her contemporaries as a "woman of superior understanding whose disposition was frank and generous, with manners bland and unaffected; although possessing an open and engaging countenance her features singly could not be called beautiful." Red hair, big brown eyes, well-shaped nose, generous lips, and firm chin made up these features. We are assured by this same person that her secret charm and cordial expression of truth and sincerity, with an added genial grace, endeared her to all in New Bern. Her chief virtue was the practice of extensive charity.[5] Her portrait reflects this.

By this time Gaston was well established. In the April following his marriage he bought his wife a piano, paying $310 for it; a few days before, he had purchased two lots in town on Craven Street, paying £912 for one and £250 for the other.[6] The latter lot, at Front and Craven Streets, he sold in 1817 for $2,325.[7] It is not certain just where he lived then, but his mother was with them until her death in 1811, for in several letters of Hannah to William there are references to his mother's health. Between this time and the outbreak of the War of 1812 he bought three hundred and twenty-three acres on Brice's Creek for $1,000; a couple of lots in town and some other land outside it for about $5,000.[8] Besides this increase in his financial status there was a like growth of his family. The first child, a son, was born to the couple January 19, 1807, and was named Alexander. A daughter was born June 4, 1808, whom they called Susan. Another, Hannah, came March 18, 1811. Not only was the father engaging in an extensive and lucrative practice of the law but he was also establishing a reputation as a legislator "who in deliberative bodies had become as much the paragon as had been Governor William R. Davie."[9]

However, he had ample time to devote to private interests because his duties in the state legislature took up but a short period, the sessions generally lasting only a month. Although he owned a plantation and some slaves, farming was not his forte. He derived his income mostly from his legal work. As Taylor had left him a rather wide practice almost at the very time of his admittance to the bar, Gaston did not have the struggle for work and existence facing most young lawyers. His first case was Gooding *vs.* Henry *et al.* in which he served as counsel for the defendant.[10] This was probably the Henry family of New Bern, held in high regard and friendship by the Gastons.

Among the lawyers with whom Gaston practiced at this early date were John Haywood, the leader of the bar of the state with the most lucrative practice; his former teacher, Francois X. Martin; Edward Harris, also of New Bern, a very able lawyer and legislator; Blake Baker, onetime attorney general; Samuel Jocelyn, considered then as the leading equity lawyer in the state; Alfred Moore, later an associate justice of the United States Supreme Court; and John Stanly, wealthy New Bern Federalist. As was (and is) often the case in many states the lawyers were sometimes superior to the judges in legal talent and knowledge. The lawyers followed the court traveling on a wide circuit by horseback and gig.

The legislature in 1799 had passed a court law dividing the

circuits into four "ridings," and after the sessions of these superior courts were over the judges met at Raleigh twice a year in a court of conference. This law had made Morganton and Salisbury one riding; another of Hillsboro and Fayetteville; one of Halifax and Edenton; the last Wilmington and New Bern.[11] Gaston practiced in the last-named court, but seemed to have most of his cases at Wilmington in his first few years at the bar. In 1806 a new law set up a superior court in each county. While the superior courts were in session Gaston was very busy.

Sometimes he was engaged in a case with the mighty Haywood; at other times he opposed him and at least once defeated him. Once he even bested his old teacher, Martin.[12] In the court session of July, 1801, held at New Bern, Gaston defended a man accused of forging a deed. His argument was to the effect that the law would not allow the severe punishment for such an act to be incurred under an indictment not supported in all its material parts. He proved to the satisfaction of the jury that the misrecital of facts in the testimony extended beyond the deed in question and affected the substance of the case.[13] As a rule, the *Reports* do not contain the counsel's brief, although in some important cases they do. One may run across a line such as "the cause was argued at great length by Gaston and Haywood," in one of which cases Gaston defeated Haywood in an important action of injection to recover land.[14] He lost a case involving a confiscated Loyalist estate in which he contended that "those who were not born aliens could not become so by a separation of empire," and so the land in question could be transmitted by descent. Johnston, the judge, decided that the constitution of North Carolina held otherwise.[15] Gaston called upon a principle here that he was to use again as counsel in the most important case tried in North Carolina between the two wars of 1776 and 1812.

This was the famous Granville case brought by the Granville heirs against William R. Davie, Nathaniel Allen, and Josiah Collins, and tried at the June term, 1805, of the United States court at Raleigh. In colonial times the English kings were unusually generous in granting to favorites vast tracts of land in America. They also used this region to settle their debts. Charles II had given a charter to certain of his noblemen for almost all of North Carolina. In 1729 all of these proprietors, except one, had given their claim back to the crown. The heirs of this one man, the Earl of Granville, after the Revolution, brought a suit of ejectment in support of their claims. So by this action there was placed in jeopardy title to property of greater value than any other ever litigated before an American tribunal.[16] Naturally the people of North Carolina were very much interested in the case as many of them lived on the land in question, to which title was to be decided by this test case. The English heirs had placed their cause in the hands of an American agent, John London of Wilmington, North Carolina, who hired Gaston as their counsel. A correspondence between the two concerning the case began in 1801 and continued up to 1808 even after Gaston had resigned as counsel.[17] Gaston constantly had to ask for more material, such as documents and other papers for use on the case. He spent a great deal of time and effort preparing for it in the four years interval before the case was tried in 1805.

When the time finally arrived only one judge, Henry Potter of Granville, was on the bench. Potter, appointed around 1801, has been described as "blameless but not shining in his functions." Chief Justice Marshall, the other circuit judge, had declined to sit because the question was exactly that involved in the current Fairfax title in Virginia, in which he had an active interest. London was much annoyed with his withdrawal, writing Gaston that it "partakes more of political acquiescence than the dignified, official independence we had a right to expect from his character . . . it has very much the appearance of shirking to popular impression." He thought that Marshall had said enough to convince their opponents he was unfavorable to them.[18] However, Gaston did not agree with London in this characterization of Marshall. Nor was London correct in his premise, for the Chief

Justice would never shirk duty, but rather had a delicate sense of propriety and felt that he could not judge the case with justice. The state expected a decision contrary to North Carolina, and Governor David Stone asked the legislature to consider what should be done for the citizens affected in that eventuality. This was before it was known that Marshall would not judge the case. The counsels for the defense were Duncan Cameron, Blake Baker, and Alexander Martin; the latter two had volunteered their services. Gaston was aided by Edward Harris. Both sides presented their evidence and then began their arguments. The North Carolina *Journal* of Halifax stated that "the cause was opened by Mr. Gaston in his usual masterly fashion." Contrary to the ordinary habit of lawyers Gaston liked to open his cases; he believed that if he could forcibly impress the jury, those who followed would have less chance of making an impression. Cameron then replied to Gaston, and was followed by Blake Baker and Alexander Martin, former governor.

Gaston's carefully prepared argument began with an oratorical appeal to the jury. Then he continued with a statement of the facts showing that the plaintiffs had title to the land up to February 12, 1776, and concluding that unless it could be proved that the title was divested their claim was still valid. The defendants held that the Granville claim was invalid because of the Bill of Rights, the confiscatory clauses of the state constitution written during the Revolution, and finally by the very nature of the Revolution.

One by one Gaston examined these arguments. Concerning the last he stated that private rights were not suspended by civil wars or revolutions, for if this principle were admitted a strong inducement would be given to the turbulent to destroy social harmony. Moreover, a sense of justice dictated that the unoffending citizen should not suffer from his offending nation; humanity loudly complained of all unnecessary aggravation of human calamities. He argued that in no respect, except in the amount, did his clients differ from other subjects of the king possessing property in the state. Gaston held that the section referred to in the Bill of Rights secured to *individual citizens* titles held before the Revolution; that the defendants could not assume that it was intended to vest the state with rights in all the lands. Such a construction he deemed odious, by attributing to past legislatures unworthy motives. It was a principle of the law of nations that if a majority changed its government the minority could sell its property and go elsewhere. He maintained that the confiscatory laws did not extend to any person in open enmity at the time of passage but were passed to confiscate traitors' lands and to restore aliens their lands upon their taking the oath of allegiance.[19]

The counsel for the defense, Duncan Cameron, admitted some of Gaston's contentions but held that the heirs were aliens and so could not hold lands, while their action was barred also by the statute of limitation. Counsels for both sides rested their case upon the interpretation of the effects of the Revolution upon the title, and the twenty-fifth section of the Bill of Rights. Gaston argued upon right reason and natural equity without reference to municipal law, while Cameron contended that the status of Granville removed him from the protection accorded to private ownership, that he merely took the place of the king. Judge Potter in his very lengthy charge to the jury stated that the law of the case was with the defendants.[20] The jury returned the verdict according to the judge's desire.

With the return of a verdict unfavorable to the Granvilles, London wished to appeal to the supreme court. However, Gaston asked to be released from future service, for it was taking up too much of his time. London was disappointed and told Gaston that he was "sorry your private affairs do not permit you to carry suit to the Supreme Court . . . the disappointment is a serious one to me," and assured him that he had considered his services as a "Host against the adversaries."[21] Wishing to obtain a competent lawyer to carry on for him, Gaston asked a friend living in the national capital for advice on the best lawyers there. To him were recommended P. B. Key of Georgetown, Luther Martin and William Pinkney of Baltimore as the best available, with an added note that Luther Martin had the most extensive knowledge of the law and was the greatest lawyer in that part if not in the whole country.[22]

Gaston secured the services of Key, who wanted him to come to Washington and help him at the court, and also asked him for his notes on the Raleigh trial. But before the suit could be heard Key died, and in 1808 London wrote Gaston that he was dropping it at this time because "the increasing irritation between this country and England made it imprudent to press on."[23]

In 1802, while his mind was occupied with gathering the material for the Granville case, Gaston as well as the entire community of New Bern was shocked and grieved by the death of former Governor Richard Dobbs Spaight at the hand of the wealthy Federalist, John Stanly, in a duel over politics. Stanly immediately left town, and then wrote Gaston for advice on what course to follow, and asked him to consult with Judge Taylor about the question. Gaston told him to remain out of town until some adjustment was made. He thought it might be necessary to make an application to the general assembly for a pardon, but felt that the governor had the power to grant one. As this power had never been exercised before in the state the governor might be reluctant to set a precedent in this respect, was the final opinion of Gaston. Among Governor Williams' last official acts was a pardon for Stanly.[24]

Although Gaston aided his friend and townsman as much as possible in this affair, and although he himself several times almost became involved in the Code Duello, he was at all times very much opposed to the practice. Among his manuscripts is a copy of an essay on dueling which probably was intended for newspaper publication and may have been submitted. Although not dated it was probably written between 1802 and 1805 and may have been suggested by the Stanly-Spaight duel. In it he asked "how long this monstrous idol which delighted in human sacrifice would be adored." To him it was a "monster of cruelty existing through the pride and vanity of man."

Naturally few of his cases were as important as the historic Granville one. Many involved merely the collection of debts. He acted as agent for several firms outside the state; one such account amounting to $2,600 he collected for a firm in Philadelphia. These cases were lucrative, for his commissions ranged from $50 and $100 on up, depending upon the amount collected.[25] Although not historic, some that he argued greatly concerned the public welfare through the decisions rendered. Such a case Gaston won in 1809 in the July term of the superior court, the opposing counsel being Alfred Moore.

The question at issue was whether a posthumous child would take a distributive share of the estate. Gaston argued that it would on three counts; through the statute of distribution, the design of the legislature, and the doctrine of the law on analogous subjects. Regarding the first clause, the statute directed that the surplus, after the widow's share, be distributed by equal portions to the children. The inquiry depended then, he thought, upon the construction of the word "children." This word embraced those born after as well as before the father's death. He argued that the legislature would not add to the miseries of a posthumous child by forbidding it any part of its parent's personal estate, for according to the feelings of nature as well as the principles of equity it was a universal will to give an equal distribution to those equally dear. He found in analogous cases that in all instances children in *ventre sa mere* were considered when they came into being as having the same rights as the rest.[26] The injustice of attempting to deprive a child of its inheritance irked him so much that he later introduced a bill in the legislature to settle the matter, and had the satisfaction of seeing its passage.

Through intensive study Gaston was well versed in the most minute matters of law. Most of his cases are liberally sprinkled with citations from the current authorities as well as from like cases in other states and in England. He excelled in land cases, but was also a good criminal lawyer.

His agility in seizing a weak point is well demonstrated in a case which he argued before Judges Marshall and Potter in the federal circuit court at Raleigh. Two men who were charged with passing counterfeit notes had retained him. As was his custom he took the first argument. Instead of reading a brief in defense he turned to the judges to obtain leave "to ask a single question of the prosecution's witness and so save the court's time." He then asked the witness if the note on which the indictment was drawn was in the same condition as when he had received it from the prisoner. The reply to this was in the negative; the witness went on to explain that the note had been perfect when given to him, but now some of its parts, among them the date, were missing. With this Gaston turned to the judges and bowed. The court immediately discharged the case, holding that the note should have been presented when perfect.[27]

In another criminal case which he undertook shortly afterward he was less fortunate. Early in May of 1810 New Bern and the entire seaboard region along there was shocked by the discovery of the body of a young boy, which was washed up from the sea on the beach at New Bern. The very foundation of the town rocked with indignation against the person accused of the crime, a Captain Edward Tinker. So great was the fury aroused that mob action was feared; no jury could be formed for no one could be found with an unbiased view. The case was thereupon removed from Craven County to Carteret County. The murdered boy had been cabin boy in a ship belonging to Captain Edward Tinker, who was accused of the crime by his mate, Peter Durand. Through want of a jury Tinker languished in jail from May 3, 1810, to February 7, 1811, when he filed off his *irons*, opened the door with an iron bar, and made his escape, but was soon recaptured. However, the frantic mariner again escaped on February 21 and it was not until a month later that he was retaken in Philadelphia.[28]

Lost causes were not hopeless to Gaston, and in this case his sense of fair play and justice was outraged, for the prisoner could not obtain even a lawyer not to mention a fair trial and unprejudiced jury. The trial was held before Judge John L. Taylor. Isaac Guion and Edward Graham, both of New Bern and good friends of Gaston, prosecuted the case for the state. Gaston was sole counsel for the defense.

With every point of law at the command of an attorney, with every tactic known to the power of an orator, he pleaded with and cajoled the jury; with the cold majesty of a judge he confused and terrified the prosecution's witnesses. A spectator at the trial later stated that this plea was equal to some of his great legislative addresses. Appealing first to the jury for sympathy Gaston said that the countryside had made it seem to be a crime even to assist the accused in his ordinary privilege, and that passion instead of understanding swayed the community. He attacked the evidence of the mate, Durand, showing that he had committed perjury on at least one occasion and finally accused him of the murder. He pointed out that the evidence was circumstantial, that Tinker's actions before and after the crime were unimpeachable, that at least two witnesses had contradicted each other. He told the jury that it was better for ten guilty to escape than one innocent man to suffer.

Guion had spoken first, Gaston next, and then Graham last; the drama did not close until eleven-thirty o'clock at night. The crowd that had sat through it all, thrilled by the power of the advocates' tongues, leaned forward tensely upon the return of the jury to the courtroom ten minutes after it had filed out. Guilty![29] The outcome almost had been assured; Judge Taylor was forced to sentence his brother-in-law's client to hang by the neck until he was dead. The excitement throughout the region over the event was so intense that the printers in New Bern were able to take advantage of it, publishing the full account of the trial in pamphlet form.

Gaston's personal relations with his companions at the bar

seemed to have been always good. On only two occasions were there hints of anything else. In March of 1807 he had printed his argument in a case and sent it to Judge Baker, explaining to the judge that he would not have done this had his opponent not taken such action, and that this left him no choice in the matter of justice to his clients.[30] In the other case Haywood left North Carolina suddenly for Tennessee, leaving his affairs in utter confusion. His friends had to divide up his pending cases among themselves so as not to inconvenience his clients. From Nashville Haywood wrote to Gaston he had heard that the latter published a letter declaring him insane as well as accusing him of taking exorbitant fees. This Gaston vigorously denied, and as Haywood went on handling the litigation over Gaston's lands in Tennessee he must have been convinced.[31]

Many lawyers from outside the state wrote to him for advice on certain cases or to learn points of law as interpreted by the courts of North Carolina. From New York to Virginia such requests reached him. The well-known Virginian, Littleton Tazewell, placed several of his North Carolina cases in his hands. Concerning one, which came up at the outbreak of the war, Tazewell wrote, "I hope that the interests of my friends will be in your hands, but if you can not serve me, engage a counsel you prefer." Expressing his gratitude for Gaston's attention to other applications he had made to him he said, " . . . though I haven't the opportunity of a personal acquaintance with you . . . yet there are few persons I would rather have one with."[32]

While engaged in the arduous duties of the legislature and the bar William also found time to train future lawyers. He accepted students as early as 1804 when young John London, the son of the agent of the Granvilles, came to him. William Barry Grove placed one of his protégés under his care soon afterward. In 1808 John R. Donnell, brilliant lawyer and judge, came to him at New Bern when but seventeen to sit at the feet of "one of the greatest of our lawyers." To all his pupils Gaston devoted himself unsparingly and patiently, giving each his earnest attention and courteous consideration. The thoughtfulness with which he treated one, William B. Meares, was typical of his actions toward the rest.

After Meares had left his office Gaston wrote him that his fond hopes anticipated the day Meares would be an eminent lawyer, a great and good man, for he had the talents, and, with a disposition properly cultivated, the blessings of God would conduct him to this goal. He admonished him of the immense value of the coming five years, with the importance of improving upon it.

To gain the qualifications of an illustrious lawyer Gaston laid down four requisites. It was necessary to devote much time to study, knowledge being evanescent. He must acquire a thorough knowledge of legal science, a facility in expressing thoughts clearly, correctly, and agreeably and so arrange them as to illustrate, convince, and persuade; he must give an unremitted attention to the interests of his clients and finally have an incorruptible integrity. Gaston advised him to make plain, short briefs at first, and always to go to original sources. He must read the classics to aid his style. Finally, he warned him that the most dangerous pest of society was the wicked unprincipled lawyer, whose reason was a slave to his appetite, whose honor was but a fashionable honor, whose religion was pride, revenge, and sensuality. He felt that vice and its temptations held out more than usual allure to lawyers.[33]

Gaston was at this time in his thirtieth year, and already Luther Martin's remark of less than ten years before was accomplished. A new generation was coming on; many of the older lawyers were leaving the scene forever, while many others, like John Haywood, left the state. Blake Baker died during this time, and Edward Harris of New Bern, who had so many times been his opponent at the bar, died just before the War of 1812. Gaston argued as many cases as any of them, and more than most. His fees netted him ample means to support his young family in comfort and style. He was well on the road to wealth and honor.

## NOTES FOR CHAPTER TWO

1. J. F. McLaughlin, "William Gaston: The First Student of Georgetown College," *American Catholic Historical Society Records,* VI, 225–251. Cited hereafter as *A.C.H.S. Records.* Martin made this remark to a Dr. Potter in Baltimore.

2. "Letter from Hamilton C. Jones the Elder" (Feb. 2, 1819), *North Carolina University Magazine,* XXIII, April, 1893.

3. Raleigh *Register,* Sept. 19, 1803.

4. John W. Moore, *History of North Carolina,* p. 433. Moore cannot be depended upon as he is very inaccurate. It is valuable in its reminiscences of forgotten incidents, and is really more a compilation than a history.

5. Raleigh *Register,* July 13, 1813.

6. Deed Book of Craven County, XXXVI, 795, 803.

7. *Ibid.,* XXXIX, 749.

8. *Ibid.,* XXXVII, 919; XXXVIII, 217, 284, 285, 300, 301, 389.

9. Moore, *op. cit.,* p. 453.

10. Statement in Gaston *MSS.* I have not been able to find the case in any of the court *Reports* at my disposal.

11. Moore, *op. cit.,* p. 431.

12. "Hunt v. Williams & Miller." *Martin's Reports of the Superior Court 1799–1802.* New Bern, 1802, p. 318.

13. "State v. Street." *Ibid.,* p. 158.

14. "Wells v. Newbolt." *Ibid.,* p. 166. Also in Cameron and Norwood, *Reports,* p. 375.

15. John Haywood, *Reports in the Superior Courts . . . and Federal Court 1799–1806,* II, 138.

16. Henry G. Connor, "The Granville Estate and North Carolina," *University of Pennsylvania Law Review,* LXII, no. 9, 1914, p. 671 ff. Judge Connor of the North Carolina supreme court gave a most complete and able account of the case.

17. Albert J. Beveridge, *Life of John Marshall,* IV, 156, makes a statement concerning Gaston and this case which is not only a guess but untrue. He did not and could not have known the facts upon which he based this statement as he did not have the use of the Gaston *MSS.* Beveridge says: "Finally on Feb. 4, 1817 . . . the case was stricken from the docket. The reason for this action undoubtedly was that William Gaston, counsel for the Granville heirs, had been elected to Congress, was ambitious politically, was thereafter elected judge of the Supreme Court of North Carolina; none of these honors could possibly have been achieved had he pressed the Granville case." As a matter of fact Gaston was no longer counsel, hav-

ing given up the case by Oct. 6, 1806, so by the time mentioned by Beveridge he had practically forgotten about the case. It was not until seven years after he had dropped the case that he was elected to Congress. When the case was finally given up he had already retired from national politics through his own desire. Politics had absolutely nothing to do with his severance of connection with the case, and Beveridge's assumptions are unjustifiable. The author of this great biography of the Chief Justice seemed not to have been aware of the very intimate relations between Marshall and Gaston, as the latter is mentioned only once in a footnote.

18. London to Gaston, July 8, 1805, Gaston *MSS.* Also in Henry Connor, *op. cit.*

19. Brief of the Granville case in the Gaston *MSS.*

20. *North Carolina Journal* (Halifax), Jan. 27, 1806.

21. London to Gaston, Oct. 6, 1806, and April 2, 1806, Gaston *MSS.*

22. E. B. Caldwell to Gaston, Jan. 24, 1806, Gaston *MSS.*

23. London to Gaston, Jan. 4, 1808, Gaston *MSS.*

24. Gaston to Stanly, Sept. 10, 1802. Stanly *MSS.*, Hawks Collection, New York Historical Society.

25. Gaston to Willings & Francis, May 31, 1805. *Misc. MSS.*, Wm. Gaston Folder, New York City Public Library.

26. "Hill v. Moore & Watters." V, *North Carolina Reports*, 248.

27. Raleigh *Register*, Nov. 15, 1810.

28. *Ibid.*, May 3, 1810; Nov. 8, 1810; Feb. 7, 1811; March 21, 1811.

29. *Trial of Edward Tinker, Mariner, For Murder of a Youth Called Edward . . . Carteret Superior Court, September 1811.* New Bern, 1811. The pamphlet was over fifty pages. In North Carolina University Library.

30. *Den on demise of Wm. B. Sheppard & Wife vs. J. Relfe. Pasquotank Superior Court, March 1807. Argument by William Gaston.* In North Carolina University Library.

31. Gaston to Haywood, Jan. 13, 1808; Haywood to Gaston, Nov. 30, 1809, Gaston *MSS.*

32. L. W. Tazewell to Gaston, Oct. 4, 1812, Gaston *MSS.*

33. Gaston to W. B. Meares, June 23, 1808, Raleigh *News & Observer*, July 26, 1884. There are several letters in the Gaston *MSS.* by Meares complaining of ill health. However, he did become well known as a lawyer, and served in the legislature of North Carolina during periods when Gaston was also a member.

*The national government was established by the people and not by the states.* — WILLIAM GASTON

## CHAPTER THREE

# The Young Legislator

IN THE period of practically fifteen years between Gaston's admission to the bar and the outbreak of the second war with England, American life and policy was dominated by foreign affairs. Naturally Gaston's political career was shaped by the resulting events. The young man entered politics in 1800, at the age of twenty-two. In the face of the strong Republican trend of the early nineteenth century, and in a state largely Republican in its temper, he became a Federalist. The revival of Federalism brought about by the French crisis of 1798 was short lived. It was buried beneath the avalanche which, starting slowly under the skillful hands of Thomas Jefferson, had moved forward imperceptibly until its momentum had gathered enough force to drown all but the roar of triumphant Republicanism. The election of 1800 brought Jefferson to the presidency on March 4, 1801, only after the celebrated deadlock with Aaron Burr was broken in the House of Representatives, when enough honorable Federalists decided Jefferson's Republicanism was preferable to anything Burr had to offer. This administration was marked by the famed Louisiana purchase.

Jefferson began his second term in office in 1805 with George Clinton as vice-president; he had obtained one hundred and sixty-two electoral votes to the fourteen of his Federalist opponent. From the very first moment affairs moved forward rapidly toward a break with the two great belligerents, England and France.

These two mighty powers had renewed with increased vigor the struggles known as the Napoleonic wars, which lasted from 1793 to 1815. During the course of this struggle the United States as one of the great neutral carrying powers suffered from the depredations of both nations and probably one million tons of shipping was forced into idleness here. When war seemed just imminent in 1807 as a result of the Leopard-Chesapeake affair, President Jefferson put in motion one of the greatest experiments ever attempted by a president, the Embargo. Even some of his ardent followers, such as Albert Gallatin, secretary of the treasury, preferred war to this measure. The South, all but ruined by it, still gave loyal support to Jefferson. Such immediate havoc came from the measure that in 1808 the Federalists captured the legislatures of New England, and in the national capital the House decided to repeal the act, and actually did so on February 27, 1809. Then the milder Non-Intercourse Bill was passed by a vote of eighty-one to forty. A few days later Jefferson left the White House to his successor, James Madison, who continued to have the same difficulties with the two nations. During the course of this affair southern opposition in the House came chiefly from Georgia and North Carolina.

Yet, the latter state was controlled by vigorous followers of Thomas Jefferson, for Republicanism seemed more natural here to the great majority of the ordinary farmers and backwoodsmen. Only after eleven other states had ratified the Federal Constitution, so leaving North Carolina isolated, had she seen fit also to do so, on November 21, 1789; and then by a second convention convened because the first had failed to arrive at a decision. Only a minority of the public of the state believed that the new order would be safer than the old.[1] Samuel Johnston and Benjamin Hawkins, both prominent Federalists, were sent to the Senate of the United States, while to the House were sent two Federalists and two Anti-Federalists. The next election saw the defeat of one of these latter by William Barry Grove, uncle of Gaston's first wife. At the same time Nathaniel Macon began his thirty-seven years' service in Congress. The assumption of state debts met with violent opposition in North Carolina; the legislature instructed the state congressmen to vote against it. Soon after this Federalism began a rapid decline in the state, although given a short reprieve by the French war scare. Jefferson was not certain he would secure its presidential vote in 1800, stating that "the medicine for that state must be very mild and secretly administrated." Upon election Jefferson wisely tried to convert the most influential Federalists by giving them Government positions. His party also showed its political sagacity by persuading Joseph Gales to set up at Raleigh an administration newspaper. Under these conditions William Gaston began his career in politics as a Federalist.

During the spring of 1800 he announced through handbills his candidacy to represent Craven County in the Senate of North Carolina. Late in June he enclosed one of these handbills with a letter to General Samuel Simpson, in which a phase of the campaign was discussed. Gaston was worried over the fact that handbills had appeared notifying the freeholders of the county that the former Senator Henry Tillman was also a candidate. He felt sure these had appeared without that individual's knowledge because the latter had been in Virginia for a month and was still there; besides Tillman had stated "in the most solemn manner to fifty different people that he would not be again a candidate." Gaston thought these bills would be disavowed upon Tillman's return, but if not they were in for a "tug of war." The young candidate declared to the general that much as he disliked to be in a contested election he could not retreat. With youthful naïveté he said, "To do so would betray a want of proper spirit in me and also a want of confidence in the strong assurances of those, at whose application, and upon whose encouragement, I became a candidate."[2]

Although Gaston had been engaged in many legal cases in the preceding two years this was practically his first public appearance before the people of the county. His address at New

Bern to St. John's Lodge, No. 3 of the Masons, on the "distressing death of the late worthy brother, George Washington," hardly could have brought him much attention in the county.[3] Nevertheless, he was elected by the county to the Senate, and James Gatling and John S. Nelson to the House of Commons, while the borough town of New Bern was represented by George Ellis.[4] This assembly contained a large majority of rabid Republicans. John Haywood, state treasurer for many years, declared that never before had he seen such a talentless assembly;[5] William Polk, a prominent Federalist, was "disgusted with the collective ignorance of the body," feeling that no Federalist had a chance of obtaining any office in the assembly's gift.[6] His predictions concerning this were only too true. Gaston himself wrote a friend during the session "a very severe account of our present legislature."[7] Congratulating Gaston upon the results of this election, his friend Frederick Beasley noted that despite the fact of "shameful corruption which prevails too generally at our elections in the southern states, merit is not obliged to stoop in order to mount into posts of honor," and that "some respectability was now given the deliberative councils of North Carolina" because of the election of Gaston.

The assembly convened on Monday, November 17, 1800. In the Senate the Republicans started off in triumph with the election of one of their number, Joseph Riddick of Gates County, to the speakership over Stephen W. Carney, a Federalist from Halifax County. The only exception to the rule of spoils was the election of the veteran and able Samuel Johnston to a state judgeship and the re-election of Governor Benjamin Williams (the governor was elected for but one year, but the custom was to keep the same man in office for three years). An apprehension had existed that jealousy between the East and West might influence the choice of the judgeship. One of Gaston's correspondents hoped that a wise choice would be made despite this and expressed his opinion that "Johnston and Wood would be proper." A Republican senator, David Stone, was sent to Congress in preference to the very capable and experienced William R. Davie by a vote of 94 to 72. The state printing was given to Gales by a majority of twenty-four votes, although he had but just arrived in the state.[8] Montfort Stokes, who later became very influential in the state, was made clerk of the Senate.

Despite his Federalism and youthfulness (he was only twenty-two) Gaston must have had some reputation for ability and common sense, as he was kept fairly busy for a novice. He was appointed to the Committee of Privileges and Elections as well as to that of Propositions and Grievances.[9] Two days after the convening of the session, on his motion, a joint committee of both Houses was appointed to inquire if any and what alterations were necessary in the law regulating the mode of conducting disputed elections. To this committee Gaston, Basil Gaither, and Hector McAlister were appointed for the Senate.[10] He served on the joint committees named to amend the penal laws of the state, and to divide Rowan County.[11] The young legislator and William McKenzie were named to examine for the Senate the engrossed bills passed during this session.[12] By motion of Levin Watkins on December 1 he was added to the Committee on Finances.[13] He was also on the joint committee to which was referred a letter from the president and the bill to repeal the law enabling the university to take the lands of confiscated property. Peter Forney, with whom he was later to serve in Congress, was also on this committee. The young man must have felt some elation when he was appointed, toward the end of the session, chairman of three different committees. One of these was to inquire what sum should be allowed Joseph Gales for the public printing. The report of the last-named committee gave Gales £75 for the printing of the session, as well as £50 for nine hundred copies of the militia law, and this report was adopted.

The most important act of this assembly was the action taken against the university. At first both parties had supported this state institution, although both the faculty and trustees were ardent Federalists. The trustees were inclined to appoint as fellow members those of their political faith. The Republicans charged that none but Federalists held positions there, while the youth of the state were inculcated with Federalist doctrines. Previous assemblies, more kindly disposed, had given the university land escheated to the state as well as the unsold, confiscated land.[14] These sources of income the Republicans determined to take away. Gaston was very active in his opposition to this measure. He had served on the committee appointed to draw up the bill, but was able to accomplish nothing in the committee room. He had also presented the petition of the trustees concerning it. When the bill was reported providing that all confiscated property of the university not sold should revert to the state he moved to amend this by the phrase "not legally sold" or else to amend it to read "all confiscated property of the university not reduced into their possession." His amendment was lost by a vote of twenty-nine to twenty-one.[15] The original bill passed by a vote of thirty-two to twenty-three, Gaston having required the yeas and nays to be put on record, and of course voting with the minority. This was done five days before the close of the session.

Naturally the Federalists were wild with rage. Besides writing in the New Bern *Gazette* that he felt this law was inconsistent with the state constitution Gaston also expressed his wrath to friends. At least the Federalists were pleased by one action of this assembly—the decision of the two Houses to buy two portraits of George Washington, the purchase of which was postponed for a time because of the expense. Gaston complained that the assembly had wasted its time in passing private laws.

December 20, 1800, the state legislature adjourned, having been in session thirty-four days. A couple of members of the Senate had not appeared at all; some had been able to remain but a short time. Gaston was there every one of the thirty-four days; as a salary for this time he drew £53:3:6 besides five shillings for ferriage, with a mileage of two hundred and fifty miles. The Speaker, Joseph Reddick, was also there every day, reporting a mileage of three hundred and ninety miles, and drawing £55:4:0

besides four shillings for ferriage. Joshua Williams drew the highest amount, £67:16:6, his mileage being six hundred miles. The members in the Lower House from Craven County and New Bern drew practically the same amount as Gaston. One from the county reported a hundred miles more than the others.[16] This mileage was, of course, figured for both ways. William held no office for six years after this term in the state Senate. He became a member of the House of Commons in 1807.

In the presidential campaign of 1800 Gaston took little or no active part. To one of his young friends he reported that he did not figure on more than five votes for Adams from North Carolina. Even this was an overestimation for that state gave Adams only four of its electoral votes. In his reply to Gaston the friend lamented that violence was increasing in the country, and that "the democrats are constantly sounding the alarm and preaching up the rights of the people."[17] Adams was completely defeated by Jefferson and Burr. The bizarre proceedings in the House resulting from this defeat of Adams and tie vote for Jefferson and Burr had been entirely unforeseen. In the voting of the House to elect a president the Federalists as a general rule supported Burr. North Carolina supported Jefferson throughout the thirty-six ballots, although the four Federalists: Archibald Henderson, William B. Grove, William H. Hill, and Joseph Dickson, voted most of the time for Burr. Nathaniel Macon, Benjamin Williams, Richard Stanford, Willis Alston, David Stone, and Richard Spaight, voting each time for Jefferson, gave him their state's vote. On the second to last ballot the Federalist, Dickson, declared it was time for a final vote and that he would support Jefferson thereafter.[18] As other Federalists reached the same conclusion, on the next ballot Jefferson was elected.

During the next eight years Jefferson faced many attacks, but none more bitter than the one launched against him by all Federalists, both great and small, because of an expression of his high regard for Thomas Paine, "the pen-man of the Revolution." Paine, the writer of the Revolution's classic *Common Sense*, after our Revolution went over to France to aid that country in hers. Even he was horrified by the excesses of the Frenchmen, and as a result landed in prison. While there he wrote *Rights of Man*, a deistic pamphlet. Not satisfied with the flurry caused by this attack on religion, he also made a very savage, scurrilous, and cutting attack on President Washington. When President Jefferson learned that he wished to return to America he offered to place at his disposal a United States ship for the return home. This became the occasion for a Federalist outburst. Gaston took part in this by writing an open letter to the president in the Raleigh *Minerva* under the signature "A North Carolinian." He asked the president whether it was possible so infamous a person as Tom Paine could have received such an invitation from the head of the country; whether it was possible his character was unknown to him. He maintained such an action was unworthy of the president's character and degrading to the country's honor, besides being an indignity to the late president, Washington.[19]

Jefferson was more fortunate in another important matter, as his diplomatic handling of the Leopard-Chesapeake incident brought him praise from all over the nation. Editors, plain farmers, and practically every Republican who could write more than a plain *X* rushed to the cupboard for writing materials to address the president. The legislatures of the various states joined the movement, voting addresses of praise to him. Among these was North Carolina, but here it took three weeks to frame a proper message. For a legislature that remained in session but a month this left little time for needed state business. This was especially true of North Carolina, which consumed so much time passing private laws, even having the task of granting divorces. Besides this address about the only other thing done during the session was the election of a Federalist governor by the Republicans over the Republican then in office because of the latter's criticism of a court rule.[20]

After his absence of six years from politics Gaston had been elected in 1807 to the House of Commons. The fireworks were heavy there during this session. John Hamilton of Pasquotank County started them off with a resolution which bestowed the most fulsome praise upon the president, and asked him to run for a third term. Federalist anger was aroused by the phrase in the resolution which condemned them in no uncertain terms as a "party which seeks to subvert because they cannot direct." This was struck out in the final address. Blake Baker, J. J. Daniel of Halifax, and Henry I. Toole, lawyers all, whom Gaston had met and was to meet many times in opposition at the bar, supported Hamilton. The Federalists were led by Gaston and Archibald Henderson, both representing borough towns. The latter did not think Jefferson should be so endorsed because he had allowed the navy to decline (a pet peeve of the Federalists against Jefferson), and had bought Louisiana which, Henderson thought, because of its vastness would lead to disunion. Gaston was opposed to any address at all, and on December 11 spoke against the proposal. He maintained that the language of the address was "better suited to the trembling slave who falls prostrate at the feet of his despot than to the legislature of a great, free, and independent state." The insulting clause directed toward his party he branded as "calumniating audacity which attributes to virtuous men villainous conduct." Two reasons were generally given by the proponents of the measure for its passage. One, that Jefferson was an illustrious character; the other, that since the incident of the two warships addresses had poured upon him from all sides. To these Gaston replied:

> I do not entertain this extravagant admiration. He possesses talents and virtues . . . something to approve and much to censure. . . . But is the legislature of North Carolina bound to address him because he is an illustrious man. . . . Shall we sit in judgement (as a legislature) upon the executive. *The national government was established by the people and not by the states.*[21]

His last argument was the favorite of the Federalists in their stand. They held that the legislature was not authorized as a constituent part of the union to sit in judgment on the conduct of the national executive and even if it were to have this right, it should be used with extreme caution and only in great emergency. During the course of this speech Gaston caused some stir in the House and throughout the town by stating that he was of "the proscribed sect of Federalists."

In a hurried note to his brother-in-law, Judge Taylor, concerning the stirring events of the day he spoke on this resolution:

> . . . Nothing of great interest here except Hamilton's resolution. After weeks he called it up and brought forward an amendment infinitely more exceptionable than original. Harris next day proposed an amendment; decent and moderate with no fault except that it contained a general approbation of the president's public conduct and particularly his behavior toward Great Britain. Friday a long debate on the two amendments. Then on motion made by me for papers stay on table indefinitely, and finally on Hamilton's resolution the fulsome address was finally carried, and Harris Resolution lost by six votes. Baker, Daniel, and Hamilton only Democrats who took part in behalf of violent proposition. Baker proposed one of his eccentric measures. Poor Baker shows mortification plainly, frets and complains that those "Federal lawyers will not let him do any good." Hamilton left House and went home.[22]

John R. Donnell, graduated from the University of North Carolina in 1807 at the age of sixteen with first honors, destined to be a wealthy lawyer and a well-known judge, had just arrived at New Bern to study law under Gaston, but found that his teacher had little time for him at this period. Donnell, writing to a friend, stated that he did not find New Bern a good place to study. He may not have cared too much about this or the prolonged absence of the teacher for he also reported that "the female society was good and rather inviting," but he "hoped to brave all attacks from that quarter." In this same letter, written shortly after the above-described debate, the seventeen year old Donnell said of Gaston, "I have heard it said that he was not very popular in the House, but must confess that I am highly pleased with his conduct as a Legislator. His speech against Hamilton's address to the President was such as would have done honor to a better cause. . . . "[23]

With many of the other legislators, Gaston took a hand in drawing up a resolution concerning the *Leopard-Chesapeake* affair. However, in his draft there was no praise of the president, but rather it expressed the indignation of the state and promised that North Carolinians were ready to make any sacrifice for the Union. Gaston preferred war over this incident to the subsequent embargo. However, neither his nor any other than Hamilton's was passed. The latter's resolution passed in the House by a vote of eighty-three to thirty-five; in the Senate its majority was thirty-six.[24] Naturally Gaston voted against it. There was a very lively discussion about it outside the assembly; the papers were full of the topic. The Edenton *Gazette* of January 20, 1808, and the Raleigh *Minerva* printed Gaston's as well as Henderson's entire speeches. The only other event of any moment at all during this session, according to Gaston, was the passage of the bill giving the superior courts concurrent jurisdiction. This was passed in the Senate by the casting vote of the speaker, and in the Commons by only a small vote.[25] Concerning this Gaston wrote an article for the *Minerva* in which he expressed his strong dislike for the "present system of county superior court." He wished to see it "improved and tolerable" as it was improbable it would be changed. Gaston held that the business of the courts was unequally divided between the county and the superior court, and wondered why judges should be sent all over the country with no business to do.[26] The courts were really in a mess, many lawyers were displeased with them, and not a few left the state because of them. In 1819 Gaston was to serve his state well by the new court system which went into effect then through his efforts.

While this earnest discussion was going on in North Carolina the Congress of the United States with little opposition passed Jefferson's Embargo, which had almost missed being tried because of the anger of the people over the *Chesapeake*. The following year was the fifth time the people were to go to the polls for a presidential election. Despite the Embargo the president still held control of his party and named his secretary of state, James Madison, as his successor. He would retire to become the "Sage of Monticello."

The Embargo was the main issue of the campaign. The news of the measure was received everywhere with mixed emotions. The seaports were hardest hit by it. Young Donnell's statement that the merchants of New Bern were a good deal ruffled over the Embargo was logical. Just after its passage in Congress he said, "We are in doubt concerning the cause of the Embargo. It is the opinion of many that we shall have a war with France; which opinion is corroborated by the declaration of Bonaparte that there shall be no neutrals."[27] So the town talked.

The state as a whole remained loyal to Jefferson, although North Carolina felt the pinch severely because of her dependence upon exports. The coastwise trade there was in just those articles proscribed; in fact almost the entire trade of the state was in those commodities. Special conditions differentiated it from the commerce of other states.[28] Although reports from the state were encouraging and affection for Jefferson strong, nothing prevented the North Carolinians from violating the measure. Colonel William Tatham of New Bern wrote Jefferson that the planters around the town were in a mood to tax themselves voluntarily for the benefit of injured commercial men, *if only the amounts could be justly ascertained*,[29] although the commercial men were generally opposed to the government. He said, "So far as I can judge the majority of our citizens in town are as loyal subjects to John Bull. . . . "[30] This was not only too strong but also rather hard on the townsmen and merchants who were now selling rice at nineteen cents a bushel which had before brought a dollar;

tar at forty-five cents a barrel which before had brought $1.75, with a like drop in other commodities.[31]

Gaston entered the campaign actively, running for the office of presidential elector in his district against General Bryan Whitfield. He announced his candidacy in a seventeen-page pamphlet devoted especially to the lack of qualifications of James Madison, and an attack on the Embargo. It was only after sixteen pages that the reader was informed for whom he would vote as president; his choice for the vice-presidency was not revealed.

He pointed out that the presidency had been held by different types of men but that every important measure proposed by them had been carried out. After damning Madison with faint praise, Gaston noted that although he was an excellent writer and theorist he would make a poor administrator. This prophecy concerning Madison and his administration was borne out by events. Finally, Gaston attacked the Embargo, Jefferson's administration, James Monroe, and the caucus method of nominating Madison. Charles C. Pinckney was the Federalist choice for the presidency.[32]

Gaston was answered in a pamphlet of forty-four pages signed "A Republican." In this the author states that Gaston's contentions were entirely the creatures of his own imagination; an acknowledgment of ignorance on the subject. He asked if it were true that British seamen were lured off their vessels. If this were so "it is a charge against the merchants of the United States, and to them we leave the settlement of the affair with Mr. Gaston."[33]

This "Republican" stated that Congress would not have passed nor Jefferson recommended laws which they foresaw would involve them in difficulties if it could have been avoided. He knew that if the Federalists raised the Embargo the country should have a French war, and so the Republicans were forced to choose between the two. That Madison was once a Federalist he branded as a most unfounded and imperious insinuation. On the whole, this reply was weak and contained several items of misinformation. The author proudly pointed to the fact that

Jefferson had saved three million dollars by reducing the army, navy, and other military appendages.[34] The time was not so far away when this economy was to become a bitter pill.

Another Republican, signing himself "Julius," in the Raleigh *Register* of October 20, 1808, denounced Gaston and "his seventeen pages of old hackneyed tales of Federalism." However, Gaston's address was widely circulated. From Washington E. B. Caldwell wrote that it was highly spoken of there. Some time before this he had asked Gaston if the latter would favor Monroe were a bargain made for a Federalist vice-president. Gaston indignantly repudiated the suggestion, and Caldwell admitted that it was "not honorable by intrigue to elect a president," nor did he think Monroe had a chance as he had so little talent.[35] There was, nevertheless, a very strong move in North Carolina to vote for Monroe and Clinton instead of Madison.

On November 11 eleven Madison electors were named to three Federalists. Gaston had won in the New Bern district by a majority of less than two hundred. The other Federalist districts were Fayetteville and Hillsborough. So on December 7 Madison and Clinton received eleven of North Carolina's votes while Pinckney and Rufus King had three. Since the vote of the Hillsborough district was disputed, the legislature of 1808, which convened soon after the electors were chosen, decided to investigate the matter, but Gaston who was again in the House representing New Bern, was able to prevent any action.[36]

However, in another strictly party measure Gaston was not so successful. The Republicans decided to send another address to the president, but wished to make it much stronger than the one of the previous year by not only condemning British conduct, but even by endorsing the Embargo. Gaston tried to substitute a weaker resolution expressing indignation over the violation of rights by belligerent powers, whose "naval way of war operated indirectly against themselves and directly against neutrals," and stating that the "legislature was prepared to support measures in vindication of national honor." However, his resolution was

Hannah McClure Gaston
Gaston's Second Wife

COURTESY OF MRS. GEO. VAUX

Wm. Gaston
Upon Graduation From Yale

BY JAMES PEALE
COURTESY OF MRS.
JAMES CROMWELL,
STAMFORD, CONN.

GASTON'S DAUGHTER, KATE
(*Daughter of Eliza Worthington*)

COURTESY MISS MARY G. HAWK

GASTON'S DAUGHTER, SUSAN
(*Daughter of Hannah McClure*)

COURTESY OF MRS. JAMES CROMWELL

allowed to lie on the table, while James Wellborn's was passed in the House by a vote of seventy-nine to twenty-nine. This legislature again refused to arm the militia properly.

Despite these party rancors Gaston was able to aid in bringing about some constructive legislation. On December 2, as chairman of the committee to inquire into the expediency of amending the law of descent, he reported a bill to effect this, which was then passed by the House and sent to the Senate. In his report Gaston stated that the various acts were replete with ambiguities, while certainty in this law was important. He believed that all this difficulty had arisen because the legislature had tried to define with minuteness the cases which might occur instead of laying down certain general principles. He thought only four rules were necessary to secure to the family the labor of the father, and read them into the bill. As chairman, he also reported in favor of a bill to make provisions for children born after the making of a father's will.[37] This, too, was passed in the House. Both these reforms were very dear to his heart, and he had averred their need several times in his arguments of cases before the courts on the very same issues. It was said that he was as proud of these laws as of any action of his entire career. During this session he attempted introduction of other bills to reform the superior courts; served on the committee to consider the governor's annual message; and was chairman of the committee on military land warrants.

December 16, the speaker, Joshua G. Wright, resigned, as he had been appointed a judge of the Superior Court of Law and Equity. Jesse Pearson proposed Gaston for the vacancy and the House unanimously concurred.[38] This was a personal triumph, a mark of his growing popularity in a House so strongly Republican. However, he held the speakership only a week, as the assembly adjourned December 23, after a month's session.

The next session, in 1809, was to be devoted to an entirely different issue, as the Embargo was repealed late in February and the much milder Non-Intercourse Act substituted, designed to stop commerce with England and France until they should remove their offending laws. Gaston was again representing the borough town of New Bern in the North Carolina House which convened November 20.

When the usual contest for the speakership took place Gaston was nominated by Daniel Glisson, while J. H. Bryan nominated Thomas Davis. The latter, a Republican, was elected by a vote of ninety-five to twenty-nine.

One of the minor events of the session was the attempt by Hugh C. Mills to unseat Jacob Henry, a Federalist, on the grounds that as he was a Jew his presence in the assembly violated that article of the state constitution which forbade anyone not believing in the truths of the Protestant religion to hold a state office. The entire day of December 6 was spent in consideration of this.[39] Besides himself, Henry's main support came from Gaston, who argued for religious liberty and tolerance. It has been said that Henry's able defense, one of the best ever heard in a state legislature in defense of religious liberty, was written by the learned Judge Taylor, Gaston's brother-in-law.[40] The motion to unseat Henry was lost.

The real fight in this session was over the banks, and such a fight it turned out to be that bloodshed was averted only by a thin margin. Banks were having their troubles in other states around this time; a couple years previously Henry Clay was having a hard fight in Kentucky to preserve that state's financial institution from destruction. North Carolina, alone of the thirteen states, had had no banks before 1804; in that year the assembly chartered two private banks, the Bank of Cape Fear at Wilmington and the New Bern Bank. These banks were in Federalist districts, with Federalist directors and shareholders. (Gaston had been just re-elected a director of the New Bern Bank early in January of 1809.)[41] An attempt made to establish a state bank in 1805 met with failure so these two remained for some years the only financial institutions of the state. There was some question of the soundness of their operations, so the Republicans decided upon closer regulation.

The bill introduced by William Drew of Halifax contained two important provisions; one to extinguish the old paper currency, the other to apply the interest from the stock North Carolina held in funds of the United States to redemption of the notes. The notes of the banks were to be taxed 2 per cent. Then W. W. Jones made a motion to strike out the part relating to the Bank of Cape Fear. Drew had spoken before on his measure, and had made some very cutting remarks about the bankers.

Jones made his motion on December 16 and the fireworks began. Gaston then rose to express his surprise at the motion. He maintained that "the miserable clamor against the New Bern Bank had no foundation but in ignorance and malignity"; that he perceived no reason for distinction between the two. He had not opposed the original act of Drew's because he thought all sections of the bill were either unconstitutional or unjust. However, as he represented the commercial town of New Bern and as he regarded the honor and interests of his constituents he should feel interested for the reputation of this institution. The New Bern Bank did not fear scrutiny.

Then Gaston referred to some remarks of Drew's. He charged him with being unacquainted with the subject, and having made assertions which had no foundation in fact. One of these statements was that the capital of the New Bern Bank was 50 per cent less than that of Cape Fear, while Gaston stated it was 100 per cent greater as New Bern's was $200,000 while Cape Fear's was but $100,000.

> He states the two banks act in concert. My own interest in the bank is not large but as a manager I can speak from *facts.* The gentleman from Halifax implied they acted in concert so the more effectually to injure the community. The only way the banks acted in concert was to receive the notes of the other on the same par as its own. . . .

> The gentleman stated the New Bern bank shaves its own notes . . . the facts were not so . . . repel with indignation that suggestion.

With some sarcasm he described the directors of the bank as men of honor to be compared even with the gentleman of Halifax. Thereupon, someone reminded him of the question, so he sat down. Drew asked the House if he or the gentleman from New Bern had wandered the most. He then stated he was well acquainted with banks and their directors, and believed them generally avaricious; although he had not said the Cape Fear Bank shaved notes, he had heard another bank did so. The only other bank was that of New Bern, so the insinuation was evident. Drew was called to order for becoming too personal.[42] Feeling ran high, tempers were on edge, so Jones made a motion to adjourn for the day on the plea the debate was too warm. His suggestion was wisely followed; the bill being in its second reading.

This took place on a Friday; the following Monday the debate took a less personal turn as the members were cooler. The reporter for the *Register* noted that "Mr. Gaston was back in his place today, after mutual explanations from the members of Halifax and New Bern for some warmth that had taken place last Friday."[43]

Gaston spoke again, but with moderation, more sense, and with real objections. He approved of the provision to redeem the paper money, asserting that if the sinking fund tax had been collected regularly no inconveniences would have been suffered. However, the second clause of the bill was not a good thing, for he thought the balance in the treasury was not more than sufficient to defray the expense of the government. If the $44,000, the interest of the stock, be diverted an additional tax would have to be laid to produce this from another source. The problem was in what manner the treasurer should redeem the paper currency in the banks. Gaston was in favor of the course recommended by the governor and treasurer and introduced a bill providing for it. This directed the treasurer to apply the dividends arising from the shares owned by the state in the two banks to the redemption of so much paper currency. By his bill the provision to appropriate the money of the state in the United States stock was struck out. Gaston's bill was agreed to in a vote of eighty-three to thirty-two.

Meanwhile the proposed tax of 2 per cent had been reduced to 1 per cent. Gaston stated that this was the first time such a proposition had been submitted to the legislature; that it was a breach of contract and invaded a principle of the Bill of Rights. He felt that the property of a corporation was not liable to any tax to which the property of natural persons was not liable and referred to several cases of such attempts in other states, notably Georgia and New Jersey. He thought such a tax had been declared illegal by the Federal Court. Had the fourteenth amendment been in effect then, he would have had no difficulty in making his point. Gaston contended that anyone could be stripped of his property by calling an act a tax, and asked what magic there was in the word. Defining tax, he stated this act was but a call on two corporations to pay the state certain money and so deprive them of part of their property.

> It may be said . . . this was done by the law of the land. Any act of the legislature comes under this. The law of the land means the *legal decision of a competent tribunal.* If the General Assembly has the power to invade property of individuals security is gone.

He finished his peroration by asking the state not to be so perfidious as to break its contract. If it did so by passing the bill in question, the state would receive 17 per cent in dividends while the shareholders got but 9 per cent.[44] He was listened to, and the proposal was dropped.

Gaston left the session early to be home with his wife who was not well. In the nine years of the new century he had been in the assembly five times, but in 1810 he decided to try for bigger game, the Congress of the United States. During the summer he began his campaign by scattering broadsides through the district.[45] His Republican opponent was William Blackledge, who had already served in Congress. Hannah, Gaston's wife, took an active interest in the campaign. While he was on court circuit she wrote him concerning the political picture. However, Blackledge defeated him by a majority of 480 votes; only three of the seven counties giving Gaston a majority. His own county, Craven, gave his opponent a majority of 249 votes.[46]

The Federalists were very much disappointed in Gaston's defeat. The congressional campaign of 1810 was especially violent as the nation was speeding toward the final break with England. The New Bern Federalist toast during this time was expressive: "The Freemen of New Bern District, may they by their suffrage on the 10th of August next, place William Gaston where he should be, in the councils of the nation; and again leave William Blackledge where he ought to be, in domestic retirement."[47] The bitterness of the time may be judged by the regret expressed by J. A. Cameron who wrote his brother, Duncan, that "with yourself, every rational man, everyone who regards the prosperity of the nation, must sincerely lament the issue of the New Bern election. When worth and talents such as Gaston's are postponed for the bloated ignorance, the arrogant presumption and the poisoned politics of Blackledge, well may the friends of order inquire into the dangers of their situation. . . . French politics have so far gained the ascendancy that the godly precepts of Washington are no longer remembered. . . . "[48]

So the usual cry of French influence rose against the Republicans. However, there is no question but that both parties had American interests first in mind, although each misjudged the other in their plans to carry out those interests. Both parties made extravagant statements about the other. Archibald Henderson told Gaston that the dismissal of the British minister Francis Jackson, for antiadministration activity and propaganda[49] would

COMMUNITY MASS Sunday 6/25/89

PROPER: Twelfth Sunday OT

INCENSE: Entrance/Offertory

GLORY: Yes

CREED: Yes

E.P.: III

PREFACE: Sundays

P.C.: Fr. Regis

A: Fr. John

B: Fr. Jerome

and must lead to war, and that no insult had been offered by Jackson. He felt it strange that the wise of the nation had been imposed on by the tale of British insult.[50] However, Jackson's recall was not only just but probably necessary in view of his policies. No self-respecting nation would have allowed him to remain. Henderson's observations could have little comforted either the rejected British minister or the defeated candidate.

In 1812 Gaston was back again in the assembly, this time in the Senate, having been elected by a majority of 135 votes.[51] The war with England was on and this was the presidential election year. One of the causes for conflict this year in the assembly came out of the new electoral law. The census of 1800 had given North Carolina credit for a population of 563,526, and it was expected that the decade would show an increase of about 85,000. However, the legislature would not meet before the presidential elections, so the state could not be redistricted. The Republican assembly of 1811 turned the coming election over to the following legislature. Gaston tried unsuccessfully to have this law declared evil in so many words so as to castigate the legislators responsible. The exact provisions of the new reapportionment act of Congress were not known until after the adjournment of the 1811 assembly, so the presidential electors would be chosen before the next meeting of the assembly. Under these conditions the assembly of 1812 acted as an electoral college and chose the electors. Although Gaston's attempt in the Senate to have this law specifically condemned met with failure, as did John Steele's in the House, it was repealed and the state laid out in new districts. The Republicans profited by the change; Gaston's attempt to gerrymander in favor of the Federalists had little chance of success.[52] Naturally under these conditions there was no presidential campaign. Gaston received letters from many outside the state on the outlook in North Carolina. The Committee of Federalists from New York wrote him for information on the chances in his state. Caldwell spoke of Marshall's chances. William Polk wanted to run Nathaniel Macon as vice-president the Federalist newspaper and carried Federalist speeches in full.

22. Gaston to Judge John Louis Taylor, Dec. 13, 1807, Gaston *MSS.*

23. John R. Donnell to A. D. Murphey, Jan. 3, 1808, W. H. Hoyt, *Papers of Archibald D. Murphey,* I, 16. Cited hereafter as *Murphey Papers.*

24. *House of Commons Journal, 1807,* pp. 40–42.

25. Gaston to Taylor, Dec. 13, 1807, Gaston *MSS.*

26. Raleigh *Minerva,* Dec. 31, 1807.

27. Donnell to Murphey, Jan. 8, 1808, *Murphey Papers,* I, 16.

28. Sears, *op. cit.,* p. 86.

29. *Ibid.,* p. 63. (Italics mine.)

30. *Ibid.,* p. 97. May 6, 1808.

31. *Ibid.,* p. 229. Quoted from *Minerva.* Lincoln County in Dec., 1808, petitioned Congress for relief from the bill.

32. *To the Freemen of the Counties of Wayne, Green, Lenoir, Jones, Craven and Carteret.* William Gaston. New Bern. Sept. 19, 1808, p. 17. The address also appeared in the Edenton *Gazette,* Oct. 13, 1808.

33. *Remarks on Mr. Gaston's Address to the Freemen of the Counties of Wayne . . . ,* Oct. 21, 1808, New Bern, p. 10. This pamphlet is signed: *A Republican.* The copy in the Library of Congress Rare Book Room is inscribed: Author Mr. Woods — a man of sound morals, opinions, principles. The Mr. Woods may have been Benjamin Woods of New Bern. The printers, Watson & Hall, were of New Bern.

34. *Ibid.,* p. 57.

35. E. B. Caldwell to Gaston, Nov. 26, 1808, Gaston *MSS.*

36. *House of Commons Journal, 1808,* p. 27.

37. *Ibid.,* p. 22.

38. *Ibid.,* p. 42.

39. Raleigh *Register,* Dec. 7, 1809.

40. See John H. Wheeler, *History of North Carolina,* II, 74, for this version and Gaston's part in it. Wheeler, a contemporary, who knew these men gives Taylor the credit for this speech of Henry.

41. Raleigh *Register,* Jan. 19, 1809.

42. Raleigh *Register,* Jan. 4, 1810.

43. Raleigh *Register,* Dec. 21, 1809. This was reported for Dec. 19, but was not printed until two days later. On this day a bare survey of the events was given; the debates were not printed until Jan. 4 and Jan 11, 1810.

44. Raleigh *Register,* Jan. 11, 1810.

45. The only copy of this broadside that I know of is in the hands of Dr. Archibald Henderson of the University of North Carolina.

46. Raleigh *Register,* Aug. 16, 23, 1810. The first date had incomplete returns, the latter gave the following:

*Return of Majorities:*

| *County* | Blackledge | Gaston |
|---|---|---|
| Johnson | 234 | . . . |
| Wayne | 64 | . . . |
| Lenoir | 275 | . . . |
| Green | . . . | 83 |
| Jones | . . . | 55 |
| Craven | 249 | . . . |
| Carteret | . . . | 204 |
| Majorities: Total | 822 | 342 |

Only two Federalists were elected; one of these was Jesse Pearson.

47. Gilpatrick, *op. cit.*, p. 177.

48. J. A. Cameron to Duncan Cameron, Aug. 27, 1810, Cameron Collection, University of North Carolina.

49. See Josephine Fisher, "Francis James Jackson and Newspaper Propaganda in the United States, 1809–1810," *Maryland Historical Review*, XXX, 93 ff.

50. A. Henderson to Gaston, March 7, 1810, Gaston *MSS*.

51. Gaston to A. D. Murphey, Aug. 16, 1812, *Murphey Papers*, I, 63.

52. *Senate Journal, 1812*, p. 28.

*The greatest of the great men of the War Congress was William Gaston. I myself came along after him.*
— DANIEL WEBSTER

*Mr. Gaston's conduct seems to me to be in the true spirit of an honest opposition . . . for it comports with the conduct of a good citizen.* — JOHN C. CALHOUN

# CHAPTER FOUR

# In the War Congress

THE War Hawks! There was more than mere romance in the appellation, for the men enrolled under this banner at last had gained control of the destiny of their nation. Mostly frontiersmen, impetuous, eager, and ready for a good scrap, these men were as young in years and spirit as their country. It was they, led by Henry Clay, who had forced the hesitant Madison into a declaration of war against England.

The disgrace of the Eleventh Congress had been forgotten by the action of its successor. The Eleventh Congress, composed largely of old Congressional troopers, with no program and little wish for one, had expended time in vain debate and puerile action. The most pressing issue before it had been that of finding a substitute for the discredited Non-Intercourse Act. Instead of taking any action against France and England for violating our neutral rights Congress wished only to exclude their warships from our waters. Attacked, reproached, and ridiculed, the legislators closed their session early in May of 1810. The country was so disgusted that in the next election Congress was placed under different leadership. Young men from such western states as Kentucky and Tennessee and other frontier districts, impatient to vindicate the honor of their country, lashed the people into a show of courage. Leadership of the Republican party passed from the executive and his officers into the hands of Congress. Federalist leaders and editors raved against the "young hot-headed Westerners," who seemed to desire nothing more than an invasion and annexation of Canada. Besides this accusation it was charged that the war hawks would withhold the nomination from Madison if he did not give them war. With these powerful forces at work Madison had little chance, and it was a matter of surprise to no one when on June 18, 1812, he signed the act to set in motion the "Second War of Independence," sometimes also known as "Mr. Clay's War." Madison called the Thirteenth Congress to meet in a special session on May 24, 1813, after finding that the previous Congress had not taken adequate action to carry on the war.

In North Carolina the elections for this War Congress were bitterly contested.[1] Gaston was elected over William Blackledge to represent the fourth Congressional district of North Carolina, which included Wayne, Greene, Lenoir, Jones, Carteret, and Craven counties. Blackledge had at first declined to run, but finally entered the contest a few days before the election.[2] Gaston, like Federalists all over the country, conducted his campaign upon an antiwar basis. In a pamphlet distributed over the district he told his readers that America had cause for complaint against both France and England. He felt we were forbidden by our own interest to fight England; that from a continuance of the war we had nothing to hope for, but everything to fear, for all trade would be destroyed except that permitted by the enemy. He did not believe that seamen's rights would be protected by an invasion of Canada, although he would continue to prosecute the war to obtain freedom from impressment if it were necessary to do so. By inference Jefferson was brought into the general condemnation of the administration with the remark that " . . . the gallant little navy — remnant of a sounder policy — was only slighted until it fought its way into notice."[3]

Gaston's colleagues from North Carolina were the veteran

Nathaniel Macon; William R. King, who later became a vice-president; Willis Alston, best known as an object of John Randolph's wrath; John Culpepper, described by William B. Grove as good for nothing except logrolling; the brilliant lawyer, Barlett Yancey; Peter Forney, Meshack Franklin, William H. Murfree, Israel Pickens, Joseph Pearson, William Kennedy, and Richard Stanford. The last four supported Federalist policies.

In general this Congress was made up of men not only younger than those who had usually been sent, but also more active, more able, and more spirited. Both sides of the House were represented by some of the finest intellects in the country. The administration had a workable majority, 114 Republicans to 68 Federalists. One of the Republicans, Charles J. Ingersoll of Pennsylvania, who was to be an influential chairman of the House Committee on Foreign Affairs under Tyler and Polk, stated that "the division of parties was so intense there was little personal intercourse among many members of opposite sides. The Federalists and Republicans did not sit together, except a few Republicans overflowing among the Federalists, occupying the speaker's left . . . and debate ran high." Young Henry Clay of Kentucky, known to his ardent followers as "Harry of the West," was immediately elected speaker. Autocratic and bold, clever but not learned, charming although impetuous, the tall, thin, gray-eyed, plain Clay was more likely to be governed by emotion than reason. Second only to him was the profound, logical, and dynamic John C. Calhoun of South Carolina. A gentleman by every mark, he was fierce in debate although never personal nor offensive. Other remarkable Republicans included Langdon Cheves, later speaker of the House and then president of the second bank of the United States; William Lowndes of South Carolina; George Troup; and John Forsyth, who was to be Andrew Jackson's secretary of state.

Among the Federalists was "Black Dan" Webster, there for the first time, who found his seat marked for him by a friend "in good company." This company included William Gaston, who sat on Webster's right,[4] Alexander C. Hanson, caustic editor of the *Federal Republican,* who had been severely injured by a Baltimore mob in an attack upon his offices incited by his pro-British policies, Joseph Pearson of North Carolina, and Thomas Grosvenor of New York.

Gaston arrived at the capital by May 24, making the journey by mail coach, gig, and horseback, traveling for days through the lonely forests. His disagreeable trip over the bad roads was made even more hazardous by heavy rains.[5] His young family remained in New Bern as Mrs. Gaston had the three babies to care for, and was expecting another in a few weeks. Few of the congressmen brought their wives with them. Washington, "the city of magnificent distances," was not a very agreeable place in which to live. It was a dismal place, with a few shanties, uncompleted public buildings, endless stretches of mud with no sidewalks. Its population was but a fraction over five thousand. The president's house had been completed only in 1809. The north and south wings of the capitol were in use by 1813, but the space between, the future dome, was only roughly boarded over. Three hotels in its neighborhood were all the capital could boast. Gaston, like most of the congressmen, lived in a boarding-house. Social life was not too lively, even outside of wartime. The population momentarily expected to see the British, for Admiral Cockburn had come up Chesapeake Bay but a short time before to burn Havre de Grace.

This was Gaston's first extended sojourn away from his family. He was naturally lonely for them, although his wife wrote him as often as she could, telling him of their daily life and concern for his welfare. Each letter contained news of the children, such as the following:

> The little plagues . . . answering their questions to Ma . . . but they are well and speak constantly of you. . . . They were abusing George for keeping the horses away so long. . . . They are my best companions. . . . Margaret has had several crying spells when she thinks she sees you and then is not

noticed. Alexander is reading and Susan wants some muslin, a new frock and a book. . . . Don't forget to get a large trunk. . . . I both wish and dread your absence at a certain time, for I have more uneasiness than I ever had before at the approach of a like event. . . . [6]

In this first session Gaston was appointed to serve on several relatively unimportant committees. He actively entered the first clash occurring between the two parties on the floor. George Richards, reporter for Hanson's *Federal Republican,* had been excluded from the floor of the House by Speaker Clay, who stated that as there was room for only four reporters he had assigned those in order of seniority. Three of these wrote for Republican papers, and the one employed by the Federalist newspaper did not write out the debates.[7] Robert Wright of Maryland supported Clay with the sneering remark that the *Federal Republican* was in the British pay anyway. This caused the excitable Hanson to indulge in some very plain language. During the course of the affair Hanson invited Wright to an exchange of shots. The subject then was taken from Clay's control and given to the committee of the whole. This was the occasion of Gaston's maiden speech in Congress, and marked his first brush with Clay and Calhoun. In this he said:

> . . . The subject is worthy of every attention because it is intimately connected with the first principles of a Republican government, freedom of discussion and publicity of proceedings. Majorities are frequently tempted to exercise their powers with a high hand. Minorities always suspect them of a disposition to oppress. . . . Forbearance on the one hand will inspire courtesy on the other . . . and a spirit of generous contest will forbid all unnecessary altercations or wanton opposition.[8]

After Calhoun had given his opinion Gaston rose again to examine the arguments of the gentleman from South Carolina, which he declared to be "pervaded with fallacy as Mr. Calhoun had not exercised his usual critical acumen." Although the committee of the whole voted to exclude Richards, a select committee, of which Gaston was a member, was appointed to investigate the matter and arrangements were then made to accommodate more reporters in the galleries instead of on the floor.

When this trivial matter was disposed of, the Federalists moved to attack their opponents in a more serious way. The duke of Bassano, the French minister of foreign affairs, had stated that Napoleon's revocation of the Decrees of Berlin and Milan had been sent to their minister in Washington to be transmitted to the State Department. The Federalists suspected that the president had received but suppressed this important information. Therefore, on June 10, Webster submitted resolutions calling for papers upon the subject. This brought on a very fierce debate. On June 18 Gaston entered the fray.

The ugly, acid-tongued Felix Grundy of Tennessee had accused the Federalists of being in favor of the enemy. Gaston disliked Grundy, and felt that his remarks upon this occasion were directed at himself. He told Grundy that the bare supposition was untrue, and then turning to the House, remarked that this gentleman reminded him of the animal that muddies the water through which it glides, thus finding safety in the confusion. With flashing eyes he continued:

> It will not be deemed egotism, I trust, to add, that baptized an American in the blood of a martyred father; bound to my native land by every moral and natural tie that can fasten on the heart of man; with not one motive of interest, of passion, or prejudice to seduce the loyalty of my affections; never can I separate myself from the cause of my country, however that cause may have been betrayed by those to whose care it was confided.[9]

He maintained that a shameful fraud upon the people had been somewhere perpetrated by the declaration of war; that although the character of the government needed no protection, a determination to believe everything right connected with authority and so to applaud without examination was characteristic of folly and servility. Thereupon, he discussed the general question of the decrees and their operation upon this country. He felt that the duke of Bassano's assertion was false, and that the president was guilty of no wrong action. The Republicans soon realized that the inquiry could not be stifled, so the resolution went to the president. It was found that the suspicions of the Federalists were unfounded, for the first intimation this government had had of the revocation came some weeks after the declaration of war. Gaston's speech was well received not only in his own district but throughout the country. A newspaper of Raleigh noted that the quotation of Gaston's given above had been used by an orator on July 4 at Princeton, and stated that "this expression which suits well the whole American people has peculiar propriety and force in the mouth of this accomplished statesman and orator."[10] The talented, eccentric John Randolph of Roanoke, speaking to Francis Scott Key of it said, "I am much pleased with Mr. Gaston's speech on Webster's motion. Chief Justice Marshall had taught me to think highly of his abilities; and my expectations, altho raised, have not been disappointed."[11] During the remainder of this session Gaston spoke on a few other minor matters, but before its adjournment on August 2, 1813, urgent necessity called him home.

The British had carried the war into North Carolina. Near the coast, New Bern was felt to be too open to the enemy, so in May the bank removed its specie, amounting to $80,000 to Raleigh. The town also made some attempt to construct defenses in case of attack.

On July 13 the long-awaited invasion became a reality, for on that Monday evening word was passed swiftly from house to house that the British were once more marching on New Bern. A hurried knock, excited speech, scampering feet, and dismay spread over the town. Mrs. Gaston was visiting a neighbor, the Dunns, when the news reached her, "communicated in an improper manner," and she immediately hurried home. She became more and more nervous as the long evening passed, so that around eight o'clock she was seized with violent convulsions. The family physician, Dr. Peter Custis, was called, but they could not be stopped, and at three o'clock in the morning she died, taking with her the unborn child whose advent she had so dreaded. John Donnell took the remaining three children to Gaston's sister in Raleigh.[12] That same day Gaston was speaking in Congress on the necessity of having a fixed date to hear the report on foreign relations. He was still in Congress on July 19, as the news had not yet reached him. The enemy had actually never reached New Bern. A small naval force had appeared in Ocracock Bay, seized a few men, and cleared the surrounding countryside of livestock.[13] Before the end of the month Gaston was in Raleigh, from which he soon returned sadly to his own home, there to remain until the next session of Congress that winter. Four days before the death of Hannah, Alexander had written his first letter to his father, asking him to bring home some "white allies and some marbles," and telling him that he had things "put away for you to go a gunning with your own affectionate son." But it was a lonely summer as he rode over the plantation.

With the exception of the debate on Webster's resolutions there had been little action in this first session as the two parties were feeling each other out. By the beginning of the second session, which convened on December 6, the individual members possessed better knowledge of one another's personalities and qualities. From then on Gaston became the leader of the Federalists in the House. Of him Charles Ingersoll said, "Mr. Gaston, an handsome man of pleasing address and speech . . . was one of the ablest and most pleasing speakers of the House, a leading member of the opposition."[14] Ingersoll stated that Webster during this Congress did not make any of the great speeches on which his reputation rose. George Ticknor in 1815 declared that Webster had been in Congress only two years but "was already among its foremost men, and stood with Gaston and Hanson to lead opposition in debate, on the floor of the Lower House."[15]

As the congressmen returned to their post the state of the nation was cause for grief. With the exception of Oliver Hazard Perry's naval victory on Lake Erie the American arms had suffered heavily. Hull, Van Rennsselaer, Smyth, and Dearborn were defeated by the British in a series of shameful fiascoes unequaled in our annals for military incompetency. Gaston voted with the majority to inquire into the causes of the failure of American arms. During the rest of the year the session was uneventful.

However, at the very beginning of 1814 Gaston rose to speak in favor of an amendment to the Constitution which had been introduced by Pickens of North Carolina. It owed its origin to the action of the state legislature which in the last presidential election had given the task of choosing electors to the succeeding legislature. The proposed amendment directed a uniform method of appointing the electors throughout the country. Gaston felt that by this mode the voice of the people of the Union would be fairly expressed and fully felt; that when each state was made to throw all its votes in one scale there was no evidence of the sanction of the majority, for when electors were chosen by states the minority in each state was without weight. He objected to nomination through congressional caucuses made by the very men the Constitution specifically forbade to take such action, members of Congress.

He disliked the idea of a few leaders directing all things, for then pre-existing bodies of men and not the people made the appointment. He stated that our government partook both of the national and federative forms; that state attachment must continue but must not swallow up all attachment to the general government. He felt that were the amendment to pass it would not put an end to all cabal, intrigue, and corruption, for states might endanger the perpetuity of the confederacy by their combinations or by their quarrels, but those dangers would be stripped of half their terror when citizens felt they had a common country and were linked together by the strongest bonds of connection, brought about by the election of a president by the majority of all the people.

His intense love of the Union and Constitution, which was strong and energetic throughout life is seen in every line of this speech, in which he said:

> There breathes not a man who views the sacred character of the Federal Union with more reverence than myself. No one can more sincerely or ardently deprecate any innovation on its principles. However, this is not to introduce new, but to invigorate old; to rescue it from abuse and perversion. . . . Nothing can contribute more effectually to the permanence and stability of any institution than that its essential forms should be stable. Time and customs have an effect upon opinions and feelings which render them distinctive and characteristic. It is the part of political wisdom to strengthen and create the union between affections of people and the forms of their government. You so consecrate these forms in their estimation and establish a solid basis on which government rests.[16]

After a fierce debate in the Committee of the Whole the proposal was voted down. During the second session of the next Congress, on December 18, 1816, he tried again to have this passed. With true statesmanship he questioned the wisdom of renouncing the benefits of experience in respect to the Constitution, saying, "Shall the beacon of practical experience be in vain? Such was not the design of the framers. They were aware that time would manifest defects in it which could not be foreseen, and provided for them."[17] However, nothing was done at this time either about the question.

On January 18, 1814, Gaston presented a resolution to the effect that "pending the negotiations with Great Britain it is inexpedient to prosecute military operations against the Canadians for invasion or conquest," for he felt that the cause of humanity forbade what he expected would be a useless effusion of blood. His resolution was voted down.

In most of these debates the Republicans had been able to control matters much as it pleased them; whenever they tired of listening the Federalists were silenced. In February a new loan bill came up and by the rules of the House it had to be discussed in the Committee of the Whole, at which time discussion could not be stifled. The Federalists determined to take advantage of this situation by covering every subject not hitherto allowed in general debate. Webster wrote his brother that "on the loan bill we hope to get a blow at them . . . Gaston and Grosvenor are prepared to give great speeches on the subject."[18]

Following a very vicious attack on the Federalists by Grundy, Gaston began his "blow" at the administration. He claimed that the old Federalist Alien and Sedition Acts were grossly misrepresented; that the idea of punishing truth when published against the officers of the government was reserved until more recent times, "until the abused acts had expired and the champions of a free press were safely in power." As proof of this charge he cited the case of a certain Harry Croswell, who had been jailed during the Jefferson administration.

Gaston maintained that if the desired loan of twenty-five million dollars was necessary for the honor or welfare of the country, it would meet with no opposition from him, but that considerations of humanity, justice, and national policy objected to an invasion of Canada. He contradicted Calhoun's statement that the war was one of defense, saying, "so fatal is war to the best interests of the human family that a tremendous responsibility always rests upon the nation that commences it." Throughout the speech he claimed that the war was not waged because of seamen's rights but rather for the conquest of Canada. He asked the war hawks what could be done with Canada if it were taken, for he doubted that the slaveholding states would allow it to be incorporated into the Union. He stated that there was not one impressed seaman from North Carolina, and that their number in general had been greatly exaggerated. Warning his hearers that England would never give up any of her maritime rights because of her jealousy of us he directed attention to what has always been the central feature of British policy with these words, "were Canada a thousand times more important to Britain than it is, it were yet of less value than her naval power. For the sake of it she would never yield a principle on which that naval power depends." Noting the avidity of the Westerners for the possession of Canada he said:

> It is a very different question whether the Canadians have armed the Indians to join in a defense against a common invader, or had, previously to war, instigated them to hostilities against us. There is no evidence of this last charge. Over the affair of Tippecanoe, the commencement of the Indian war, there hovers a mystery which ought to be dissipated, but which the Government will not dispel. I have honestly sought for information. From private sources, friendly to this war and connected with the Western feeling and interest, I learn the great cause is to be found in our cupidity for their lands, and their jealousy and distrust of our superior intelligence and force. General Harrison's treaty of 1809 was the mine of the great Indian explosion. . . . [19]

It took Gaston two days to finish his passionate denunciation, but this was nothing as the floodgates of oratory were now open in the hall of the House. The administration paper, the *National Intelligencer* said that "every sentence is interesting, every word important as the best speakers on both sides are engaged, and neither spares the other."[20] The debate on this bill brought almost everyone who could at least stammer into the fray. Macon wrote a friend that "it was as much improved as ever I knew one, especially the speeches of some of the Feds, of whom I took notes. . . . I find some of the Republicans pretty warm this morning and a little violent."[21]

The Republicans had been hard hit by some of the shafts

aimed by their opponents and several revealed that these wounds hurt. Gaston drew the fire of many. John Forysth voiced their annoyance when he said:

> Mr. Gaston has recommended moderation, liberality, and forbearance, but he has not given us an example. He has not shown either that moderation or liberality. His language is correct, gentlemanly and polished. No harsh terms deform the smoothness of his periods. It matters not, though, whether the victim is struck down by the butcher's cleaver or a glittering Spanish blade.

Forysth's remarks had aroused the anger of Gaston, who at the close of the day's session sent the Georgian a stiff note to inquire if there had been any personal meaning in his words. Among the different messes throughout the capital ran the rumor of an impending duel. The next day Forysth returned his answer, declaring that Gaston could think as he pleased about the affair.[22] Friends intervened then and nothing came of the exchange. In the meantime Calhoun had noted the storm and sought to soothe Gaston's ruffled feelings with these words:

> Mr. Gaston's conduct seems to me to be in the true spirit of an honest opposition. . . . It is thus we may divide among ourselves and the national strength not be impaired . . . for it comports with the conduct of a good citizen.[23]

Calhoun went on to say that Gaston had claimed that Congress had become merely a registering body for the executive and that this was untrue in fact. Gaston leaped to his feet at these words and hotly denied that he had used such a term. Then in ominous calm he turned to the South Carolinian and in cold, measured tones "of unmistakable significance" demanded to know in what sense he had used the term "untrue." The House grew strangely quiet as its members watched this prelude to a duel. However, all relaxed as Calhoun quietly answered that he had meant the fact was not as Gaston had stated it, for he had too much respect for him to have an allusion to any other sense. This incident did not disturb the friendly relations existing between the two men.

A few days later the *National Intelligencer* stated that "we regret we cannot conclude Mr. Gaston's speech on the Loan Bill . . . from which we will not withhold the meed of plausibility and ingenuity, although we deny the claims of the orator to correctness."[24] This bare statement has a sequel told by the editor's wife. She states that the Republicans feared the speech might do some injury, and therefore it was not published in their paper. The Federalists regarded it with much favor and various ones called upon the author with the request he write it out for the *Federal Republican.* Finally Webster came to him and would take no denial. When Gaston complained of weak eyes Webster said, "That shall be no obstacle. I will act as your amanuensis; walk across the floor, and I will write as you dictate." With no excuse now Gaston started to pace across the floor as Webster sat at the desk writing furiously. He had barely started, though, when Webster interrupted him with the cry, repeated again and again before the finish, "Gaston, won't one of those words do? I make it a rule never to use two words when one will answer as well."[25] Among other Federalists, Abijah Bigelow wrote his wife that there had been many good speeches on this occasion, but none which better suited his taste than Mr. Gaston's.[26]

One of the first acts of this Congress had been a new Embargo, at the urging of Madison, covering the coastwise trade of the country, and forbidding commerce by water even between ports of the same state. In March Gaston asked that this be repealed as it was very hard on the people of his section. He felt that the collection of the war taxes from the farmers would be practically impossible since the Embargo was keeping them from their market. Although his motion was negatived by a vote of 86 to 58, the president soon afterward called for the Embargo's repeal as it was seen to be unprofitable and unworkable. With no other choice it was repealed by a decisive vote. The situation thus created is described in an amusing manner by Macon:

> I have not for a long time seen the feds look in so good a humor, they have all a smile on their countenance and look at each other as if they were the men which had brought this great and good work about, in fact, that they are the wise men not only of this nation, but of the world; the Republicans have not the most pleasing countenance.[27]

A few days later the session came to a close. Gaston addressed a circular to his constituency, in which he claimed that no one had believed the capture of Canada possible and complaining that the majority had given his resolution to stop the war no consideration at all.[28] He then returned to New Bern to spend an uneventful summer, except for a trip to Raleigh and to the university at Chapel Hill. An intended trip to Tennessee had to be postponed because of the confusion of his own financial affairs. The loss of his wife made the summer a lonely one, and the disasters suffered by the nation did not lighten his gloom.

The fall of Napoleon had allowed England to devote all her resources to America. Most of the seaports were blockaded; many of the legislatures and governorships in New England were in the control of the Federalists who did not support the war; the currency was in a state of disorder; the loan voted by Congress failed; and finally the administration was becoming panic stricken. In August the crowning misfortune came to pass; British regulars landed in Maryland, overwhelmed the Americans at the battle of Bladensburg, and with little resistance marched into Washington, burning the Capitol and other public buildings.

In the meanwhile President Madison had called an emergency session of Congress to meet in September, confessing that the treasury was practically bankrupt. Washington had never been such as to gladden the vision of any beholder, but the sight of the burned city that met Gaston on his return was more than ever doleful. For the next few days he wandered among the ruins. The only place that could be found for Congress to meet was an old ramshackle building on Seventh Street. What stories this unpretentious shelter could have told! It might have sighed over memories of old friends, of births and deaths, for it had been a boardinghouse; it could have told tales of lust and greed, of laughter and sorrow, for it had been a tavern; it might have spoken of its plays that had aroused the emotions of the great and humble of the city, for it had been a theater; it would have uttered with awe the names of far-distant places and of every strange thing under the sun, for it had last housed the General Post Office and Patent Office. The only suitable room that could be given the Lower House was so small that not all members could have desks. Yet every spot was used to advantage, even the window ledges and the fireplace. Naturally, all were very uncomfortable. They began their deliberations by seeking to place responsibility for the capture of the city. Gaston thought the inquiry should be made general instead of confining it to particular details, but this the administration would avoid at all costs.

Gaston was appointed to several committees, the most important being that on Ways and Means. When certain Federalists tried to annoy the administration by a proposal to remove the capital, Gaston not only voted against the measure but vigorously opposed the move as he thought it would involve both individual injustice and public mischief.[29] During December he made a few short speeches against a measure for military conscription which the administration in vain tried to pass. On January 27, 1815, he presented a petition of the president and directors of Georgetown College asking for authority to confer the usual degrees.[30] On February 4 such a bill was reported, read three times, and passed. Gaston, the first student of the college, was thus given the honor of obtaining its charter from Congress.

Meanwhile, the president's plea for funds was meeting almost the same fate as that for men. Congress simply did not know how to meet the situation, so little was done outside of inane bickering. Gaston feared that things were coming to a crisis and advised friends to free themselves of debt so they might have enough to live on.[31] The original bank of the United States, organized by Alexander Hamilton, had not been rechartered in 1811.

The bill which was proposed by the administration would have established a "paper money" bank, with a capital of fifty million dollars, and by its terms the bank was to be controlled by the government. It was sponsored by the secretary of the treasury, Alexander J. Dallas, who did everything possible to insure its passage. During the course of this session as well as in the next Congress Gaston spoke several times on the question, and also served on the committees considering the bill. He objected to several features of the first bill as he felt that the bank should have the confidence of the people. However, he claimed all elements of its formation under the discussed plan would excite distrust. He objected to the extent of the capital, the limited proportion of the specie and the power of the president to suspend even that limited amount. He stated that the plan amounted to mere stock jobbery, that "to revive public credit by imparting an extraneous value to stock seems about as wise as to restore health by an artificial coloring of the cheek." In January it was brought to a vote in the House, where the roll call revealed 81 in favor and 80 against the bill. Langdon Cheves, now speaker, after explaining his action in a few words, cast his vote in the negative. Thus the bill was lost by a tie vote.

On January 21 John Eppes, the son-in-law of Jefferson, read a letter of Secretary Dallas to the House. The Democrats were dismayed at its final revelation of national bankruptcy. Eppes read it with growing bitterness and chagrin to the attentive House, and when he had finished threw it down upon his table with a violence all too eloquent of its meaning. Then he turned to Gaston and said, "Well, sir! will your party take the government if we give it to them?"

"No, sir!" replied Gaston in earnest tones, "No, sir! Not unless you will give it to us as we gave it to you."[32]

However, the Federalists did help to draw up another bill for a bank, which passed both Houses only to be vetoed by President Madison. Another designed to meet his objections was introduced, but news of the Treaty of Ghent reached these shores in

February, interfering with the debates to such an extent that nothing was accomplished when the session came to an end on March 3, 1815.

Reviewing his congressional policy for the people back home Gaston pointed out that in the treaty of peace there had been no mention of impressment, and that the nation was not even restored to the state existing before then, as the fisheries were lost; while the national debt had increased from $45,154,189 to $125,688,305.[33] The following June he announced his candidacy for re-election in a circular which contained a note of apology. In this he stated that he could not have hoped to give universal satisfaction or to escape error, as his position had been difficult and embarrassing.[34] However, he was a "man whose abilities so commended themselves to all factions that he was re-elected . . . without opposition." The Raleigh *Register* of August 18, 1815, reported that Gaston had received 2,900 votes.

Gaston took his place in the fourteenth Congress on December 5, 1815. He was again appointed to the Committee of Ways and Means. Once more the nation had sent to the House some of its most talented men. Among these were William Pinkney of Maryland and Joseph Hopkinson of Pennsylvania, two of the foremost lawyers of America. The latter soon became a firm and lasting friend of Gaston. Clay who had served as one of the commissioners negotiating the treaty with Great Britain, once more occupied the speaker's chair. Congress met this time in a plain brick building on the corner of A and First Street, N.E., which had been erected during the summer and leased to the government as a temporary headquarters.

With the end of the war the Federalists were deprived of their main issue, and there was little excitement during debate. The foremost problems concerned questions of currency and tariff, and these were discussed on their merits as economic measures. Nor was Gaston as active for he confined himself to short speeches. When Tennessee tried to obtain from Congress a preference for her citizens in establishing claims to pre-emption rights in that state, Gaston reminded them that in making the cession North Carolina had done so on the condition that no such action would be taken.[35] He became involved in a quarrel with Clay over an interpretation of the treaty, during which he stated that if a certain law desired by the latter were passed it would cause a conflict between the legislative and judicial branches of the government. He denied that his contention supposed a supremacy of the power to make treaties over the power to enact laws. He opposed internal improvements "as the Government was confederated for certain general objects and ought to leave these improvements to the municipal regulation of states,"[36] and spoke against the appropriation for the Cumberland Road. He spoke for about an hour in opposition to the act introduced to protect "infant industry," but this tariff act received the support of Calhoun and Lowndes.[37] During the height of the tariff controversy in Jackson's time he was proudly to point to his opposition to this original protective tariff bill. He assisted in drawing up a more satisfactory bill for a national bank.

During this session, he voted against the measure for raising the pay of congressmen from $6 a day to $1,500 a year. Practically the entire body of North Carolinians voted against this bill. Although it passed there was such an outcry against it that the next Congress repealed the so-called "Salary Grab." Gaston's most important action during this Congress was his famous speech on the "Previous Question," delivered on January 19, 1816. This was a device by which the majority could call for an immediate vote on a measure, and so automatically cut off debate on that subject.

A short time before, Speaker Clay had defended this procedure and Gaston began by declaring that if this gentleman's ingenuity and zeal combined could form no other defense than the one the House had just heard, it was clear that the "Previous Question" could not be defended. It invested power in the majority to forbid a member to speak, but could only be admitted when demanded by a majority of members present.

> Liberty of speech is here in its Citadel. Yet even here it is to be strangled. The delegation of sovereignty was not the revocable, precarious, grants of a courteous majority. Can it be that the people selected as guardians of their rights those who should have no right to assert them?

Gaston then gave a long and detailed history of this procedure. He proved that no sanction had been given this custom by British tradition, for in England the House of Commons had deprived no member of the right to amend the main question. It was, he caustically observed, reserved for us in this age of illumination and in this freest of all free governments to adopt a rule which sets common sense at defiance and prohibits the exercise of an undoubted parliamentary right. With earnestness he concluded:

> Dispatch in lawmaking is inconsistent with deliberative freedom. Five times in the course of the last session "necessity" for speedy legislation forced the previous question. Yet so purely imaginative was this that no legislation took place upon them.[38]

Gaston's study of the question had been careful, detailed, and scholarly, and with no warning Clay had been caught so unprepared that he was unable to form an answer. This so mortified and enraged the Kentuckian that it was long years before he again spoke to Gaston. More than twenty years later William W. Seaton, friend of both, arranged a meeting.[39]

## NOTES FOR CHAPTER FOUR

1. *Murphey Papers,* I, 68. Stanford and his opponent, Mebane, spent a week in Raleigh, "electioneering with all their might."
2. Raleigh *Register,* May 7, 1813.
3. *Circular to the Freemen of Wayne . . . ,* March 15, 1813. New Bern.
4. Claude M. Fuess, *Daniel Webster,* I, 152.
5. Mrs. Hannah Gaston to Gaston, May 18, 1813, Gaston *MSS.*
6. Mrs. Hannah Gaston to Gaston, May 10, 31, July 5, 1813. Gaston *MSS.* On the letter from his wife, Hannah, dated May 10, William Gaston has written the following: "After her dear Mother's death she was baptized

by name of Hannah Margaret." He is referring to their second daughter, who had been called Margaret before this event. On writing to Donnell on Aug. 7 he stated that only his faith in the revealed truths bore him up, and that his wife was no sufferer from their separation.

7. *Annals of Congress. Debates and Proceedings,* Thirteenth Cong., first sess., p. 111. Cited hereafter as *Annals.*

8. *Ibid.,* p. 119.

9. *Ibid.,* p. 239.

10. Raleigh *Star,* Sept. 3, 1813.

11. Hugh A. Garland, *Life of John Randoph of Roanoke,* II, 17. Randolph to Francis Scott Key, July 17, 1813.

12. Peter Custis to Gaston, July 16, 1813; John Donnell to Gaston, July 13, 1813. Gaston *MSS.*

13. *National Intelligencer,* July 22, 24, 1813.

14. Charles J. Ingersoll, *Historical Sketch of the Second War Between the United States of America and Great Britain,* p. 207.

15. Fuess, *op. cit.,* I, 178.

16. *Annals,* Thirteenth Cong., second sess., pp. 835–844.

17. *Ibid.,* Fourteenth Cong., second sess., p. 334.

18. Webster to Ezekiel Webster, Feb. 15, 1814, *The Writings and Speeches of Daniel Webster,* XVII, 240 (National Edition).

19. *Annals,* Thirteenth Cong., second sess., p. 1570.

20. *National Intelligencer,* Jan. 17, 1814.

21. Macon to Nicholson, March 3, 1814, Nicholson *MSS.*

22. John Forysth to Gaston, Feb. 24, 1814, Gaston *MSS.*

23. *Annals,* Thirteenth Cong., second sess., p. 1691.

24. *National Intelligencer,* March 16, 1814.

25. Josephine Seaton, *Life of William W. Seaton,* p. 300.

26. "Letters of Abijah Bigelow," *American Antiquarian Society Proceedings,* n.s., XL, p. 381.

27. Macon to Nicholson, April 5, 1814, Nicholson *MSS.*

28. *Circular* . . . , April 19, 1814, Washington.

29. Gaston to John Burgwin, Sept. 28, 1814, Gaston *MSS.*

30. *Annals,* Thirteenth Cong., third sess., p. 1106.

31. Gaston to John Burgwin, Sept. 28, 1814, Gaston *MSS.*

32. Eliot & Hillard, ed., *Life, Letters, and Journal of George Ticknor,* I, 31.

33. *Circular* . . . , March 1, 1815, Washington.

34. *Circular* . . . , June 12, 1815, New Bern.

35. *Annals,* Fourteenth Cong., first sess., p. 394 (Dec. 21, 1815).

36. *Ibid.,* p. 871.

37. *Ibid.,* p. 1313.

38. *Ibid.*, pp. 699–718. Years later James Kent, chancellor of New York, concerning it said to Gaston, "I have found your speech on the Previous Question in one of the volumes of my pamphlets. . . . I have read it again this morning and permit me to say it is a masterly and conclusive law and constitutional argument, with the most diligent examination and keen critical analysis of the documentary authorities. It is an admirable production. I put a value upon the volume above all price. . . . " Kent to Gaston, Nov. 14, 1833, Gaston *MSS*. This speech has been published in the *Congressional Globe* in our own time.

39. Seaton, *op. cit.*, p. 295.

CHIEF JUSTICE JOHN L. TAYLOR

COURTESY NORTH CAROLINA DEPARTMENT
OF ARCHIVES AND HISTORY, RALEIGH

GASTON'S LAW OFFICE IN RALEIGH

PAINTING BY JACQUES BUSBEE
COURTESY OF MRS. GEO. VAUX

GASTON HOME IN NEW BERN

*To hear the voice of love whispering peace and comfort to the heart when it is oppressed and dissatisfied with itself is indeed happiness of such exquisite nature that language cannot do it justice.* — ELIZA WORTHINGTON GASTON

*I go where human comforts can only reach me through news of my children's well doing. . . . Let my solicitude and toils be cheered by learning that my darling daughters are running the race of virtue and knowledge. . . .* — WILLIAM GASTON

# CHAPTER FIVE

## Raising a Family

DURING the Fourteenth Congress society began to have more attractions for the handsome, young widower. In later years, after sorrow had again placed its mark upon him, he was to look back with nostalgia upon this period and exclaim to Webster:

> I fancy that I shall never laugh again as I have done with Lovett and Vose – and never unbend with such social ease as I was wont to do with Mason and Goldsborough and Hulbert and yourself over a glass of hot toddy in a cold winter night at Crawfords. If we had not much wit . . . we had much hearty mirth.[1]

With less to do in Congress he had more time for the various parties, balls, outings, and boat rides upon the Potomac River. During this winter friends began to notice his preference for the company of one of the daughters of Dr. Charles Worthington, and it probably did not surprise Eliza Worthington too much to receive this letter announcing his love:

> It is to your goodness, Miss Worthington, I throw myself for forgiveness in presuming thus to address you. In vain have I

> sought a fit occasion for personally communicating to you the holy secret of my soul. In society only have I the happiness to meet you and then I *dare* not even by a look intimate the emotion . . . which it is torture to suppress. . . . I flatter myself this declaration will not be a shock . . . others have perceived it . . . can it have escaped you . . . that I hang with delight upon your conversation. . . . I thought it a feeling that could no longer animate a heart which has been accustomed to glow with the warmest affection, but which calamity had rendered torpid. If hope is illusory . . . a simple blank return. . . . [2]

Gaston had enclosed this letter in one to her father, asking permission to speak to his daughter. The next day he received an answer from the physician telling him to call, and that he would be received "in a manner you are entitled to from the preference by which you have distinguished my daughter." In a short time the question was settled and he became a daily visitor at the Worthington home in Georgetown.

A few days after his avowal to Eliza that April day of 1816 the first session of the fourteenth Congress adjourned. Gaston remained in Washington for about three weeks, then left for Raleigh where he had several cases to handle. Hannah had been dead for three years, and during this time the children lived with his sister in Raleigh. The thirty-eight year old widower started a steady stream of letters back to his fiancée. These told of his activity of the moment and of past events. The first was written from Richmond. After telling her about the society there and a few minor incidents in which he had a part, he said:

> There are a thousand things I'd like to tell you if I were near you, but cannot in writing speak to you . . . as when seated in the corner of our favorite sofa when any and everything possesses charm. You may be sure that eight o'clock was never forgotten, but I can scarcely say that the rememberance of you was more intimately connected with that than any other hour. The living day was an eight o'clock.[3]

Eight o'clock must have had a very special significance to the two, for a reference to that time constantly occurs in their letters. Perhaps it was the time she had become engaged to him or it might have witnessed their first kiss.

A week after writing this letter, May 5, 1816, he was in Raleigh where he arrived weak with a fever. The country through which he had passed was parched with the drought, and the dust was thick almost to suffocation. His daughters saw him in the distance, and their screams of delight brought Judge Taylor and his wife running to the road. Gaston remained in the capital long enough to attend the session of the court and then went on to New Bern, where he received his first letter from Eliza. Warning him not to write when he felt ill, she continued:

> I dreamed of you as pale and languid and couldn't sleep. For the sake of those who love you so *dearly* take care of yourself. . . . Don't you think it was indiscreet to travel sixty miles when sick. . . . I was flattered you did stop on account of me. . . . As interested is a favorite word of yours I'll use it. When you were here I thought I could not freely write to you, but now I have to hold myself back. . . . Remember your tremulous accents on the evening of your departure and "remember eight" . . . a new and delightful sentiment is now in my heart, which is so much your own.[4]

On that same day Gaston wrote her to "congratulate Miss . . . . on her marriage this spring, which is a good season to marry in but her best friend seems to like the fall of the leaf . . . in May is the season nature invites as you would know had you listened as I did to the mocking birds here. . . . "

While he was in North Carolina Eliza was vacationing at Annapolis with a party of girl friends, whose charms were so alluring that Eliza confessed she would not introduce him to them until he was hers. There, even in the gaiety of the Maryland capital she thought of him, "stealing away from the party below to write to him. I cannot be happy from your side. Never till now did I know how much I loved. There are fifteen of us here. Tonight there will be a large party of all the belles and beaus of Annapolis." Toward the end of June while at a dance at the governor's mansion she slipped away from the floor, and in high glee related, "The girls think I am writing Papa and don't know what an interesting occupation I am engaged in."

After a hard day at court Gaston relaxed in the evening at the Taylor's, where he played and talked with his children, telling them of Eliza, to whom he described their reactions at some length. He warned her not to think "because I speak of Susan more she is my favorite . . . Hannah is intelligent, affectionate, and unaffected, and bears a striking resemblance to her mother, but Susan's age and reason. . . ." He spent a great deal of time between Raleigh and New Bern. Once he heard that his sister was very ill, so he hurried from New Bern to Raleigh in twenty-four hours, boasting to Eliza that this was "probably the shortest time it was ever done."

It seems that a certain Major Lewis figured prominently in their love affair. His name was often mentioned by both. Asking about him Gaston became reminiscent:

> He has been uneasy for us for two years as he knew my anti-matrimonial stand and saw how we were becoming attached. I wish he would settle down. . . . Do you remember the evening at Mrs. Tayeves . . . of the chess party the next night and of *the night after*, of the meeting at Mr. Carrol's . . . of the Birth-Night Assembly . . . of the steamboat party and the gaiety . . . Mr. Mill's hints and Mrs Lee's stronger ones . . . how Matilda Chase noticed the interest of each other's society we ourselves scarcely noticed.

A charming letter of June 21, 1816, deserves some quotation. It is headed Summer Hill.

> . . . To hear the voice of love whispering peace and comfort to the heart when it is oppressed and dissatisfied with itself is indeed happiness of such exquisite nature that language cannot do it justice. . . . What a valuable and blessed privilege it is that two hearts should be so united as to admit of such a

delightful intercourse. . . . Letters have drawn us nearer each other. . . . I wish I could feel worthy of such devoted love. . . . The clock is striking midnight. . . .

From Germantown Eliza informed him that she would have four bridesmaids, so he would have to make arrangements for two more attendants. She suggested her brother, Dr. Nicholas Worthington, and Lieutenant Rodgers, who "was almost an agent of the affair in the beginning." Major Lewis and a Mr. Lee were to be the other two. The wedding was to take place in the Worthington home, with only intimate friends present. Gaston left North Carolina late in August, and on Tuesday evening, September 3, 1816, the two were married by Father de Grassi, president of Georgetown College.[5] If arrangements previously entered into were followed, the couple then left Washington for New Bern the middle of the month, arriving there about ten days later.

When the second session of Congress convened Gaston brought the entire family back with him, and they lived during this time at his father-in-law's in Georgetown. During this session he took little part in the business of Congress. At the end of this time he left that body never to return. His reasons for this decision are unknown, although there is a tradition among his descendants that his inability to control his temper there was a deciding feature. However, his young and growing family, together with his recent marriage, made it imperative for him to give more attention to his own financial interests. As a member of the minority party during a war he had little chance for any constructive legislation. He followed the usual Federalist party line, except when he thought it unsound on particular points such as the removal of the capital. He gave some of the greatest speeches during the War Congress, such as those on the Loan Bill and the "Previous Question." Daniel Webster had not yet made his great reputation, so that Gaston stood out in this Congress. He opposed the first protective tariff as well as the acquisition of Canada, so was more consistent than Calhoun. His demands for free speech, his support of a sound financial institution, and his opposition to a war of doubtful expediency revealed sound statesmanship. Had he remained in Congress, or had he accepted the offers of national office proffered him, his reputation would without doubt have been as great as that of Clay, Calhoun, and Webster. Several years later one of the congressmen from Ohio asked Webster, "Who was the greatest, of the great men, of the War Congress?" Webster replied, "The greatest man was William Gaston," and with a smile he added, "I myself came in along after him."[6]

Before the close of the session Gaston had to return to Raleigh but left the family behind. Eliza took the children's education into her own hands. All rose at six, and from nine to eleven o'clock she taught them. Susan practiced with her music lessons for an hour. In the evening they rode or walked either for a visit or for pleasure and fresh air. On September 27, 1817, their first child, whom they named Eliza, was born in the Worthington home.

On her return to New Bern the third wife of Gaston found a warm welcome among his family and friends. Gaston's financial status was in such a good state that he could afford to buy a fine home for his bride. On April 17, 1818, for $6,000 he purchased from J. Groenendyke the beautiful colonial home, built around 1767, located on Craven and New Streets, with a lot 121 feet by 142 feet. The double veranda had a delicate railing, cunningly wrought, considered by many to be superior to that of the famous Stanly home.

That summer Eliza returned to Washington for a visit. In the late fall she was back in New Bern, from where she wrote her husband, who was at the state capital, that "the change in the weather has produced acidity again, which plagues me not a little, but I live upon magnesia which I find is the only remedy. I am too important a personage now to neglect anything that will keep me in tolerable health. You know the all important period is a month later and I am so apprehensive."[7] January 6, 1819,

Catherine Jane was born in the Gaston home. After the event anxiety was high as Eliza did not recover as she should; thirteen days later apprehensions were realized for despite frantic efforts of their physician she quietly slipped into a lasting sleep. She was buried from Christ Church, the Reverend Richard S. Mason, Episcopalian minister, officiating at the funeral.[8] The latter had also baptized her child, Nicholas Worthington, Jane Taylor and Susan Gaston being sponsors.[9] The blow was almost more than her husband could face, until he sought comfort in his religion. At forty-one he was widowed for the third time.[10]

At this time Alexander was twelve, Susan eleven, Hannah eight, Eliza Ann not yet two, and Catherine but a baby of two weeks. Gaston sent the two oldest girls to school at St. Joseph's in Emmitsburg, Maryland; Alexander to Mt. St. Mary's, and the babies were taken to his father-in-law's home in Georgetown. From this time dated Gaston's dependence upon his favorite child, Susan. His letters to her and the others are characteristic of the man. Not long after their departure for school, from the lonely home in New Bern, he wrote his eldest daughter:

> Remember, my dear Susan, that I look to you as my great and efficient coadjutor in the instruction of your sisters. You are charged not only with your welfare but theirs. . . . I go where human comforts can only reach me through news of my children's well doing. Let me have this consolation. Let my solicitude and toils be cheered by learning that my darling daughters are running the race of virtue and knowledge and are growing daily in grace and favor with God and man. Guard against melancholy which is a foe to mental vigor and bodily health and is a species of treason against the divine law.[11]

Gaston kept them in this school of the renowned and virtuous Mother Seton until 1822, at which time the two were separated. In August he visited Philadelphia to make arrangements for Susan's further education, while Hannah remained at St. Joseph's. Before his visit Gaston had written Joseph Hopkinson, telling him of this project and asking his aid. Hopkinson, son of a signer of the Declaration of Independence, author of *Hail Columbia,* one of the foremost lawyers of his time, had been in Congress with Gaston, and the two soon formed a close friendship. Writing about Susan he further said:

> I had designed visiting Washington during the session of the Supreme Court and promised myself much pleasure from meeting with you there. But this promise like many other more important schemes in which I have been accustomed to indulge my fancy was but the harbinger of disappointment. A special criminal court called at this place about the end of January compelled me to forego the gratification of seeing my children and talking with all my friends. In the number of *these* I need not say that you are included. To use the homely but expressive phrase of my country "I took to you mightily from the first." You may be assured that I shall not pass through any place you are without giving you a call.[12]

Susan was received with love and kindness whenever she visited the Hopkinson home during her school days at Philadelphia. Gaston was delighted that his fifteen year old daughter had found a place in their hearts, telling them "dear to me is my blue-eyed Susan." On January 4, 1823, in answer to Hopkinson's query he stated:

> I thank you for your friendly letter of December 16th, which I yesterday received at Raleigh. The kind things you say of my child come home to my heart and favorably as I have always thought of your judgement I now set it up as unerring. You must take care therefore not to ask anything from me about her which you are not confident that it will be proper to grant. That she should occasionally and without [ — ] mingle in your family circle would afford me high gratification. But I believe it would be better that she should not frequently have this enjoyment. When a girl sees much society her mind is liable to become dissipated – serious studies are regarded as irksome and she is too apt to fancy herself a woman. My dear daughter has years yet in which I wish her to be considered

and to consider herself a child. As to the Theater – I could not refuse her permission, if she asked it, to see a play or two in the course of the season, but I could be quite as well pleased that she did not ask it. Such amusements can add nothing to her happiness and may give her an early fancy for dress, vanity, etc. I am engaged here in attendance on our supreme court and will probably be here detained throughout the month. Whether I can visit Philadelphia before next summer is as yet uncertain. Few things would give me greater enjoyment than to spend two or three weeks there. To see my child every day and to mingle familiarly with the delightful society of your city, with the learned and the gay and the polite, is among the highest gratifications which my fancy can conceive.[13]

He was troubled over the expense of his daughter's education, which he considered excessive. Entries upon his accounts, such as $230 for Alexander, $270 for Hannah, $300 for Susan, $500 for Hannah, were frequent. Concerning this worry, early in 1823, he confided to Hopkinson:

The charges attending my daughter's education are indeed inconveniently high – more especially when I am solicitously engaged in paying off debts which a neglected profession, a mismanaged estate and confidence rashly bestowed caused to grow during my public career. I grudge them not – if they are necessary. Any plan which you or Mrs. Hopkinson will have the goodness to suggest by which they may be lessened will be gladly received. As I can not expect to see you earlier than July or August I would ask the favor of you not to postpone writing. If the excessive discount on state paper could be prevented it would be something.

Then, turning to the subject of his daughter's welfare, he continued:

I rejoice to hear that Susan is well. Should you discover anything relating to her which you deem not exactly as it should be, in mind, manners, habit, fear not to let me know. My parental partiality deceives me much if she have not the *material* out of which an amiable woman may be educed. Skill and care in management are necessary – perhaps in regard to her, particularly necessary.

However, this expense became so burdensome that later in the year he asked Archbishop Maréchal for advice about schools in Baltimore. He told the bishop he would like to have the two girls together so that the younger might by her sister's example correct an indolence of disposition, but the exorbitant price at Mrs. Sigoine's school in Philadelphia, where Susan was placed, prevented the attendance of both there.[14] The advice of Roger B. Taney was also sought, but no satisfactory solution was found so the twelve year old Hannah remained at Emmitsburg.[15]

After Susan's vacation that summer in New Bern, Gaston was particularly anxious that she receive the best of care, for as he told his friend in Philadelphia:

> The coming year is of vast importance to Susan. It will be the last which she spends in school. . . . Intent as she is on improvement she needs nothing but fit instructors and a proper plan of studies. Removed as I am from her I cannot enter into the details of her education. I ask it of your friendship from time to time to enquire into them – to ascertain what are the studies to which her attention is directed, whether she has the proper facilities, books, maps, etc., for prosecuting them, whether her teachers are of the best sort and use due diligence in instructing, and to direct such changes and give such orders for such help as a father on the spot would deem himself authorized to make. Occasional inquiries about her health I beg may not be neglected.
>
> I will not apologize for thus troubling you for were I near one of your children and you far distant I should be vexed at the doubt which an apology for charging me with its welfare would imply. Alexander goes home in two months and spends the winter with me. He is wonderfully grown. . . . If I can succeed in converting a passion for military glory into an ambition for forensic distinction I hope to make something of him.[16]

Another problem soon was placed before the anxious parent by his friend, and his reply was probably not unexpected, but rather characteristic:

> I had the pleasure a few days since of receiving your kind letter. The interest you have the goodness to take in the welfare and improvement of my daughter is such I had expected from your friendship. I long to hear of your visits to her and of your opinion in regard to her progress. No change can be made which will diminish the expense of her education and as these are to continue but one year more I will submit to their extravagance without repining. No doubt you have in Philadelphia libraries of all sort to which access may be had for a small charge. I wish Susan to have an opportunity of reading the best works of Bourdaloue, Massillon, and Bossuet in the original and have recommended them to her for her Sunday reading. Will you be good enough to put her in the way of procuring them. With a good voice she has an almost invisible repugnance to singing in company. As you may have the means be kind enough to use them for conquering this diffidence. You will see how freely I avail myself of your permission to trouble you with her concerns.
>
> On the subject of Susan seeing company I have a difficulty in forming a definite opinion. I am well aware that many advantages may be derived from it which she needs. Were I with her so as to be able to check at once any excess which an association with the fashionable and gay might threaten I would delight to bring her more into society. But as this cannot be, and as the main object of her stay in Philadelphia is the cultivation of her mind I fear to hazard this by exposing her to the dissipation of amusements.[17]

At the end of the summer of 1824 Susan's school days were over, and she came home to become the mistress of the Gaston house in New Bern. For the next three years she retained this position until she found romance in the person of Robert Donaldson, a young Scotch merchant from New York City, who had financial interests in North Carolina. In giving his permission to the match Gaston told Donaldson, "I have confidence in the judgement of my daughter and cheerfully give my approbation. She is a gift the value of which none can know as well as I. Long has she been my pride, joy, and solace."[18] They were married in Gaston's home on February 14, 1828, by Bishop John England.[19] The twenty year old girl and her husband lived at Fayetteville during the winter, and in summer at his home in New York on the Hudson River, near that of Chancellor Kent.

Hannah finished her education at a private school in Baltimore, and then returned to take Susan's place in the household, until her marriage to Mathias E. Manly, which took place on February 16, 1832, in the Gaston home; the ceremony was performed by Father R. S. Baker.[20] Manly was a young lawyer, well liked by his father-in-law, who held his legal talents in high respect. After Gaston's death Manly served on the bench of the state supreme court. A year before Hannah's nuptials, Alexander had been married in Christ's Church by the Reverend J. R. Goodman to Eliza Jones, the daughter of Dr. Hugh Jones.[21] In the meanwhile Eliza and Catherine were attending school at the Georgetown Visitation Convent, where their bill for a year amounted to over $1,000.

After his appointment to the state supreme court in 1833 Gaston had much more leisure time, so he used to go to New York each fall to visit Susan. While there he would spend long evenings with Chancellor Kent, and if possible would go farther North to visit other old friends. Story and Tichnor asked to be given "the earliest notice of your arrival in Boston," and a friend from North Carolina informed him that "Jeremiah Mason's beautiful daughter tells me that he frequently speaks of you as one of his favorite friends."[22]

With the marriage of his three eldest children Gaston now devoted most of his parental efforts to the two youngest, who were with him. When Manly became involved in a political contest with a friend of the Gastons, the judge expressed relief that the latter had withdrawn and warned his daughters not even to allude to it as "nothing is more unfeminine as to take part in any political strife." Governor David L. Swain often visited Gaston and the girls.

The three spent much of their time on the plantation, going there at least a day or two every week, especially so after the death of Hannah, who expired March 16, 1835, leaving two daughters, Jane and Hannah Manly. The week following this sad event the three spent in the country; rising every morning with the sun, they breakfasted at seven, and then rode horseback over the fields and hills until noon. Every afternoon they took a long walk, and tired out with their long day retired at nine o'clock. For some time Gaston had his son, Alexander, running his plantation on Brice's Creek. His cotton often was shipped to Donaldson for disposal. Although Gaston was very proud of his rural standing, he was not much of a farmer, as an incident related of him by an old farmer indicates. It seems that Gaston took a neighboring planter out to his plantation to view the work, and proudly pointed out how neatly the irrigation ditches were laid out. The farmer chuckled and to Gaston's chagrin demonstrated that although they looked very nice they were impractical as they ran in the wrong direction. Another amusing incident about him, often related by himself, occurred as he was riding in his gig past a schoolhouse and stopped at the sight of a small boy by the road; Gaston spelled out loud, B–A, ba, K–E–R, ker, BAKER, to which the boy immediately replied, D–A–M, dam, F–O–O–L, fool, DAM FOOL.[23]

The joy and delight he experienced in his children was well expressed by him to his old friend, Dr. Beasley, "I rejoice to learn you are so blessed in your children. An old man, surrounded by affectionate children whom he has trained up to virtue and usefulness, and by whom he is regarded with gratitude and reverence is to me one of the most interesting objects in the world."

## NOTES FOR CHAPTER FIVE

1. *The Writings and Speeches of Daniel Webster*, XVI, 90.
2. Gaston to Eliza Ann Worthington, April 4, 1816, Gaston *MSS*.
3. Gaston to Eliza Ann Worthington, May 5, 1816, Gaston *MSS*.
4. Eliza to Gaston, May 19, 1816, Gaston *MSS*.
5. *National Intelligencer*, Sept. 5, 1816.
6. M. E. Manly, "Memoir of William Gaston," *North Carolina University Magazine*, X, 196.
7. Eliza to Gaston, Dec. 3, 1818, Gaston *MSS*.
8. *Register of Baptisms, Burials, and Marriages, Christ's Church*. New Bern, N. C., p. 75.
9. *Ibid.*, p. 1.
10. May 23, 1814, Gaston wrote to the bishop of Baltimore for advice concerning a possible religious impediment to a marriage he was contemplating, which depended "on the probability that the individual with whom I might be disposed to form a union would not merely make a virtuous and agreeable helpmate, but also a faithful and affectionate mother to my bereaved children. To one individual my mind has been very forcibly directed as a person peculiarly fitted to secure both these objects. In infancy she was the playmate, and in more mature life has been the companion and bosom friend of my late inestimable wife. . . . Her childhood was passed under the pious care of my venerable Mother, by whom at the request of a dying father she was educated a Catholic. . . . I seriously looked forward to a declaration of my wishes when an obstacle suddenly presented itself which I had never anticipated." Gaston then asked the bishop if the impediment was too serious for removal or if it existed at all. It seemed that the lady in question was godmother of one of his children, which was the difficulty in question. The bishop's answer is unknown, but Gaston thought better of taking the step. A couple of months later he told John Burgwin that he had thought for a while of doing this because of the children, but finally decided that the risk involved was not worth while. Baltimore Cathedral Archives, 3Y4.
11. Gaston to his daughter, Susan, Feb. 20, March 21, 1820, Gaston *MSS*.
12. Gaston to Joseph Hopkinson, March 22, 1822, Hopkinson Collection, Pennsylvania State Historical Society.
13. Gaston to Hopkinson, Jan. 4, 1823, Hopkinson Collection.
14. Gaston to Archbishop Maréchal, Aug. 12, 1823, Baltimore Cathedral Archives, 17C2.
15. R. B. Taney to Gaston, Aug. 7, 1823, Gaston *MSS*.
16. Gaston to Hopkinson, Aug. 26, 1823, Hopkinson Collection.

17. Gaston to Hopkinson, Sept. 21, 1823, Hopkinson Collection.
18. Gaston to Robert Donaldson, June 2, 1827, Gaston *MSS.*
19. *Records of St. Paul Roman Catholic Church,* New Bern, N. C.
20. *Ibid.,* 1832.
21. *Register . . . Christ's Church,* p. 134.
22. J. S. Jones to Gaston, Nov. 8, 1833, Gaston *MSS.*
23. I am indebted for these incidents to the Honorable R. A. Nunn of New Bern. An old farmer, whose father knew Gaston, related the incident to him. See the June 14, 1917, issue of the *Gastonia Republican,* published at Gastonia, N. C., for an address of Judge Nunn's on Gaston.

*He is one of the most distinguished of American lawyers in the highest sense of the phrase; eminent as a statesman and as a private gentleman is all that one could wish for or desire. . . . He is truly a doctor of laws, whom to know is to respect. . . .* — JUSTICE JOSEPH STORY

*All eyes were turned upon Mr. Gaston, then in the zenith of his fame and popularity.* — JOHN H. WHEELER

CHAPTER SIX

# Enhancing a Reputation, 1818–1828

WHEN Gaston returned to New Bern after his final congressional session he had no difficulty in finding clients, for his reputation had been greatly enhanced by his public career. Business came to him from every part of North Carolina as there was not enough in the neighborhood to keep him actively engaged. New Bern had grown but little in the years since the war. In 1818 the *Carolina Sentinel* estimated its population to be three thousand.[1] However, it was larger than the capital as the Raleigh *Register* in 1821 released the following figures: New Bern: population, 3663; whites, 1475; slaves, 1920; free colored, 268. Fayetteville had 1918 whites, 1337 slaves, and 277 free colored; Raleigh was given third place with 1177 whites, 1320 slaves, and 177 free colored.[2]

Many of Gaston's cases were simply the prosaic collection of debts. His letter book revealed that in 1818 he received a commission of $339 for the collection of various debts amounting to $6,436. The next year he collected a debt of $13,306 for which he received $300.[3] Trying to collect $5,905 from John G. Blount for Captain Peter Lamb of Philadelphia proved a difficult undertaking. Gaston wrote Lamb that "there is no man of property in our state from whom it is more difficult to get money from as from Mr. Blount."[4] However, he managed to obtain this sum and much more in various other debts from Blount.

His various friends freely sought his advice in their moments of dilemma. Dr. Beasley asked him to handle a case of inheritance involving nearly $300,000; Haywood sent him $100 for his aid as "a small token in no proportion to your real service," but Gaston returned the money with the remark that it was enormously too much for a service which he had not intended to be professional. A former classmate, John M. Berrien, asked for information on the practice in the courts of equity of North Carolina. Although Gaston had all the business he could handle, Hopkinson wished him to practice in Philadelphia because "the bar is bare of men calculated for the first grade of business. They will welcome you and give you business of a grade you are entitled to . . . in a theater worthy of your talents."[5] Although he did not take this offer it was a pleasure to visit in the East. Whenever he attended the sessions of the supreme court in Washington he was sure of a warm welcome from many old friends. John Randolph told him, "To be remembered by you is very grateful to me. I have never omitted an occasion of making inquiry after you since we separated. . . . I shall enjoy the double pleasure of seeing you and . . . Marshall at the same time."[6]

Gaston won two cases in the May session of the state supreme court. In the first, an admiralty case, he insisted, for the defendant, that the Court of Common Law had no jurisdiction in the case as a fundamental law of the land gave it solely to a national tribunal.[7] In a more important case concerning a matter of inheritance Gaston in "an able argument," according to the *Reports* stated that "when an ancient dogma is itself abolished the tenets grounded upon it must fall too, unless they are preserved from a superstitious reverence for antiquity."[8] Bedford Brown, leader of the bar before the appearance of Gaston, lost this case to him. In 1818 Gaston was told that the North Carolina members of Congress intended to ask the president to appoint him a circuit judge, but Gaston did not care to assume the added burdens of this office.

In the June term of 1820 Gaston appeared in every case of any importance. The school at New Bern owed much to him. Moses Griffin, a resident, had freed his slaves by his will and ordered the remaining proceeds from his estate to be applied to establish a free school. The will was contested and Gaston, one of the executors appointed to look after its integrity, argued and won the case. He denied that estates could be so limited that devisors could not sell them, declaring that the purposes to which the profits were to be applied could have no effect on the will, for the law would never prohibit the present owner of an estate from disposing of the profits in charity. He maintained that this was a most sacred trust for the entire community as it was a charity of a most beneficial kind.[9] The Quakers also sought his aid in a case very important to them. Archibald Murphey told them "there is too much at stake for the case to rest upon my exertions alone, and I earnestly recommend you to engage Mr. Gaston and Seawell. They are eminent and have long been acquainted with the case. . . . "[10] This was done, and it was not the last time Gaston was to be of great service to that sect.

After his return from Congress Gaston was honored by many different societies. In 1817 the American Philosophic Society in a meeting at Philadelphia elected him a member; in 1819 the American Antiquarian Society made him a counselor for the state of North Carolina (each state had one), to which office he was re-elected each year; two years later the American Academy of Languages and Belles Lettres announced his election to that body. Joseph Delaplaine of Philadelphia asked for his portrait to be placed in his National Gallery with those of Wirt, Adams, and others. Delaplaine was willing to pay half the expense of a thousand dollar painting. In 1823 the Cliosophic Society of Princeton elected him president of its meeting at the graduation exercises of that year, and requested that he make the regular address at this time. Professional duties made it necessary for him to refuse, as was the case again in 1826 when the Literary Society of Nassau Hall made the same request. The latter society made him a vice-president then, John Quincy Adams being made president.

In 1819 the University of Pennsylvania conferred upon him the honorary degree of Doctor of Laws.[11] Gaston learned of this honor through the newspapers, and immediately wrote to his old classmate and friend, Dr. Beasley, assuring him that he knew to whose partiality he was indebted. He told Beasley, "You, my boyhood friend, have drawn attention to my humble name. It is an honor of high value but the pledge of your unabated affection is dear to me."[12] Beasley acknowledged that it had been his intention for several years to do this. In 1825 Harvard University conferred the same degree upon him and William Sullivan. Gaston asked the latter "in confidence, what is expected of him so honored?"[13] Gaston again learned of the event through the newspapers; this time the honor was due to the distinguished associate justice of the supreme court, Joseph Story. Story told Sullivan his reasons for naming Gaston were that:

> He is one of the most distinguished of American lawyers in the highest sense of the phrase; eminent as a statesman and as a private gentleman is all that one could wish for or desire. . . . Hitherto North Carolina has not shared our public honors as she deserved. . . . He is a Catholic and I was most anxious that a Protestant university should show its liberality by doing homage to a gentleman of a different faith and so honor itself by a fair exhibition of Christian virtues. . . . The honor is on ourselves and not on Gaston. . . . He is truly a doctor of laws, whom to know is to respect. . . .[14]

Reporting the episode the *United States Catholic Miscellany* expressed a belief that Gaston was the first native Roman Catholic to whom Harvard had paid this tribute.[15]

During this time Gaston had also been concerned with the making of the laws of the state. In 1817 James Monroe became the fifth president of the United States, and the period during which he occupied that office has been designated as the "era of good feelings." At about this same time party politics in North Carolina disappeared.[16] Bartlett Yancey was elected speaker of the Senate for the next ten years, not so much because of personal popularity as through the absence of party alignments.[17] Despite this beneficial condition of affairs the state made no great headway in constructive legislation. Too much time was spent in petty bickering over the election of state officials, among whom was the governor. The penal code was in a sorry condition, but instead of rectifying it the assembly wasted its brief period in reviewing divorce proceedings. Archibald Murphey, the state's greatest exponent of internal improvement and education, bitterly complained of this. The greatest achievement of the assembly during this period was the establishment of a new reformed supreme court, which North Carolina owes to the persistent urging of Gaston.

Craven County sent him to the North Carolina Senate during the two terms of 1818 and 1819. In the latter year his campaign seemed to have been confined to a simple statement in the papers that, "We are authorized to say that William Gaston will serve in the next Senate, should it be the wish of the freeholders of Craven County."[18] Party politics had indeed disappeared. In that year he was elected over Colonel John S. Smith, who was not even a candidate, by a majority of eighty-seven votes.[19] His friend, John Stanly, without opposition was elected to represent New Bern in the House.

At both sessions he was appointed by Yancey chairman of the judiciary committee. He was not in Raleigh at the beginning of the session of 1818 as his wife was ill, and although this created delay, the position was reserved until his arrival.[20] Governor John Branch had recommended the establishment of a separate supreme court, and an increase in the salaries of the circuit judges. That part of the governor's message relating to the judiciary was referred to his committee.

Under the leadership of Gaston a bill was reported for a supreme court to be composed of three judges, distinct from the circuit judges, having appellate duties only, except that the superior courts could order equity cases removed before hearing upon affidavit showing its necessity for purposes of justice. In this report Gaston dwelled upon the evils of the judiciary of North Carolina. Pointing out the faulty organization of the supreme court then in existence, which was made up of all the judges of the circuit courts, he advised that another was needed to compel all the inferior courts to adhere to the same exposition of the public will. He stated that "under the present order property is insecure and liberty endangered, rights are ambiguous and law unknown. The judges of the superior courts, as circuit judges, travel from a thousand to fifteen hundred miles, are absent from home twenty-two weeks of the year. Their heavy expenses and insufficient salaries compel them during the residue of the year to apply themselves to other pursuits which aid in the support of their families." He concluded the report by declaring that the supreme court must have men of ability and integrity in order to obtain respect as well as uniformity. Also he demonstrated that the efficiency of the superior courts would be greatly increased.[21]

The bill was passed by both houses in record time. It fixed the salary of the supreme court judges at $2,500, which was $500 more than the governor received. Chief Justice John L. Taylor, Leonard Henderson, and John Hall, three of the ablest men ever to occupy the bench [in North Carolina] at the same time, were elected to the new court. Of these men, the learned and eminent Governor David L. Swain said, "Taylor was the Mansfield, while Hall was proverbial for integrity and common sense, and Henderson in genius, judgment and power of fascination was without a peer."[22] As predicted the immense labor of the superior courts was decreased, although the judges were still overworked. This act gave tremendous relief to the equity docket of the superior courts, for these cases could now be sent to the supreme court. Before, it had not been unusual for a suit to be continued over such a long period of years that it was handed down from father to son.[23]

In the next session an attempt was made to cut the salaries of the judges of the supreme court. The instigators of the move must have known that this would have ruined the court, for the incumbents would have resigned, and in order to fill the vacancies inferior and incompetent men would have to be appointed. In opposition to this move Gaston said, "The court is ready to receive those weighty and numerous equity suits, which have for so many years slept unheard on the dockets of the courts in the West. . . . Sufficiently long have the parties been mocked with a promise of hearing. In this court they will be heard, and it is in this court only that they can obtain this boon." He proved that the new court had done very well, since for the first time in several years the West had no cases waiting to be heard, and although but one year had gone by, it had done more than the old one had managed to accomplish in twenty years. With no other duties these judges acted finally and without delay, and appeals on all questions of law were placed in their hands. Although time would suggest improvements, he urged that the salaries not be lowered for the judges were entitled to a fair emolument, and there was a contract between them and the state. According to this plea of Gaston the best talents of the state were needed to secure respect for the court. His words were heeded, the bill being tabled by a vote of thirty-four to twenty-six.[24]

Although he had been concerned primarily with the supreme court bill in the session of 1818 Gaston also had taken a vital part in other issues. He voted in favor of a bill "to establish and regulate schools in the several counties," and introduced a bill "to prevent the abatement of actions by the death of the parties thereto." However, much of his time was devoted to the difficulty North Carolina was having in obtaining satisfaction from the United States concerning certain rights to titles of land in Tennessee, which forms an episode in the long and litigious history of land titles in the old Southwest. North Carolina in colonial times had claimed a large section of the present state of Tennessee, and in common with certain other states had ceded these western lands of the Confederation Congress so as to bring unity and peace to the Confederated States. However, in ceding the territory in question to the United States North Carolina had made certain reservations which were not recognized by the United States Congress. While in that body Gaston had attempted to have the state's claims adjusted. Now he was chairman of the committee appointed to consider the matter. Before submitting the report to the Senate Gaston wrote Justice Marshall for advice on the matter. In a confidential reply the latter stated:

> Your letter of the fifth has reached me. . . . One might obtain land by some other title than possession . . . in Tennessee by patent. . . . I could not concur in astute reasoning which construed the Act of Congress into a sanction of the whole. . . . As I do believe the decision is much more beneficial to claimants under North Carolina than one which would have continued conflict I was secretly gratified my opinion did not prevail and took no pains to support it. We all understood that there would be no difficulty if not created by North Carolina in obtaining an act of Congress which would enable her citizens to derive titles from Tennessee and we all thought though she lost a point of honor she gained substantially a point of interest.

After discussing this question Marshall told Gaston, "I rejoice that you are in the legislature of your state, since you determined to withdraw from that of the Union . . . and I am glad that the spirit of party . . . is not blind or so fiercely vindictive."[25]

Gaston's committee reported that it believed the state had done all it ought to do, and that the United States would no doubt recognize its obligations. Copies of this report were sent to the state's representatives in Congress.[26] Two years later the legislature empowered the governor to appoint an agent on behalf of the state to attend Congress to "lobby" on this affair, and Governor Branch named Gaston. The latter declined the office under the plea that the object contemplated could not be achieved, for the question was not a legislative but a judicial affair. He also thought Congress was then in the midst of such a vital topic — the Missouri Compromise — that no attention would be paid such an agent. The university also had land interests in Tennessee, and according to the indignant protests of Archibald Murphey, who was handling its affairs there, a leading member of the committee had proposed to give Gaston $5,000 to go to Tennessee and argue the case of the university before the legislature of that state.[27]

In 1821 Gaston was not in the legislature and although the supreme court was doing its work very effectively he feared for its safety so asked Barlett Yancey to guard its interests, warning him:

> The Supreme Court has its enemies to encounter, and I think has much to apprehend from their hostility at the next session. The plan will be, I think, to make a mob court of it by getting the Ct. judges on it and thus destroying its most valuable feature, its perfect separation from the tribunals whose decisions it revises. Daniel is busy about Halifax. He can't bear that his adjudications should be reversed, and he fancies *himself* competent to sit in judgement of the opinions of all men. Seawell is a candidate for the Assembly in Wake and will probably be chosen. Henderson, Sanders, Iredell will not be in the next session. There will not be a man from our section of the state who can render the court any effectual aid. In the meantime Murphey and Ruffin have failed, as they ought, to publish the reports. There seems to be an evil genius that tries to thwart anything that is attempted for the increased reputation and prosperity of the State. If enemies of the Court cannot put the circuit judges *there,* they will try to bring down the judges of the Supreme Court to the circuits. It will be enough if they can make a break thro' the dam. . . . [28]

Yancey replied that he felt the present court was safe although there was much conversation on the intention of certain individuals to overthrow it. He reported that a plan was afoot to place the present judges on the circuit and to elevate all the circuit judges to the court, but if this succeeded his intentions were to have all the laws concerning it repealed.[29] Nothing occurred during this session, but in 1824 Willis Alston introduced a resolution to abolish the court, and immediately became the target of a newspaper attack all over the state. In the first ten years of its existence the court was to undergo many such trials.

Gaston also called Yancey's attention to a subject on which he felt a little legislation would prove useful. In the Act of 1782 establishing courts of equity it was provided that matters of fact which came into issue between the parties should be determined by a jury in the presence of the court. A difference of construction leading to a difference in practice had arisen upon this provision of the law. Therefore, said Gaston to Yancey:

> . . . The judges in the Supreme Court asked the Bar for their opinion on the question whether a jury must pass upon *every fact* on which the parties do not agree in the Bill and Answer as being a fact in issue – or whether a jury in the presence of the Court were to try those issues which the Court, proceeding according to the uses of Chancery might direct, instead of their being tried in a law court as had been the case before the passage of the law. Mr. Mordecai thought every part of the defendant's answer was put in issue by the complainant's replication, and all the allegations in complainant's bill were to be deemed in issue which defendant's answer did not admit. Mr. Henderson and myself thought the Act proscribed a different mode of trying issues of fact than had theretofore prevailed, but left the making of issues of fact where it had been before in cases where the Conscience of the Chancellor required information. . . . The court have hitherto deemed it safest to have issues in every case. This practice is very inconvenient and exceedingly at variance with the nature and spirit of a Court of Equity. Where there is one great question of fact, or a few great questions of fact, controverted between

> the parties, there is no difficulty in making an issue or two and impanelling a jury to try them, but in the complicated and multifarious matters which a Chancery suit sometimes involves to have the matter broken up into fifty issues, and to have a dozen squabbles as to the wording of these issues and to dispute about the admissibility of the testimony as to some issues and to task the patience of the court to explain them to the jury and ultimately to have the findings of the jury set aside because of their not comprehending the subject is anything but useful and decorous. As there is a prospect of getting all our chancery suits determined a short explanatory Act of Assembly might remove such inconveniences. It might enact that all issues of fact in every matter of equitable cognizance should be tried by a jury in the presence of the court having cognizance thereof, and that issues of fact should be made up at the discretion of the Court, and according to the usages of Chancery to satisfy the conscience of the Chancellor concerning doubts as to facts. I submit the subject to your judgment.[30]

Yancey was entirely in accord with the suggestion and informed Gaston he would do everything possible to have this done. He asked the latter to let him know of any other legislation Gaston thought either desirable or necessary, so was informed that in the fifteenth section of the Act establishing the courts of the United States there was an admirable provision with respect to parties being compelled to produce books in evidence which should be incorporated into the state's system of jurisprudence. Concerning this he wisely observed:

> Everything that has a tendency to bring out fully the merits of a case when under judicial examination is very desirable.— Now, unless the party will produce the books, in nine cases out of ten evidence of their contents is not to be had.[31]

Another project in which Gaston was interested was a plan fathered by Virgil Maxcy of Maryland to appropriate the public lands for the several purposes of education. His resolutions concerning this were passed by the legislature of Maryland, and Maxcy asked Gaston to obtain the co-operation of North Carolina. Maxcy reported that the administration in Washington favored it, and that Congress also would if its attention were called by several state legislatures.[32] Gaston felt the scheme would succeed if the Atlantic states would support it and asked Yancey to act on the matter. In 1822, under the latter's direction, the assembly made a favorable report on the subject.[33]

With the approach of the historic presidential election of 1824 strictly state measures were crowded into the background as the qualities and policies of the five candidates were considered, discussed, and supported. The state and congressional elections of August, 1823, were regarded vital in view of the prospect that the General Assembly of 1823 would form the electoral ticket. Secretary of State John Quincy Adams was the northern candidate; Secretary of War John C. Calhoun and Secretary of the Treasury William H. Crawford of Georgia were southern candidates; the West offered Henry Clay and General Andrew Jackson.

Friends of these men began their campaign as soon as the election of 1820 was a matter of the past; in North Carolina William H. Crawford was regarded as most likely to receive the fifteen electoral votes of the state.[34] However, a serious threat to his chances soon developed in Salisbury, where Charles Fisher became the organizer and director of a state-wide Calhoun campaign with the aid of the newspaper, the *Western Carolinian*. Such success attended his efforts that Calhoun became interested in his chances in the state and began to encourage Fisher and his helpers. The following year Calhoun persuaded General Joseph G. Swift of New York, who was well known in North Carolina through marriage and a previous residence there, to conduct an extensive correspondence with leaders in the state.[35] Swift and his friends were surprised and gratified by the outcome of the August elections in this district. Although Crawford was supported by most of the political leaders and federal and state officeholders, a large number of Calhoun men were sent to the legislature from the counties west of the Yadkin River. General Swift contacted Gaston late in the fall, and must have been well pleased with the latter's reply which read:

> The high opinion which I entertain of Mr. Calhoun's merits, of his understanding, integrity, firmness of purpose, devotion of views and devotion to his country's welfare, added to in a moment of bitter party hostilities and fondly cherished since these have ceased, cause me to take a deep interest in behalf of his claims to the presidential chair. When indeed he was first announced as a candidate I feared that there was no chance of success and would not permit myself to indulge any solicitude on the subject. Since, however, I have perceived a possibility, if not a probability that the exertions of his friends may not be unavailing I have not hesitated to give such an expression of my opinions and wishes as might operate where they were likely to have an influence. If I should discover a more active participation in the contest will advance his interests I shall not hesitate to make the necessary exertion. In this district of the state he is decidedly the favorite candidate. Throughout the state his cause has recently been gaining ground and that of Mr. Crawford (the only competitor to be feared in North Carolina) has been losing. I trust this process will go on and that if we have not now a majority of the state with us, we shall have a majority when the choice of Electors come on.
>
> . . . I cannot say who are the leading men in North Carolina. The discipline or machinery of faction (thank God) never was complete here and of course individuals have not obtained with us artificial consequences.

The rest of the letter to Swift was devoted to a list of the men in various parts of the state "whose opinions would be respected in their several neighborhoods."[36] As for New Bernians Gaston advised that although Stanly preferred Adams he would support Calhoun rather than Crawford; that Calhoun would find a warm and useful friend in John H. Bryan, that year representing Craven County in the Senate, who "left my office but a few years since and is a young man of character and talents and has always been of the Democratic party"; and that the *Patriot,* a Calhoun paper edited in New York, should be sent to Daniel Shuckelford. A few months later Swift's brother complained that Gaston was too inactive in the campaign, and asked if there were no way to devise means "to bring out Stanly more generously" for the South Carolinian.[37]

From other parts of the Union there came pleas to Gaston for information concerning the probable result in his state. Among these Maxcy reported that in Maryland the electors were divided between Adams and Calhoun, although Clay might get one in the western part of the State; but all the commercial men of the East were afraid of the latter.[38]

Crawford drew the fire of his opponents because of his nomination by a caucus of members of Congress. The objections to the caucus system were kept before the public by newspapers, broadsides, public speakers, and every other means. Opponents to the system declared the contest to be a democratic crusade by the people to gain control of elections from the domineering minority. The Crawford people alleged that the cry was not against the principle but rather against the result.[39] Rufus King of New York, old Federalist statesman and onetime candidate of the party for president, earnestly denounced the method, and sent Gaston his speech in Congress on the subject, asking at the same time for his views. Gaston's record was clear in this regard for his opposition to it was consistent and continuous. In his reply to King, with old-fashioned courtesy, he said:

> Accept my acknowledgement of your kindness in sending me a copy of your late speech in the Senate. Before I received your communication I had read your remarks in the National Intelligencer, and (suffer me to say it) read them with gratitude and delight. The warning voice which you have raised against the unconstitutional and dangerous central power which now would control the election of a President, and hereafter may aspire to control all the operations of the

government may not at present be heard with the reverence which it ought to command. But when the excitement of the moment is over it must produce its proper effect. Hereafter your admonitions will be recurred to by the thinking and the upright as a legacy of political wisdom bequeathed to the country by one of its most faithful servants at the moment of closing his public career, and at that moment, "as in all the past," exhibiting in all its force the principle which ever characterized his conduct, a preference of the People's good to the People's favor. Pardon me for speaking thus to you. I probably shall never see you more, and as you are about to leave Congress never again hear from you. The moment of parting has its privileges. It is then permitted to give vent to feelings of reverence and attachment which the decorum of society had before required to be suppressed.

God bless you, Sir! May the residue of your days on earth be peaceful. May you be happy hereafter.[40]

At first the candidacy of Jackson was not taken seriously by the others but he revealed an amazing strength. In March of 1824 Calhoun was eliminated from the contest when the Pennsylvanians swung to Jackson. The issue was confused in North Carolina where a People's Ticket was pledged to vote against Crawford for the stronger candidate – Adams or Jackson – but no means were at hand to decide which of the two had that distinction. In April Gaston told Webster that while there had been a prospect of electing Calhoun he had felt a strong interest in his success, but now preferred Adams to the other candidates. He felt that the struggle in his state would be between Crawford and Jackson, with the former having the better chance of success. He asked Webster whom he thought would be chosen if the election went to the House.[41] In reply Webster stated that he believed it would go to the House, and that it would be vain to conjecture concerning the results, although he thought Adams had the best chance as he had the support of New England.[42]

The vote cast in this presidential election in North Carolina was disappointing, for it was only 36,036 or about two thirds of that cast in the state election.[43] This result was attributed to the general understanding that the election would go to the House of Representatives. The western counties had given the People's Ticket the victory with a vote of 20,415 to the 15,621 for Crawford, contributed mostly by the eastern and central counties. On December 1 the electors met in Raleigh and cast the fifteen electoral votes of North Carolina for Jackson as president and Calhoun as vice-president. However, John Quincy Adams was elected by the House on the first ballot. The vote of the entire delegation of North Carolina was given to Crawford. This election had special significance in North Carolina, for a successful revolt from Virginian leadership bolstered state pride, while the revolt of the backward western section of the state against the dominance of a highly developed middle eastern section promised a constructive and active governmental program.[44]

In his inaugural address Adams advocated a vast system of public improvements. His broad views on the powers of government under the Constitution ran counter to those of the strict constructionists who were powerful in the North, and to the solid South with its fear of legislation against slavery. The election was barely over when the defeated candidates began planning for the next one. Henry Clay had been appointed secretary of state in the new administration, and the cry raised that this was the result of a corrupt bargain between Adams and Clay gained wide credence. Every move made by Adams was attacked by the Jackson-Calhoun-Crawford forces with a view of ruining him in the eyes of the people.

One of the first attacks against him came in 1825 on his suggestion that commissioners be sent to a proposed conference of South American republics at Panama. This attack was chiefly political in character, although the racial aspect also aroused bitterness. Southern opposition was raised to a white heat, and Congress debated on the question until April of the next year. Then the appointment of two commissioners was ratified, but it was so late neither reached the session before its close.

Gaston had been in favor of the mission, feeling that it would be rude to decline the invitation, and that our presence might "prevent rash combinations affecting our interests and give a tone to the body beneficial to the world." He felt that nothing of any great consequence could result from the conference, and told his New Bern friends that as Spain was already offended at our recognition of the South American republics the offense was complete, so would not be increased by our acting up to that recognition. He felt that the great powers had no cause for complaint. Although his support of Adams had been lukewarm, it was to increase daily as he watched the old statesman's policy. To his young friend, John H. Bryan, who had started his legal career under his direction, Gaston said, "The president's message . . . has raised my estimate of his talents, although I knew his acquirements were prodigious. In this message there is an elevation of thought and dignity of conception which would not dishonor a genius of the first order. I admire his beneficial views."[45]

His friendly disposition toward the administration and his disapprobation of the "strange opposition" was very pleasing to Webster, who asked him for his views and feelings as he desired to know more "than I do know . . . of your sentiments in regard to public affairs."[46] Webster was convinced the South meant to quarrel with the president right or wrong. Adams also had Gaston on his mind, for in a cabinet meeting a few days before this he had proposed the North Carolinian for secretary of war. This, however, was opposed by Secretary of State Clay, who may have still remembered Gaston's barbed remarks in the debate on the "Previous Question," and who also wanted one of his own men in that place. Adams complained that the South had no representative in the cabinet, but that he stood alone in his opinion because the others considered "public interest subordinate to private accommodations."[47]

Jackson's whirlwind campaign of 1828 with its bitter denunciation of the son of John Adams started long before the election year, and caused Gaston to become a participant. Early in December of 1827 the Committee of Correspondence and Vigilance of New Bern announced in a circular that the administration of Adams was entitled to a second term because of its honest, enlightened, and wise regard to the honor and interest of the country. It declared that in the opposite candidate one looked in vain for civil and moral qualifications, and that his national policy was uncertain.[48] This circular was clearly the work of Gaston. He, with twenty-five others, among whom were Edward Graham, James G. Stanly, John H. Bryan, and William S. Blackledge of New Bern, were elected to attend the Anti-Jackson convention in Raleigh on December 27. This was the first party convention ever seen in North Carolina.[49] It was made up of eighty delegates, mostly old Federalists, although not entirely so, as Blackledge and Bryan were Democrats of long standing. In his keynote address Gaston declared that Adams deserved the accustomed mark of the country's approbation – a second term, because there was no well-founded or serious cause for complaint against his administration, while "custom had established firmly that no president could hold office longer than eight years."[50] The president had been approved by all his predecessors, who had used his talents for the service of the country in one capacity or other. Gaston warned the South that if jealousy were aroused on the score of Adams' northern home, it could in the future be applied against southern men.[51] Examining the qualifications of Jackson he hinted at a military dictatorship, wondered who would compose his cabinet, and worried over the danger of the general's high temper in diplomatic matters. To his mind the presidency was a trust and not a reward, and although he thought Jackson a fine and courageous soldier he was also but a "heaven taught statesman." His address was concluded with admonition that "on one side is certainly safety and probably prosperity, while on the other rests clouds and darkness."[52]

Some of the delegates wished to nominate Crawford for the vice-presidency, but Gaston spoke against this and held that they had not met with that view, and should wait the decision of the convention meeting in Richmond.[53] There Henry Clay was given this honor by the party.

The part played by Gaston aroused varied comment in and out of the state. General Swift's brother, W. R. Swift, a Jacksonian leader, wrote the general that he could not understand Gaston's stand "as a few years before he had been in their camp"; in this he must have been mistaken. Swift assured Jackson that there was no cause for worry because Gaston's opinions meant practically nothing in North Carolina, his influence being very limited, so the "flourish" made by him was probably meant to operate in other states.[54] The *North Carolina Journal* sneeringly remarked that only twenty counties were represented in this convention, with but fifty-six men in attendance. A letter in the *Western Carolinian,* which carried the address, under the signature of "Philo White" attacked Gaston bitterly as an "old Fed," whose reasons for supporting the administration were obvious. This writer felt that the address would do neither good nor evil where the author was known, but he nevertheless wished "to save honest people of being cheated by Mr. Gaston's silver-toned voice."[55] The *Carolina Sentinel* stated that it would soon publish the address, "the composition of which devolved upon William Gaston, whose legislative duties were so engrossing and his professional duties so heavy that until now he has not had time to write it out."[56] Ten thousand copies of it were to be distributed. A few days before its publication Gaston in a note of apology stated that although he had long retired from public life and was reluctant to engage in political contention he yet felt it to be a duty to support Adams. Concerning the composition of the address he said, " . . . While it justifies our choice and may carry conviction to the minds of others it will manifest a proper respect to the opinions of those who have honestly determined to support the opposing candidate."[57] The *National Gazette* of Washington spoke of the address and noted that he had been serving in the legislature of North Carolina and wished for his presence in Congress where "he would be invaluable at the present time . . . for he was one of the most able and upright men ever to appear there."[58] Gaston had been elected to the House very late in the session to fill the vacancy for New Bern created by the resignation of John Stanly, and appearing on December 10 was appointed to the judiciary committee.

His late entry upon his legislative duties in this session of 1827 is very strikingly described by a contemporary, John H. Wheeler of Hartford County, who had been a law student of Judge Taylor and was serving his first term in the House. Gaston had just come into Raleigh from New Bern, and immediately went to Taylor's office, where Wheeler was introduced to him by Taylor. The three then went to the House, where says Wheeler, "all eyes were turned upon Mr. Gaston, then in the zenith of his fame and popularity." Wheeler's first motion in the House was to present at this time Gaston's certificate of election.

Although the supreme court was now functioning well and performing a great service to the state, Frederick Nash, who was also on the judiciary committee, introduced a bill for its reorganization. The next day Gaston replied "with such force of argument and such power of eloquence in opposition that its distinguished author had few adherents."[59] Wheeler stated that this speech cost Gaston a long winter night of study. Gaston himself told his daughter that he was "occasionally worn down by efforts to prevent the mischiefs threatened by violence, folly, and profligacy." He thought this to be the most dangerous session of the legislature he had ever seen; that it was scarcely possible it would pass without some mischief, but he hoped its measures would not be as pernicious as many feared.[60]

Gaston's course in the support of the administration was brought to the attention of the leaders at the capital. From Waynesborough Jesse Turner advised Clay that Gaston's address was producing a happy effect in the state. In the meantime rumor had spread through the state that Gaston would be sent to England to represent America. Wayne spoke of the rumor, declaring that North Carolina was entitled to the appointment, while the great talents of Gaston made him deserving of it.[61] Edward Graham wrote a friend, " . . . It is with no small degree of pride and pleasure that I understand our distinguished townsman was thought of as Minister to St. James, but I fear it will come to nothing, so buried is our state in the slough of Jacksonianism that the administration will be cautious."[62]

In the meantime a Jackson convention met in Raleigh and selected the brother-in-law of Gaston, Judge Taylor, as its chairman. The Jackson campaign gathered momentum in North Carolina as in the entire Union. The press on both sides raged with a total disregard of decency. Adams was accused of stealing the public money, of making a corrupt bargain with Clay, and other crimes, while General Jackson was charged with murder, and the good name of his wife was held up to scorn with the accusation that the two had lived in adultery. And so the campaign ran over a disgraceful course to its inevitable ending. In general the two leaders had no part in this shameless activity.

Gaston was no party to such foul work. His actions like his address were models upon which a fair and honorable campaign could have been conducted. Jackson's triumphal march to the White House was aided by North Carolina, whose people gave him 23,936 votes. Adams was soundly trounced, receiving only 83 electoral votes to his opponent's 178. Jacksonian democracy was in control of the government, and the "man of the people" was in the White House. Six years after his inauguration a New York paper, commenting on Gaston's address in the Raleigh convention observed, "Can any American look at this extract from the wise forebodings of as wise a man as these United States contain, and not lament that the warning voice was not listened to. . . . "[63]

Although the new president developed an ability in his office that could not have been foreseen, the opposition to him and his policies was always strong. But the voices of fear and timidity and hesitancy were faint, for a new era was at hand and it was dominated by an old man with piercing eyes, waving white hair, and warrior's head, who struck with the swiftness of a plunging eagle, whom men affectionately called "Old Hickory."

## NOTES FOR CHAPTER SIX

1. *Carolina Sentinel,* April 11, 1818.
2. Raleigh *Register,* Aug. 17, 1821.
3. Gaston Letter Book, July 5, 1819, Gaston *MSS.*
4. *Ibid.*, Feb. 28, 1829.
5. Hopkinson to Gaston, May 11, 1818, Gaston *MSS.*
6. Randolph to Gaston, Jan. 6, 1820, Gaston *MSS.*
7. 3 North Carolina *Reports,* 279.
8. *Ibid.*, p. 380.
9. 1 North Carolina *Reports,* 96.
10. *Murphey Papers,* I, 319.
11. *Carolina Sentinel,* Oct. 23, 1819.
12. Gaston to Beasley, Oct. 30, 1819, Gaston *MSS.*
13. Gaston to William Sullivan, Sept. 29, 1825, Gaston *MSS.*
14. Joseph Story to Sullivan, Oct. 22, 1826, Georgetown University Archives.
15. *United States Catholic Miscellany,* Sept. 16, 1826.
16. R. D. W. Connor, *North Carolina: Rebuilding An Ancient Commonwealth,* I, 499.
17. *Ibid.*, p. 507.
18. *Carolina Sentinel,* July 10, 1819.
19. *Carolina Sentinel,* Aug. 14, 1819.
20. Murphey to Ruffin, Nov. 19, 1818, *Murphey Papers,* I, 121.
21. *Senate Journal,* 1818, p. 117. Report of Committee in Gaston *MSS.*
22. David L. Swain, *Early Times in Raleigh,* p. 25.
23. Johnson, *Antebellum North Carolina,* p. 638.
24. *Senate Journal,* 1819, pp. 113–118.
25. John Marshall to Gaston, Dec. 11, 1818, Gaston *MSS.*
26. *Senate Journal,* 1818, p. 127.
27. *Murphey Papers,* I, 275.
28. Gaston to Yancey, July 15, 1821, "Letters to Barlett Yancey," *James Sprunt Historical Publications,* X, 1911, p. 29. Hereafter cited as *Yancey Letters.*
29. Yancey to Gaston, Sept. 25, 1821, Gaston *MSS.*
30. Gaston to Yancey, July 15, 1821, *Yancey Letters,* p. 29.
31. Gaston to Yancey, Nov. 5, 1821, *Yancey Letters,* p. 32.

32. Virgil Maxcy to Gaston, Oct. 25, 1821, Gaston *MSS*.

33. Gaston to Henry Warfield, Feb. 22, 1822, Galloway, Maxcy, Markoe Collection, Library of Congress.

34. Albert R. Newsome, *The Presidential Election of 1824 in North Carolina*, p. 45.

35. *Ibid.*, p. 51.

36. Gaston to Gen. Swift, Oct. 25, 1823, Jos. T. Swift Papers, University of North Carolina.

37. W. R. Swift to J. T. Swift, Jan. 26, 1824, Swift Papers.

38. Maxcy to Gaston, July 7, 1823, Gaston *MSS*.

39. Newsome, *op. cit.*, p. 108.

40. Gaston to Rufus King, May 3, 1824, Rufus King Collection, N. Y. Historical Society.

41. Gaston to Webster, April 11, 1824, Gaston *MSS*.

42. Webster to Gaston, Sept. 8, 1824, Gaston *MSS*.

43. Newsome, *op. cit.*, p. 155.

44. *Ibid.*, pp. 172–173.

45. Gaston to John H. Bryan, April 1, 1826, Bryan Collection, N.C.H.C.

46. Webster to Gaston, May 31, 1826, Gaston *MSS*.

47. Charles F. Adams, ed., *Memoirs of John Quincy Adams*, VII, 546–547.

48. *Carolina Sentinel*, Dec. 1, 1827.

49. Connor, *op. cit.*, I, 511.

50. *Address On The Administration Convention . . . Raleigh . . . December 20, 1827*, p. 5.

51. *Ibid.*, p. 8.

52. *Ibid.*, p. 15.

53. Edward E. Graham to John H. Bryan, Jan. 2, 1828, Bryan Collection.

54. Swift to Jackson, April 8, 1828, *Jackson Correspondence*, III, 398.

55. *Western Carolinian*, March 25, 1828.

56. *Carolina Sentinel*, Feb. 9, 1828.

57. *Ibid.*, Jan. 5, 1828.

58. *National Gazette*, Dec. 22, 1827.

59. John H. Wheeler, *Sketches of North Carolina*, p. 116.

60. Gaston to Hannah Gaston, Jan. 5, 1828, Gaston *MSS*.

61. Jesse Wayne to Clay, March 23, 1828, Henry Clay *MSS*., Library of Congress.

62. Edward E. Graham to Bryan, Jan. 2, 1828, Bryan Collection.

63. New York *American* quoted in the New Bern *Spectator*, April 4, 1834.

*There has been for several years, and there is now, among some of the leading bold and artful politicians on this side of the Potomac, a settled design to establish a separate Confederacy. . . . I entreat you preserve that country, uphold that Constitution. . . .* — WILLIAM GASTON

*Such men as Gaston are too rarely found in any country to justify leaving them in retirement. . . .* — *"Washington Republican"* of Jonesboro, Tennessee

## CHAPTER SEVEN

# Banks, Internal Improvements, and Nullification

IN THE next few years the attention of North Carolinians was directed to those paramount issues which were receiving unbounded and heated interest from all classes of people in the United States – financial institutions, internal improvements, and the tariff. The last named was most vital and pressing, indicating and stressing the divergent interests of the North and South. The people watched with amusement the drama of the petticoat war waged by the ladies of the capital over and with Peggy O'Neale Eaton, resulting in the breakdown of Jackson's first cabinet and the advancement of Martin Van Buren; approved the old hero's challenge to the Bank of the United States when Clay sought to make it a political issue by persuading its president, Nicholas Biddle, to seek a recharter before the necessary date; and hotly supported the vice-president, John C. Calhoun, in his doctrine of nullification of the tariff by South Carolina, or else joined the president in denouncing the movement as having disunion for its object.

Before the tariff controversy reached the climax that almost brought about civil war, another issue became dominant in the state – the status or even the existence of the banks. In 1819, as a result of overexpansion and speculation there began a national depression which lasted over three years. One of the major factors in this had been the second Bank of the United States, which under unwise direction had taken part in the orgy of overspeculation. However, under better management it had sought to bring an end to this financial situation by calling in loans and other such measures. These actions frequently ruined insecure state banks and aroused the bitterness and hatred of the western people. There then followed the attempts on the part of several states to force the branch banks of the Bank of the United States out of existence through taxation. This culminated in the famous case of McCullock *vs.* Maryland, wherein Chief Justice Marshall declared these projects unconstitutional.

In North Carolina the branch of the Bank of the United States was in Fayetteville. About 1825 it began to put pressure on the various banks of North Carolina to resume the payment of specie, which had been suspended. The United States Bank had outmaneuvered the private banks, secured large amounts of their notes, submitted them with the demand for specie, and the banks were forced to comply with the request. The banks were then forced to call in their loans, which amounted to about $5,500,000 and their notes in circulation had shrunk to less than $1,500,000. Consequently, debtors were forced to meet their obligations and this had caused panic throughout the state. Affairs finally reached such a point that the governor of North Carolina in his message to the Assembly of 1828, recommended an investigation of the banks. A joint committee of the assembly, appointed for this task, reported that the condition of the banks was improved, so the payment of specie should be resumed. A minority report, filed by the chairman of the committee, Robert Potter, recommended dissolution of the banks and prosecution by the attorney general, maintaining that the officers of the banks should answer to the law for abuse of trusts and their frauds. Potter magnified the indiscretions and violation of banking rules by the banks into extortion.[1] A bitter debate in the House, lasting for nine days, grew out of this report.

Gaston was elected to represent New Bern and appeared in the House on September 17. Some three months before he had been appointed president of the New Bern bank, so when the speaker, Thomas Settle, asked him to serve on this joint committee he declined, but accepted the chairmanship of the finance committee.[2] The report of this committee, returned some time before that of the investigating committee, declared that the charters of banks were too vague, while the checks imposed upon them were too feeble. The legislature must compel the banks either to become specie paying or else close down, but any interference to hasten either would produce impoverishment of debtors, sacrifice of property, and general distress. It warned that the collection of debts should be lenient; terms should be consistent with the rights of creditors and the interest of stockholders.[3]

The debate over the bill presented by Potter to prosecute the banks began on December 29, 1828, and lasted until January 6, 1829. The leaders of the opposition were Gaston and David L. Swain. Robert Potter, Charles Fisher, and William J. Alexander were the most prominent men seeking to pass the bill. Potter was a demagogue of the worst sort who "sought popularity by magnifying the evil of the day and appealing to the people for reform." He served several times in the General Assembly and in Congress. Combining shallowness of mind with a viciousness of spirit, he was "run out" of North Carolina after cruelly maiming a relative of his wife, and was finally killed in a gun fight down in Texas. Charles Fisher of Salisbury, however, was a different type of man, who served his state well in many public capacities. He had been a leader in North Carolina of the Jacksonian forces in the election of 1824.

Gaston was the first to answer the charges of Potter and in a long refutation gave a detailed history of banking in the state. He pointed out that during the war all the banks in the South had suspended specie. Then when the banks of Cape Fear and

New Bern had asked to be rechartered, the state had demanded an increase in their capital assets. The year 1818 brought back their redundant issues which were punctually and faithfully redeemed until the money in the vaults was almost exhausted. At that juncture the banks should have called on debtors for payment of considerable installments, but to have done so would have spread dismay in the state. Brokers began to buy notes of the banks and submit them for redemption in specie. Thereupon the banks had refused specie to the brokers, and this action not only received the acclamation of the people but also the sanction of the legislature. However, the brokers went to the courts and forced the banks to resume payment of specie to them. Concerning this particular point Gaston stated that he had been consulted but had not approved, for he felt there was no excuse for not paying specie as long as there was a dollar on hand to pay.[4] He invited the legislature to investigate the bank of New Bern, stating that no breach of charter would be found, only an excessive leniency toward debtors could be charged to this bank.

He declared that the state itself was concerned in the other banks, receiving profits of $326,637 from its investments in the bank of Cape Fear, and like profit from the other banks.

> Do you wish to produce a forfeiture of the charters? The effect is a dissolution of the corporations – a complete extinction of their existence. And when this takes place what is the condition of our country? Upon the dissolution of the corporation – upon its civil death I state the law to be, and I state it with an entire readiness to pledge on the correctness of the statement, my professional reputation, whatever it may be – I state the law to be, that the lands of the corporation revert to those from whom they came – that the personal chattels are taken by the state, for the want of an owner – and that all debts due to or from the corporation are completely and forever extinguished. Suppose the Bank corporations dissolved, then, and what is the condition of our country? The debtors are indeed released – they may be benefited by the tremendous catastrophe. But what of the value of the million and a half of

the bank notes in circulation? They are converted into rags. What the value of your 7,027 shares of bank stock? Where will come your available funds to carry on the operations of government? How are you from an impoverished people to raise the necessary revenue.

Turning to Potter, Gaston sarcastically asked, "Do you want, then, plunder?" Then, swinging back to his intent audience, he charged Potter with wishing to seize all the effects of these corporations and to establish a new bank owned by the state, although it would be a violation of the federal Constitution to emit bills of credit.[5] He maintained that the evils of the situation were less aggravated at this time and the prospects for their removal most encouraging. The Bank of the United States was forcing the state banks to withdraw redundant issues, to collect debts, curtail discounts, and redeem paper. Depreciation was almost gone and no bank issuing discreditable money could exist in North Carolina. After quoting figures to prove that the state was more prosperous than it was rated, he advanced a plan for improving the situation. The value of shares in the capital stock of each bank should be published; the banks should be authorized to receive these shares in payment of debts, and then the shares could be destroyed.

In reply Potter shouted that Gaston's remarks were directly at variance with the facts. "It is too bad he cannot use his talents for the people instead of these corporations. Are men who extort to the last cent to be allowed to talk of plunder," cried Potter bitterly.

He was followed by Alexander who wished to see the banks dissolved and a new one set up, even if the existing law had to be changed. He stated that its debts became the property of the state and cited as precedent the seizure of loyalist property. Swain then spoke in defense of the banks, declaring that the expansion of capital had been due to pressure exerted by the legislature.[6] Refuting Alexander, Gaston held that a corporation could not be dissolved and then re-established under different management for when its charter was taken away it died, and stockholders could not be sued because as individuals the members owed nothing.[7] He pointed out that the property of loyalists had not belonged to citizens but aliens, so Alexander's comparison was not valid. Property of citizens was protected from seizure by the legislature, and a law fixing penal consequences of an act after the act was done was unconstitutional and an absurdity in terms. He warned them that the literary fund for the education of the poor and the fund for internal improvements would be annihilated, and that the savings of innocent stockholders of all classes would suffer the same fate.[8]

Realizing that their chance of success was fading and that their original majority lessened every time Gaston rose to speak, the leading advocates of the prosecution became bitter and personal, at the same time paying tribute to his ability. Potter mournfully admitted, "had the gentleman from New Bern taken the other side of the question there would have been scarcely a dissenting voice to the course proposed."[9] After another exchange between Alexander and Gaston, Fisher, comparing the two parties at issue, observed that one wished to go to any and all lengths to obtain its end, while of the other he said:

> At the head of this party is the distinguished gentleman from New Bern, and under his shadow we see gathered, with a few exceptions, all the junior members of the profession. Lucky are the banks to have such an advocate — so able and so zealous. His displays remind me of a certain famous lawyer who not only bewildered the court, but finally even convinced the criminal that he wasn't guilty anymore.

Sarcasm was of no avail, however, for the tide was already turned. On the first reading Potter's bill to prosecute the banks had been favored by a vote of 66 to 54. As it became apparent that this bill would not pass, its authors substituted another, whose provisions were directed against only the state bank. Concerning it Nash said, "The measure now proposed pays a silent homage to the arguments of the gentleman from New Bern by abandoning the principles against which he reasoned and recognizing as true the doctrine so much disclaimed against, of the extinguishing of the debts due to and from the banks by a dissolution of their charters."[10] On the final vote the bill was lost by the casting vote of the speaker, and the fight was over.

Potter's charges were wild, but it must be said that not all of Gaston's claims were sound. His contention that offering notes redeemable in specie was equivalent to paying in specie was scarcely good economic reasoning. He also maintained that requiring those who applied for loans to pay the principal and interest in specie was not usury, but practically the burden it imposed was equivalent to usury. While this debate was raging and for some time afterward excitement was intense all over the state and opinions concerning the outcome were varied.

The Catawba *Journal* sided with the victors, admitting that the banks had in some instances passed the limits prescribed by their charters, but excusing their actions because of the peculiar situation in which they had been placed by circumstances. The editor felt it unjust to attribute all the evils of the day to the banks; he blamed the people as well, and asked that a moderate course be followed.[11] When first reviewing the different reports of the committees the *Carolina Sentinel* stated that Gaston's remedies for the evils confessed were not sufficient. However, it stamped the minority report as "drawn up with too much haste and rancor of inference and too little temperance of language to be considered fair, distinguished, or able."[12] The following February this paper published the entire speech of Gaston, with the comment that:

> . . . It is cheering to find those who carry with them a weight of talent and character like Mr. Gaston taking the lead in the discussion. . . . The speech of Mr. Gaston is the most lucid statement of the facts which we have yet seen as the report of the minority is remarkable for contrary qualities.[13]

Although this paper had at first wished to call an extra session of the legislature to consider the issue anew, when an attack was printed in its columns on Gaston in a letter to the editor, he remarked that the other side of the question was "so amply and eloquently sustained by Gaston that it would be both presumption and superfluous to add a single word."[14] The *Free Press* declared that although some papers were proposing an extra session it felt the legislature had done all it could. Its editor quoted Gaston to demonstrate that the situation was not hopeless.[15] The Raleigh *Register* published a letter from "a gentleman of New York" (one wonders if this might have been one of Gaston's friends, such as Chancellor Kent) saying that he "had never seen in all the discussions in the legislative assemblies of the states such a clear development of the true principles of banking."[16] The *National Gazette* praised "the true view . . . of one of the ablest and most distinguished of our public men."[17] In the *Yadkin* and *Catawba Journal* of February 10, 1829, Charles Fisher published his vindication and attack on the banks.

Thomas Ruffin, one of the most prominent of the state's lawyers, was made president of the state bank soon afterward, and asked Gaston's advice on closing down the bank. The latter was of the opinion that there was an injurious excess of banking capital in the state, and the only prospect of the removal of the "tremendous evil which it had occasioned to the community was by a diminution of the capital." However, without fuller information upon the details necessary to close the affairs of the bank, so as to trace the practical consequences, he was unable to form a definite answer.[18] Ruffin succeeded in keeping the bank open while he was president, until the following August, when he resigned to accept a position on the state supreme court. Gaston was asked to take over the presidency but refused.[19]

This session of the legislature was the longest on record, for it did not adjourn until January 20. Proceedings had been devoted almost entirely to the question of the banks, although Gaston had reported bills from the judiciary committee for the purpose of requiring petition in order for any man to legitimatize a child,[20] and to amend certain practices in equity, besides presenting a petition of the Quakers against bearing arms.[21] After the session he was asked by Governor John Owen to serve as one of two commissioners to prepare an act relating to executors and administrators. Ruffin had consented to act as the other if Gaston were one. The governor stated that he knew of "no two gentlemen in the state from whose hands such a work would be so well received by the legislature."[22]

Gaston was again in the House for the 1829–1830 term, "having consented to serve once more in the legislature. . . . I hope it will be the last time." Mainly through his arguments the banks of New Bern and Cape Fear obtained an extension of their charters to 1838, while a bill for a state bank was defeated, sixty-seven to sixty-three.[23]

During these sessions Gaston and Swain led the conservative financial forces in their efforts to maintain sound banking practices. In the defeat of the bill to charter a new state bank, Gaston in a remarkably frank statement thoroughly castigated the radical leaders in their attacks on the banks by stating that these men sought popularity by pandering to the ignorance of the unlearned. Partly because of these circumstances Gaston and those of like mind became anti-Jacksonian by 1832, if they had not been so previously.

In a very able defense of the high court, Gaston was also able to defeat an attempt to reduce the salaries of the supreme court judges. Several prominent public men, among whom were his friends, Swain, Nash, and Graham, asked for a copy of this speech in order to publish it.[24] Despite all his resolutions to the contrary he became thoroughly engrossed in legislative business. He felt that it required a greater sacrifice of time and mental exertions than he could afford consistently with his other duties, so resolved not again to take a place in the legislature.

In the next session he was not present, but circumstances forced his attendance in that of 1831–1832, although as late as May 11 he had publicly refused to run again. A few days before the election, under strong pressure, he consented to become a candidate for the House as a representative from the borough of New Bern. On November 25 Edward Stanly announced his withdrawal "because he owed it to the Eastern part of the state and the vast interests at stake to have the best man there."[25] The vast interests were expected legislation on railroads, the supreme court, and, most important, an anticipated attempt on the part of a few to have the capital moved from Raleigh, because of the ruinous fire which had raged there a short time before the beginning of the session. The East also feared lest the West take advantage of the situation to secure increased representation, as the West was not equitably represented.

Although he won, polling 146 votes, New Bern gave his opponent, Charles Shepard, 145 votes.[26] It was the hottest election seen in the town for a long time; Gaston was anti-Jacksonian, so the Republicans united with all the forces of the town not conservative in an effort to defeat him. His friends claimed that the sheriff's office had joined with all the rowdies in the town in this effort. The *Free Press*, a western paper, decidedly critical of his principles, discussing the results, said:

> Perhaps no better evidence could be adduced of the uncompromising spirit of republicanism possessed by the citizens of this state than the result of this election. Mr. Gaston is a veteran in political and legal contests and his superior skill and prowess have been felt and acknowledged in our National and State legislatures and in our highest judicial courts by our most eminent statesmen and jurists. His competitor is a young man of promise but unknown. . . .

Seeking a cause of this evident paradox, that such a thing could happen in "such an apparently unequal contest," the editor was not long at a loss. It was "simply because he (Gaston) is thought to be *incurably* possessed of the evil spirit of federalism – were this not the case the most exalted stations in our State and National Councils would be his." Nevertheless, the paper expressed gratification at the result.[27] In the same sense spoke the Fayetteville *Observer*, hoping that Gaston would be elected,

"Clay man and Federalist though he be," for it would give the state more dignity and interest. Gaston told Senator Mangum that he had never seen an assembly more respectable for talents nor one which could do more good for the state than this present one, were it not so distracted by sectional jealousies.[28] National events were of great interest at this time so he asked the senator to keep him informed of them, and so "gratify my curiosity to peep through the loop holes of Retreat upon the mighty Babel and behold its stir."[29]

This session of the assembly was indeed important and exciting. The House convened on November 21, but Gaston was delayed in New Bern so did not take his seat until December 5. As usual he was appointed to the judiciary committee, from which he reported a bill to allow appeals to the supreme court from interlocutory judgments, orders, and decrees of the Superior Court of Law and Equity. At a meeting held at the courthouse in New Bern the previous May he had spoken in favor of the construction of a new railroad to be known as the North Carolina Central. In the middle of December he introduced the bill to charter this railroad, with a capital of $2,000,000. It was to start near Beaufort, run through New Bern and Raleigh, and on through the central part of the state. The railroad was to be built by private means, but this was not forthcoming; only by liberal state aid was the road finally run through the center of the state.

Gaston was also on the joint committee appointed to consider the advisability of repairing Canova's statue of Washington, badly defaced in the capitol fire, and to him fell the duty of reading the resolution authorizing this expenditure. North Carolina was very proud of the equestrian work from the hands of the famed Canova, and at every opportunity, such as the visit of Lafayette and other famous persons to the capital, made a great ado in displaying it. Nevertheless, upon the completion of the report, an old man arose, and with that characteristic attitude of Nathaniel Macon and others who had won popularity from the people with the cry of economy at any cost, stammered out that he had as much love for General Washington as anybody, but that he was convinced the people did not wish to spend money in repairing his statue, for it was enough that they had him in their hearts.

Upon the completion of this hesitant appeal Gaston rose slowly, fixed a piercing gaze upon the poor fellow, and in a clear, deliberate, and emphatic manner intoned, "Out of the abundance of the *heart,* the mouth speaketh." The keeper of the people's purse spoke not another word, for the bill was carried by acclamation.[30]

Such episodes were frequent during this session. Toward the close of the year Louis D. Henry became so excited over a bill to further restrict free Negroes, which was prompted by the recent insurrection in Virginia and the abolition campaign in the North, that he used rather intemperate words toward Gaston. That evening he wrote the latter a note of apology, remarking that "I would not offend you for anything." A few days later Gaston told Spaight that his statements about another bill were not true. He was called to order by the speaker for making personal reflections, and although the matter was passed over at the moment, rumor soon spread that something was expected to come from it. Friends then rushed in to smooth the affair, one writing Gaston that he had evidently not expressed precisely what he had intended; that he supposed he had meant Spaight was too interested to be impartial, but he had used words which might reflect upon the former's veracity. This writer begged Gaston not to be hasty and not to allow pride to prevent an amiable settlement. The two did not come to blows, for the matter was settled by friends. As during the Jeffersonian administration, so now he voted against a resolution "approbatory of the administration of Andrew Jackson," which, however, passed by a vote of eighty-eight to nineteen.

The most important activity of this session, though, was the fight over the proposed removal of the capital. Sectional differences were constantly paralyzing the state's legislative machinery, sometimes on the most trivial of matters; men of the East and the West alike often acted not for the good of the state, but solely for their own section. The East itself was really divided into two sections — the Cape Fear region and the extreme East. The location of the state capital at Raleigh had always been a sore point with the Cape Fear section. They now determined to do everything in their power to secure the removal of the capital from Raleigh. Richard D. Spaight remarked that if these men could be sure of fixing the seat at Fayetteville they would give up everything else for that privilege.[31] The debate over the appropriation bill to rebuild the capitol made this clear. Toomer's remarks were characteristic of those made by the men of this section. He stated that only the people could alter the seat of the government, but that they desired such a move and public indignation would frustrate the design of forestalling the removal for the "tide of empire is marching westwardly."[32]

Gaston, in a speech declared by one who witnessed it to be the greatest ever heard by him,[33] opposed the move of the capital from Raleigh as strongly as he had opposed the proposal to remove the national capital from Washington after it had been burned by the British. He began with the statement that no proposition on which there was any difference of opinion had come under his notice in which the path of duty appeared more clear, more certain, more obvious than on this. Reviewing the history of the capitals of North Carolina he pointed out that in 1776 there had been no special place for the state government; records and officials were scattered and every town was seeking the honor. The people in convention made Raleigh the capital, and to the criticism that this ordinance was not a part of the constitution, he would reply that by the constitution of 1776 Fayetteville was not entitled to a representative, but had received this privilege by an ordinance of the convention of 1789. The Cape Fear men had said that no time was set to erect buildings, so this could be postponed from year to year. To this he replied that the ordinance had commanded Raleigh as the place for holding sessions of the assembly. No one had asked for a convention, but they were there in the middle of assembly proceedings. He felt that the people were too honest to want the ruin of the citizens of Raleigh, and too prudent to sacrifice all the public property there to local and selfish interests, even though such a desire could be created by politicians. The assembly was not a convention nor was there one in sight, neither could they wait until one was called as there was no way of knowing when this might occur, if it ever did.

Exposing the petty sectionalism of the contest he viewed the projects and tactics of each in turn. The West believed it ought to have more political power and it wished only for increased representation, but refused the appropriation in the hope of obtaining their desire in the ensuing contest. The Cape Fear party did not want the West to gain this increased representation, but only wished for a convention to obtain the capital. Fayetteville fancied that its growth would be hastened, but he branded as false the idea that it needed but the presence of the assembly to become a splendid city, for Fayetteville would not gain all that Raleigh lost. Fayetteville was in the Southwest and did not have the healthful situation of Raleigh, as was proved in the summer when every family that could left for other regions. Good roads and open communication with the tidewater was the road to prosperity there. He reproved the East's fear that their section would contribute the taxes while the other disbursed it, with an appeal to their sense of justice and understanding, telling them that every question had two sides. Demonstrating that only thirteen counties out of sixty-four had an active interest in the change, while at least thirty regarded it with abhorrence, he concluded with the masterful plea:

> Let us not leave ruins to proclaim to every passerby that North Carolina is so torn by strife she cannot even agree to erect a House for legislation.[34]

The plea was not in vain, for the West was won, and Raleigh remained the capital of the state. This was Gaston's last appearance in the legislature. However, within three years it was found necessary to call a constitutional convention.

In North Carolina internal improvement as a state activity arrived at its fruition too late to have the success wished for by the leaders of the movement. The state was badly in need of better means of communication. Roads were in a terrible state, the rivers were not navigable in many places, harbors were choked by sand bars, and other hindrances to commerce were plentiful. There was no home market, few cities of any great size, and the tide of emigration was steadily mounting. The first action by the general assembly to meet the exigency was taken in 1815. A committee was appointed to draw up a plan of general improvement, but the bill which was reported was killed in the House after passing the Senate.[35] In a series of remarkable reports Archibald D. Murphey, who became the leader of the movement for internal improvement and better education facilities, made a comprehensive analysis of conditions with plans to effect their change.[36] Although the legislature was slow to act, and a sharp conflict in that body arose over the issue, by the end of 1819 it had employed an engineer, obtained surveys of rivers and proposed canals, created a fund for internal improvement and a board to direct the new policy.[37] Gaston was in the Senate this year, and voted in favor of the bill, besides introducing a bill designed to procure speedy decisions of controversies about lands conveyed or condemned for the use of the Canal Company and other corporations. The West, in vast need of a system which would open that district to better opportunities, aided by those parts of the East whose economic interest would be advanced, committed the state to a definite policy in this regard. Although the plan aimed to avoid sectional jealousies opposition was aroused in the East.

A member of this section and often identified with its interests, yet Gaston did not feel its opposition to this policy was justified. He placed the good of the entire state above mere sections. His toast on July 4, 1825 – "A system of general instruction; the development of our internal resources; the pure and able administration of justice; let these be the cardinal objects of the policy of North Carolina"[38] – was not empty words, for he became a firm and important figure in the movement, with a prominence almost as great as that of Murphey and equal to that of Swain.

In the fall of 1827 the Agricultural Society of Craven County was formed, a constitution was adopted, and William Gaston elected its first president for a period of one year; R. D. Spaight was made vice-president, and Blackledge its manager.[39] In a speech before the society Gaston complained that agriculture had been miserably carried out in the state, but was beginning to improve through the influence of the society and Colonel John Taylor's book, *The Arator.*[40] Two months after the formation of the society a convention was held at Washington, North Carolina, for the purpose of concerting measures for the improvement of navigation at Ocracoke Inlet. Delegates to it from Craven County were Gaston and Sylvester Brown. The committee on measures to accomplish the object of the convention, which was to obtain direct and safe communication with the ocean at the mouth of Ablemarle Sound, reported that the inlet was impeded by shoals known as The Swash over which vessels drawing more than seven feet could not pass. The committee stated that the export through Ocracoke was computed to be 200,000 tons of shipping valued at $5,000,000. The charge on the ships for literage and detention was one dollar a ton, while insurance ran to $75,000 on produce and $60,000 for the ships, which the committee declared was a heavy tax on both consumer and producer. Gaston was on the committee which drew up this report, and was one of those appointed to seek aid for their project.[41]

From this time on Gaston labored hard to accomplish the object sought by the convention. He discussed with Bryan the chance of obtaining from Congress an appropriation of $20,000 to deepen The Swash. To accomplish this he wished to set up a company, incorporated by Congress, to last fifty years. The right to receive tolls was to end with the extinction of the company. He explained that the toll charge would be high because the necessary aid would not be forthcoming from the state.[42] In 1829, while in the House, he supported several resolutions on this subject. Broadly speaking, they affirmed the constitutional powers of Congress to appropriate money to all such objects of internal improvement as might be sanctioned by the state, but declared the government did not have the power to make improvements in the state except in the execution of powers delegated by the Constitution, such as the building of roads required for military or postal purposes.[43]

However, progress in these schemes was slow, and Gaston's discouragement is revealed in a letter to his daughter, Susan, in which he said, "There is a fatality attending North Carolina; all plans of internal improvement have failed, and the university is tottering to the base. Citizens are discouraged and are either leaving or are sunk in apathy. The capital is destroyed and the people are distressed about the change of the seat of government." He then went on to tell Susan that a good citizen never allowed himself to dispair of his country's fate, for the more numerous her calamities, the more vigorous his efforts.[44]

After a meeting held at the courthouse in New Bern under Gaston's chairmanship to discuss the work at Ocracoke, he wrote Mangum concerning it and asked him to try to obtain congressional aid. He told the senator that the feasibility of the project was demonstrated as work had been carried on with great success and that a channel had been made over and through the shoals.[45] Gaston also drew up a plan for a canal between Beaufort, North Carolina, and Norfolk, Virginia. He felt it would open inland navigation from Pennsylvania to Georgia, with the exception of a short run by sea from Beaufort to Charleston and, in consequence, would "give the state a distinction and consideration which would soon dissipate the contempt and slight which our sister states affect to feel for us."[46] However, the clearing of The Swash was never completed and work on a canal system began too late. The Erie Canal was opened in 1825 and drew much of the western trade to New York. Before canals could become a vogue in North Carolina, the building of railroads put a stop to all such undertakings.

July 4, 1833, when the cornerstone of the new state capitol was laid, an important convention on internal improvement met in Raleigh. It was composed of delegates from the counties of the state, and elected David L. Swain as president. During its session various resolutions were offered for the building of railroads. Gaston introduced one to construct a railway from Waynesborough to New Bern or Wilmington or both.[47] However, in the report finally adopted the convention decided it was inexpedient to recommend any specific points, but instead instructed the legislature that a liberal system of internal improvements was needed. It urged the general assembly to provide a loan so that a fund could be had exclusively for this purpose, and asked it to subscribe two fifths of the stock in any company formed. A committee of twenty members of the convention was named to prepare an address to the state and to lay before the legislature its proceedings. This committee was made up of some of the most important men in the state, including George E. Badger, James Iredell, Cadwaller Jones, Frederick Nash, John Owen, Robert Strange, William B. Meares, and John H. Bryan. Gaston was made chairman, and to him fell the task of preparing the address. In it he declared that in extent of territory North Carolina had the advantage of New York and Pennsylvania, and that before the federation it was not inferior in wealth to them, if the principal cities of the other two states were excluded; the territory now remained but nothing else could be said for it. Then he alluded to the need of colleges, railroads, hospitals, asylums for the underprivileged and deficient, and concluded by pointing out the natural advantages of the state, such as the mild winters and unmined minerals. The address won wide praise. It was republished in the *Washington Republican* of Jonesboro, Tennessee, with the following editorial comment:

> Such men as Gaston are too rarely found in any country to justify leaving them in retirement. . . . We are much mistaken if she can boast of any amongst them as well qualified by high intellectual attainments, purity of moral character, and ardent patriotism, to confer lasting glory on his state and permanent good on the nation as this distinguished . . . whom we have named. Certain we are that he has few equals anywhere. . . . [48]

Soon after this convention another meeting was held in New Bern, with Gaston in the chair, to approve the findings of the late convention and to call the attention of the legislature to the concurrence of the town.[49] The legislature of 1831–1832 chartered three railroad companies, while that of 1833 incorporated nine new companies. Soon the state saw the completion of two of these railroads, the completion of the new capitol, and the prospect of a new public school system. Gaston had a hand in this beneficial state program, and his deep interest in internal improvement of North Carolina was recognized even outside the state, as is testified in many instances such as the request of Washington Irving to him that he use his influence to obtain a position for the latter's nephew on the railroad.[50] However, the vision of a great western trade for North Carolina was doomed in the beginning, but a spirit of enterprise and aid in local development was encouraged by all these plans.

While these events were arousing the passion of their advocates and the interest of all, the more pressing issue of the tariff soon dominated the scene. American manufacturing had been stimulated during the War of 1812. At its end many desired to protect the new industries from the rush of cheap goods from Europe. Hence, in 1816 Congress passed a tariff bill in order to protect manufacturers; cotton and woolens gained the greatest advantage. John C. Calhoun, strongly supporting the measure, spoke of the dangers of disunion and of the advantage to the South and West in its acceptance. Gaston, then in Congress, with most of the other members from North Carolina voted against it.

In 1820 the protectionists attempted and failed to raise the custom duties, but succeeded four years later. It was a sectional project with the sole aim of protecting manufacturing. The entire South was against it, for that section had concluded that protectionism and slavery were antagonistic, because little manufacturing was done in the South and all the raw goods, especially cotton, were sent North for manufacturing. In 1827 another bill containing some of the worst features of the system was defeated only by the casting vote of Vice-President Calhoun, who by now had reversed himself and decided to lead the South in opposition to protectionism.

The climax was reached by the passage in 1828 of the "tariff of abominations," this being an unreasonably high bill passed solely for political reasons. These oppressive duties on woolens had increased the cost of every blanket and winter suit bought for slaves, while the tariff on hemp became a tax on common rope. Latent opposition now reached the surface. As early as 1824 South Carolina had passed resolutions denouncing the protective tariff as unconstitutional, and other legislatures condemned it. Leaders of South Carolina blamed the tariff for all the ills of the state, and especially its apparent evidence of a great decline, which forced many to leave the state for the West. These opinions soon crystallized and found a leader in John C. Calhoun, who gave them national prominence in what came to be known as "The South Carolina Exposition." The main thesis, expressed briefly and simply, was that a state had a right to nullify a federal law which it thought to be unconstitutional. Nullification would be affected by means of a special convention, and after this was done the law should be repealed by the United States Congress, or else three fourths of the states could override this single state by repassing the act. Thus, one fourth of the states could permanently veto an act of Congress, decision of the supreme court, or a treaty.

A strong force of nullifiers captured public opinion in South Carolina and, although opposed by a smaller group of prominent so-called Unionists, were enabled to have an extra session of the legislature called, which voted in favor of calling a convention. This nullification convention met on November 19, 1832, and passed an ordinance of nullification of the tariff acts of 1828 and 1832. Two years before, the president, a southerner from Tennessee whom the nullifiers thought might be with them, had colorfully announced his disapproval, but after this action of South Carolina Jackson issued a proclamation, December 10, 1832, declaring that South Carolina must obey the federal laws. South Carolina found that she was alone in her viewpoint as not a state in the Union supported her. Virginia was important because of her influence, but this state urged the nullifiers to suspend the ordinance until Congress had adjourned. While throughout the North mass meetings were held in support of the president, in South Carolina bodies of troops were raised and drilled; the state became an armed camp.[51]

The people and the legislature of North Carolina were not slow to express their distrust of the course of the neighboring state. The Fourth of July toasts were expressive of this, as one given at Fayetteville indicates.[52] It, typical of others in the same vein, read: "South Carolina. We esteem her worth, but deprecate her example. We therefore hold her in union a friend; in disunion an enemy to our political institutions." Gaston gave a toast along the same line some time later, when he received an invitation to attend an important antinullification dinner given in Montgomery, Alabama, by "the friends of Union and equal taxation."[53] He could not attend the dinner, but sent a long reply approving their aim and proposing the toast, "The Union which makes the American States one people. Political economists may try to calculate its value. We prize it as the best patrimony which we have received from our ancestors, and we mean to transmit it whole and unimpaired, as a most precious inheritance to our children." In 1830 the House of Commons of North Carolina passed a resolution which declared that the legislature did not recognize the right of a state to nullify a law of the United States, and further stated that "although the tariff laws are unwise and oppressive to the southern states we cannot concur with the extremely violent and dangerous remedies to which the South Carolina doctrine of nullification manifestly tends."[54] This resolution passed by a vote of 87 to 27, but at this time the Senate refused to commit itself. The minority was composed of extreme state-rights men, who wished to wait until the crisis became acute for such action.[55] However, when the Ordinance of Nullification was passed by South Carolina the two Houses united in disapproval, and the governor in his message to them stated that the time had not yet come for the acceptance of doctrines subversive of all order, which tended to weaken or even ruin the whole system of government.

Early in 1830 Gaston had expressed himself to the governor, James Iredell, as very uneasy over the discussion which seemed to him to have as its principal object the arraying of different sections of the Union against each other. To him he said, "These geographical divisions are to me more alarming than any other. Would that our North and South, East and West men would be to each other's failings a little blind, and to their virtues very kind. . . . Faction is destined to be the ruin of every republic. . . . "[56]

To his son-in-law, Robert Donaldson, he expressed himself more vigorously a year later, saying, "Calhoun could not but come out in favor of nullification, after having formed a party of zealous and devoted nullifiers. It is impossible for any sophistry to uphold a doctrine which involves such glaring and practical absurdities. What a pity that such a mind as his should be so warped from its rectitude by unholy passions."[57]

The following year, 1832, he finally accepted one of the numerous requests to address a graduating class of the University of North Carolina. The day appointed, June 21, Thursday, dawned bright and clear as the little village of Chapel Hill awoke to find the largest crowd ever to assemble there in its history.[58] Great numbers were attracted on the expectation of both hearing and seeing the famous orator and lawyer. The college numbered but a little over a hundred students, but most of the important men of the state, among whom were Governor Stokes, J. M. Morehead, Frederick Nash, R. M. Saunders, Hugh Wadell, William Polk, James Mebane, Dr. S. J. Baker, and Swain, were there. Gaston's daughter, Hannah, and her husband, Manly, made this the end of their vacation tour. Gaston had arrived the day before; he was the guest of Dr. Caldwell, the president of the university, and occasionally the two wandered around the grounds together, to the amusement of the student body for Gaston towered head and shoulders above the dignified president.

As the afternoon shadows settled over the peaceful and beautiful village a procession of gowned students came winding down the paths among the waving trees, headed by the Richmond Cornet Band which was blowing lustily. Next came Gaston, flanked by Thomas Ashe and T. L. Clingman; the tall, genial lawyer, attired in a black gown much too short for him, chatted gaily with the two seniors. The procession started from the old South building, right flanked to old East, and when opposite Person Hall wheeled on the left and faced the Hall, entering after a momentary pause. Reaching the rostrum, the three were taking their seats near a little table, upon which Gaston started to lay his manuscript, when Clingman's long legs knocked the table over, and, but for the hasty lunge of Ashe, table, manuscript, and Gaston might have tumbled to the floor below. The crowd then broke in, and for the next hour pushed and clawed for space within the hall.[59] However, it was not large enough, although the windows and rafters accommodated a few, and many had to stand on the outside straining to hear every word poured forth by Gaston in the next hour and twenty minutes.

The address was a masterpiece of sound advice to the young graduates, delivered in his usual grand style, written in the perfect English of which he had an unusual command. At the end of the address he sounded a fateful warning, which may have been remembered by Clingman and Ashe many years later when they donned the Confederate gray uniforms, for he spoke of the current question of nullification, saying:

> . . . Men used to be, or affected to be, at issue on questions of principle; now, Americans band together under the names of men. Then, individuals of different parties were found side by side; now parties that distract the land are by geographical distinctions. . . . Now has come a period dreaded by Washington. . . . As yet the sentiment so deeply planted in the hearts of the yeomanry that union is strength has not been uprooted. As yet they take pride in the United States. May God in his mercy forbid that I or you should live to see the day when this feeling shall be extinct. . . . But these feelings are weakened and in the end will be destroyed unless moderates frown on any attempt to alienate any portion of our country from the rest. . . .
>
> Threats of resistance, secession, separation have become as household words. The public mind will soon be accustomed to the detestable suggestion of disunion. Conjectures, what may the North do without the South; sneers and reproaches all tend to the same fatal end. What can one do without the other? They will present fields and occasions for border wars, leagues, and counter leagues. . . .
>
> If it must be so, let parties continue to quarrel with little regard to the public good. They may do the country much harm . . . destroy its harmony and impair its character. Still we have that blessed constitution, and a name revered. Such a country and such a constitution have claims on you. I entreat you . . . preserve that country, uphold that Constitution. . . .[60]

In the course of this address Gaston revealed his statesmanship and courage when he also condemned in no uncertain terms the great evil of the South, slavery. His address met with unanimous approval in the South and North. It was copied in many of the papers and went through five different editions, one of which contained a preface written by Marshall.[61]

This was not the last public occasion in which he forcibly

opposed nullification. On December 8 a large meeting, attended by many persons from neighboring counties "without distinction of parties" was held in New Bern with Gaston in the chair. The main event of the day was the chairman's speech, and, as his speeches usually were, it was very long. His devotion to the Union and the Constitution was apparent in every sentence.

He began by reminding his audience that they had met to consider a subject of universal importance, to examine into the means to keep for themselves that Union which made them a nation. The Union of the American people had been denounced and they would be faithless to their children if they did not maintain it. Then Gaston rapidly drew a sketch of the period after the Revolution, reminding them of the anarchy that had reigned when the old Confederation had no power even to pay its soldiers. Then had come the Federal Constitution, a triumph of reason, patriotism, and self-denial over prejudice, passion, and state pride. In the forty-two years since, the struggles of contending parties had been violent, but the spirit of free institutions was preserved inviolate. After outlining the advantages gained he said:

> Now there is no Prince nor People which does not respect our rights, or is indifferent to our friendship. The American name is a passport of honor in every land. . . . And we are invited to forego these blessings for some unknown, some hypothetical state of greater perfection. It is impossible to contemplate the possibility of our being broken up . . . with its consequences . . . vexatious regulation of trade by sea and land. . . . We would become like the republics of South America.

He admitted that South Carolina had well-founded causes of complaint but thought these were exaggerated, while the remedy could not be justified for the cure was worse than the disease. Revolution could not be resorted to every time inconveniences were suffered; a nation could blunder in the same manner that an individual frequently acted against his own better interests. In its case time, fair discussion, and an enlightened public opinion would rescue error before it became fatal. He told his intent listeners that the South's arguments had been urged with dogmatism and arrogance, which would render a self-respecting people indignant and unwilling to be convinced. He felt that South Carolina might be induced to pause when it saw that its neighbors, who felt as it did about the protective tariff, still rejected the course threatened by it. This state regarded itself as leading the rest and should be undeceived. He concluded with a ringing challenge:

> North Carolina has declared an unshaking adhesion to the integrity of the Union. The people may disapprove of the Tariff much, but they love the Union more. . . . When the Union is endangered . . . then all differences are laid aside and forgotten . . . they have but one voice and that voice is, the Country and nothing but the Country.[62]

Marshall wrote his friend to express his pleasure with this public expression. He commended Gaston for not exasperating prejudice, which he thought was the source of all the mischief and was something the South excelled in. The Chief Justice feared that the legislature of Virginia was contaminated by a considerable number of men who wished for a separate confederacy, and although the people were not ripe for this yet, he felt that these men were so skillful that bitter fruits would soon fall. He told Gaston that insane as South Carolina's leaders were, they would not have gone so far had they not counted on Virginia; he feared that perseverance by the state would lead to civil war.[63]

The leader of all these discontented men, the great Calhoun himself, soon appeared in North Carolina to present his case. He had resigned the vice-presidency in order to take a place in the Senate to argue and fight actively for the cause, and on his way to Washington stopped all night in Raleigh. The night before his arrival there had been a big ball in the city; one of the editors observed that it was a great pity Calhoun had not arrived in time for this event, as he would have then forgotten tariff and nullification for at least one evening.[64] However, all day Sunday he remained in the hotel lecturing on the subject, telling the crowded room that the government had remained unreformed for forty years, that no human institution could fail to require amendment after such a length of time. He maintained that the citizens of the northern and middle states were excellent allies but hard masters and should be so bound that the South could be set free.

Gaston was in Raleigh at the time, but did not go down to hear or see his old friend, and the next morning at three o'clock the ex-vice-president was on his way to the capital. Congress managed to arrive at a compromise which saved the face of the sections and their leaders and made it appear that both sides had been victorious; so another crisis in American life passed into history. The fears expressed had not been realized, but the signs of the future were ominous. Gaston had acted throughout more as a nationalist than a states-right man. However, he felt that "the strong and general expression of the American people against Nullification had not killed it" and told Donaldson:

> There has been for several years, and there is now, among some of the leading bold and artful politicians on this side of the Potomac, a settled design to establish a separate Confederacy. The tariff and nullification were seized as a means to this end. Although it failed it is not abandoned. It will be presented with unabated perseverance. The honest fears of Southern slave holders and the fanaticism of Northern abolitionists are relied upon to bring about a conviction that the interests and feelings of the different sections of our country are too contradictory to render the Union consistent with the good and harmony of the whole. Every number of Duff Green's Telegraph contains matter fitted to bring this result.[65]

His statesmanship and vision in this affair has been vindicated by the events of succeeding years, when the events against which he warned took place. Like his grasp of the slavery issue, events proved him all too right.

During these years, as Gaston's reputation rose to its zenith, his activities were increased in like manner. His usual routine was arduous – in his office from sunrise until ten o'clock; from there to the bank till one o'clock and then, after "a short solitary dinner," the whole of the afternoon was spent in reading and writing, with scarcely time to see anyone except on business. He had a hand in almost any program that looked toward the progress of the state, holding numerous positions, such as trustee of the Griffin Free School in New Bern, director of the state institution for the instruction of the deaf and dumb, trustee of the University of North Carolina.

More and more honors were thrust upon him. Among the literary societies electing him a member and asking him to speak at their graduating exercises were the Erodelphian society of Miami University; the Franklin society of Randolph-Macon College; the Philo society of Jefferson College in Canonsburg, Pennsylvania; the Ewselian society of Wake Forest College; in 1830, 1834, and 1835 Princeton University asked him to deliver the address at their commencement exercises, as did Wake Forest College and the University of North Carolina in 1834. Many times he was asked to send copies of different speeches to some editor who was making a collection of "American masterpieces" or "national eloquence."

Frequently his name was presented to the country as a vice presidential prospect. The *Carolina Watchman* of August 10, 1833, took note of this trend, but "deprecated the bad taste of prematurely thrusting him before the public as had been lately done." "We cannot speak in measured terms of the intellectual and political merits of this gentleman," said the editor. Then the writer expressed the opinion this office was below Gaston, as it was not one to give his great powers proper scope, and such attention was afflicting to this "pure patriot." "There is not a man in this nation whose private virtues and public worth more entitle him to seek even the *highest* place," was the conclusion of this writer. Similar opinions were declared in the Alexandria *Gazette* the Raleigh *Register*, the Oxford *Examiner*, and many other papers in the country. One complained that "Gaston of North Carolina and Thomas Grimke of South Carolina are two of the noblest and purest spirits of the South. Why are they not nominated for some of the honors of their country and why cannot their nomination be sustained by the whole Southern press?"

North Carolinians journeying to other parts of the Union were pleased to find him held in such high regard by great public characters, who eagerly questioned them about their old friend. William A. Graham related how Justice Story had entertained him with legal conversation and remarks on legal talent "in the first rank of which he placed Webster, Mason, Wirt, and Gaston." Frederick Blount, while in Boston, was asked many questions about him by Quincy, the president of Harvard University.[66] Bushrod Washington declared that Gaston was one among half a dozen men he would like to see with him at a table. Gaston was indeed a man to be reckoned with in his state; his talents and character were to find a new expression when his state made a new and most important call for his services.

## NOTES FOR CHAPTER SEVEN

1. W. K. Boyd, *History of North Carolina: The Federal Period, 1789–1860*, p. 126.
2. *House of Commons Journal*, 1828, p. 147.
3. *Ibid.*, p. 237.
4. *Debate On The Bill Directing A Prosecution Against The Several Banks Of The State . . . House of Commons of North Carolina from December 29, 1828 To January 6, 1829*, p. 19.
5. *Ibid.*, p. 24.
6. *Ibid.*, p. 52.
7. *Ibid.*, p. 55.
8. *Ibid.*, p. 64.
9. *Ibid.*, p. 64.
10. *Ibid.*, p. 97.
11. Catawba *Journal*, Jan. 6, 1829.
12. *Carolina Sentinel*, Jan. 10, 1829.

13. *Ibid.*, Feb. 21, 1829.
14. *Ibid.*, Feb. 28, 1829.
15. *Free Press*, Feb. 20, 1829.
16. Raleigh *Register*, Feb. 27, 1829.
17. *National Gazette*, Jan. 15, 1829.
18. Gaston to Ruffin, May 22, 1829, J. G. deR. Hamilton, ed., *Th Papers of Thomas Ruffin*, I, 499. Cited hereafter as *Ruffin Papers*.
19. P. Browne to Gaston, Aug. 20, 1829, Gaston *MSS*.
20. *House Journal*, 1828, p. 166.
21. *Ibid.*, p. 174.
22. Governor John Owen to Gaston, March 19, 1829, Gaston *MSS*.
23. W. K. Boyd, "Currency and Banking In North Carolina, 1790 1836," *Historical Papers of Trinity College Historical Society*, X, 1914 p. 79.
24. Committee of Fifteen to Gaston, Nov. 26, 1829, Gaston *MSS*.
25. New Bern *Spectator*, Nov. 25, 1831.
26. *Ibid.*, Dec. 2, 1831.
27. *Free Press*, Dec. 6, 1831.
28. Gaston to Mangum, Dec. 31, 1831, Gaston *MSS*.
29. Gaston to Mangum, Nov. 30, 1831, Mangum *MSS*, Duke University
30. Kemp Battle, "Life and Character of William Gaston," *North Carolin University Magazine*, I, 53 (April, 1844).
31. G. G. Johnson, *Ante-Bellum North Carolina*, p. 32.
32. *North Carolina Journal*, Jan. 25, 1832.
33. R. B. Creecy, who declared in the beginning of this present centur that he could find no trace of this speech, and believed it lost.
34. *North Carolina Journal*, April 18, 1832.
35. C. C. Weaver, "Internal Improvement In North Carolina Previous T 1860," *Johns Hopkins University Studies In History & Political Scienc* XXI, pp. 9–10 and 45–48.
36. *Murphey Papers*, II, 33–197.
37. A. R. Newsome, *The Presidential Election Of 1824 In North Carolin* pp. 9–10.
38. Raleigh *Register*, July 8, 1825. Quoted also in C. L. Coon, *Publ Education In North Carolina*, p. 256.
39. *Carolina Sentinel*, Aug. 18, 1827.
40. MS. in Gaston *MSS*., undated.
41. *Carolina Sentinel*, Dec. 8, 1827. The convention was held Nov. 2 1827.
42. Gaston to Bryan, March 20, 1828, Gaston *MSS*.
43. Raleigh *Register*, Dec. 31, 1829, contains these resolutions.
44. Gaston to Susan, July 10, 1831, Gaston *MSS*.

45. Gaston to W. P. Mangum, Oct. 26, 1833, Gaston *MSS.*

46. Undated MS. in Gaston *MSS.*

47. *Journal of the Internal Improvement Convention, Raleigh, July 4, 1833,* p. 6.

48. Quoted in the Raleigh *Register,* Sept. 10, 1833.

49. Raleigh *Register,* Aug. 27, 1833.

50. Washington Irving to Gaston, May 11, 1837, Gaston *MSS.*

51. Frederic Bancroft, *Calhoun and the South Carolina Nullification Movement,* pp. 1–54.

52. H. Wagstaff, "State Rights and Political Parties In North Carolina," *Johns Hopkins University Studies In History & Political Science,* 1906, XXIV, 50.

53. Citizens of Montgomery, Alabama to Gaston, Sept. 25, 1832, Gaston *MSS.*

54. *House of Commons Journal,* 1830, p. 16.

55. Wagstaff, *op. cit.,* p. 51.

56. Gaston to James Iredell, Feb. 11, 1830, Gaston *MSS.*

57. Gaston to Donaldson, Sept. 3, 1831, Gaston *MSS.*

58. North Carolina *Free Press,* July 10, 1832.

59. Reminiscences of R. B. Creecy, Gaston *MSS.* Also in Richard B. Creecy, *Grandfather's Tales of North Carolina History,* p. 84.

60. Full text printed in *United States Catholic Miscellany,* Oct. 13, 20, 1832, and in most of the newspapers of the state.

61. Marshall wrote Gaston, July 22, 1832, expressing his great delight with the address. He then said, ". . . If those who become citizens . . . would act upon the principles you recommend a republic would indeed be a Utopia. . . . Your glance at the present state of parties is not the least part of your portrait." Marshall wrote the preface of the edition printed by Thomas W. White of Richmond, Va. In it he said that Gaston's observations ". . . seem to constitute the true basis of the character to which statesmen ought to aspire." Gaston told White that Marshall was "the man who stands higher in my reverence than any other living American." White informed him that among the great number who had written him in praise of the address were Everett, Hale, Wm. Maxwell of Va., and John Sargeant of Philadelphia, who was author "of the just tribute paid you and signed G, which is copied in the *Compiler* of this city." The *Free Press* of July 17, 1832, in speaking of the address said, ". . . but to the reader much is lost; the commanding address and manner, the emphatic enunciation and action — in a word — Mr. G's delivery will not accompany it." The *Boston Daily Advertiser & Patriot* remarked, "His rank as an able, sincere, and patriotic statesman was second to none of his contemporaries. The whole nation were, at one time, as much interested in what Mr. Gaston thought and said

as in the thoughts and speeches of any of its most distinguished citizens. . . ." Quoted in New Bern *Spectator,* Aug. 17, 1832.

62. Raleigh *Register & North Carolina Gazette,* Dec. 28, 1832. Among the many who wrote him about this speech was William Sullivan who told him that there was "reason to fear it will not long continue to be our common country. . . . If S. C. perseveres in present course and disunion follows, it will draw a line, probably, far North of your native state. Many . . . consider . . . the terms of our Union are drawing to a close. We are so dissimilar in our views of policy from our Southern brethren, in many respects, that it will be more and more difficult to get on together." (Dec. 11, 1832, Gaston *MSS.*)

63. Marshall to Gaston, Dec. 20, 1832, Gaston *MSS.*

64. New Bern *Spectator,* Jan. 4, 1833.

65. Gaston to Donaldson, May 8, 1833, Gaston *MSS.*

66. Frederick S. Blount to John H. Bryan, June 29, 1831, Bryan *MSS.*

*Chief Justice Marshall had taught me to think highly of his [Gaston's] abilities; and, my expectations, altho raised, have not been disappointed.* — JOHN RANDOLPH of Roanoke

*Permit me to say it is a masterly and conclusive law and constitutional argument, with the most diligent examination and keen critical analysis of the documentary authorities. . . . Perhaps I have said a great deal too much, considering your far superior and more familiar information and knowledge on the subject of common law doctrines.* — CHANCELLOR JAMES KENT

## CHAPTER EIGHT

# Justice Gaston of the Supreme Court

I HAVE been employed for some days past in the Circuit Court of the United States where brother Gaston is all in all," petulantly declared Badger to Ruffin, "and though I have heard much and seen a little of leaning yet never saw I, or heard I of such complete supporting upon a lawyer as of Chief Justice Marshall upon Gaston. The Chief Justice seems to be but his echo, though he is not aware of it. . . . "[1]

Although Gaston perhaps may have been the "first lawyer" in the state at the time, it should not be imagined that every case placed in his hands meant victory. Some time after the above related incident, Badger and Gaston were contending counselors in a trial of important land cases at the federal court in Raleigh, where large crowds every day met to listen "to the ablest arguments on both sides ever heard in a court in this state," and this was decided in favor of Badger.[2] Yet, a client's chance of success was great, and few cared to have Gaston on the opposite side. His ingenuity is illustrated by the following episode. In a trial at New Bern the question of seaworthiness came up, as well as the strength of a mast.

There may be a partial unsoundness of particular members, which could not with propriety destroy the character of a vessel for seaworthiness, and as scarcely a vessel sails on the ocean without having some unsoundness in part of her timbers, she cannot be denominated unsound or unseaworthy merely because individual constituent parts of her hull are in a state of decay. It required an assemblage of such defects to ascribe justly to her the application of being unseaworthy; and if the brig in question was enabled to encounter the ordinary perils of the ocean she was seaworthy. . . . The strength of cylindrical beams are as the cubes of their diameters. Therefore a mast of eighteen inches through has a relative strength of 18 by 18 by 18 or 5832; if it were rotten one-third of its diameter it would still have a strength of 5616, while if it were two-thirds rotten it would still have a strength of 4104, whereas a sound mast sixteen inches through has the strength of only 4096.

The New Bern paper reporting the trial claimed that "the concluding argument made by this distinguished jurist was pronounced to be the ablest intellectual effort ever heard or witnessed here."[3]

His powers were recognized by all; even Daniel Webster did not hesitate to ask him "to run your eye over this . . . and if its view of the constitutional question be wrong, just tell an old friend that he has fallen into error."[4]

The respect for Gaston's legal talent even outside legal circles among the ordinary folk is well illustrated by the following incident. In Indiana a former North Carolinian had been indicted for murder. The case was clear – Hugh Monroe had been on bad terms with the deceased for months, and when the two had met at a shooting match, he had shot his foe while the latter was engaged in adjusting the target. Just before the case came up in court, one of Indiana's leading lawyers, O. H. Smith was in his office when "a venerable man, uncommonly fine looking, with hair as white as snow, finely but plainly dressed, entered." This was Hugh Monroe's father and he came to ask Smith to help defend his son who had already employed Charles H. Test, James Rariden, and James T. Brown, three of the finest counsels in the state. When Smith acquiesced, the father exclaimed, "Oh, if I could have brought with me William Gaston, of our state, I would have been satisfied. I offered him a deed to my farm to come with me and defend my son, but he could not leave home. I must take you, and hope for the best." However, Smith and the others managed to do rather well; they were able to obtain a verdict of manslaughter and the man later was pardoned.[5]

Hence, it is no wonder that Gaston's name was prominently mentioned to succeed Judge Taylor on the bench of the supreme court when this worthy chief justice died early in 1829. Henry Seawell wanted the place and wrote Gaston that his "endorsement would give him credit." Murphey also wrote Ruffin that if neither he nor Gaston wished the appointment he would be glad to get it. Murphey thought that Gaston, Badger, and Ruffin were the only persons of the bar qualified for the position, but had heard that Gaston would not accept it and that Badger was to become Jackson's attorney general.[6] However, Ruffin finally accepted the vacant place to which he was elected by the legislature; his appointment was to reflect honor upon the state, which he served in this position long and faithfully. Gaston's only personal concern at this time was to console his sister, the widow, attend to her late husband's financial affairs, and sell the house.

Two years later, December 5, 1832, Judge Hall resigned; many believed that this would be a signal for the destruction of the court.[7] Pearson nominated Gaston for the vacancy, but was informed by Thomas Devereux that he would not accept the appointment, so withdrew his name until Devereux could obtain a positive refusal in writing. The latter assured Gaston that it was thought he could have the place by acclamation, as Badger under no circumstances would oppose him, and it was believed neither would Strange nor Toomer. Devereux feared that "the creature Daniel" would be elected if Gaston refused, but the latter could not be persuaded from his purpose.[8]

Gaston felt that Daniel was entirely unqualified for the station, telling his daughter that he had formed this opinion not on prejudice but through sober judgment, even though the objectionable judge was then in Raleigh "electioneering in a most vulgar way." He did not believe it possible that either Toomer or Seawell could obtain the position, for although the former was an "excellent man and respectable though not profound lawyer," he had made himself obnoxious to the East by his support of a constitutional convention and opposition to the recent appropriation bill for the capitol, while the latter, although possessing equal talents, had made himself unpopular by his temper, stratagem, and manners.[9]

To the chagrin of many, Seawell withdrew from the contest and his friends voted for Daniel, who was elected and assumed his post the first of the year. Upon hearing the news Gaston groaned, "My country, O my country"; his friend Bryan told Pettigrew that the result was not too unexpected as "he had been pulling very hard for that post for a long time."[10]

Two of the original members of the court were now gone and it was not long before they were joined by the third, Leonard Henderson, elected to the chief justiceship after the death of Taylor. Henderson died August 13, 1833, and pressure brought upon Gaston became so great as to be irresistible.

He was besieged upon all sides by urgent appeals "to save the court." Governor Swain told him that the event was a crisis of no ordinary moment to the judiciary, that if any other name but his own were presented to the legislature the court would die with the late chief justice.[11] In eleven closely written pages Ruffin urged that he would see fit to join him on the bench, and declared that if he did not he would resign and the supreme court would disappear. Ruffin said that Henderson's successor must be a man "with whom a gentleman can have cordial intercourse and with whom consultations would ease labors and enlighten minds, whose talents would make it necessary to review first impressions and reconsider even settled conclusions, or in other words be a man differing in almost all respects from the person with whom I now sit." He also told Gaston that he was the first and only person with whom he had any interchange of opinion concerning his fellow member of the bench, that he had mentioned names and expressed opinions too freely for any eyes but his.[12] Gaston's friend, Devereux, assured him that the sentiment expressed in Raleigh made it absolutely necessary for him to accept the post in order to save the court. He declared that it was desirable to have a man on the court who recognized the supremacy of the federal court as Ruffin did not; dissatisfaction was felt toward the court because of the tardiness with which its business was done, its concealment of opinions until moment of adjournment, and its haste in drafting opinions.[13]

Gaston did not at once accede to these demands as there were several obstacles which he wished removed before allowing his name to be placed in nomination. By one of the articles of the state constitution no one could hold a state office who did not believe in the truths of the Protestant religion, but more than a year before this present call Gaston had concluded that Catholics were not disbarred by it. In 1832 his son had been made a justice of the peace, and before allowing him to accept the office Gaston had conferred with Ruffin concerning its meaning. Ruffin maintained that it may have been intended to exclude Catholics, but did not. He said:

> Probably the intelligent men who drew up the law in order to satisfy bigots purposely and patriotically framed the clause in such terms as to have no precise ideas affixed to them and it cannot therefore be judicially interpreted in a manner to impose the disability. . . . It is not enough to that end that it may possibly thus mean or that it was intended. The country has a right to every citizen she thinks worthy and capable. Terms ought to be perfectly clear when the country imposes upon herself restrictions. There is not the least ambiguity in other parts of the Constitution. Finally, who shall say what is the Protestant religion.[14]

This opinion of Ruffin's had been given well over a year before the question arose affecting Gaston himself. Gaston, too, felt that whatever it might have meant to do the clause in question judicially did not disbar Catholics. He had thought then that it would be an injustice to his son and to the other Catholics to create a disqualification which did not exist. He told Ruffin that:

> Until lately I had supposed it the course of my duty to decline any office under our state constitution. Whatever might be the proper construction of the thirty-second article . . . there was room for opinions that it intended to exclude Roman Catholics. I had sworn to support that constitution and it seemed safer in conscience to remain always a private citizen than to run the risk of breaking the oath by accepting an office from which perhaps that constitution excluded me. . . . I am satisfied with you however that whatever views some of the framers may have entertained, this disqualification is not plainly expressed in it – nor can it be inferred – and must therefore be regarded as not contained in it. If scruples of conscience detained me they ought all other Catholics. The consequences would be political degradation and incapacity of Catholics not contained in that constitution.[15]

Gaston felt that the most powerful point in the argument was that no one could say with assurance just what were the truths of the Protestant religion, that no tribunal could be appointed to determine that question, and, finally, that he himself believed all the truths contained in the Protestant religion. His position on this question he made very clear to Governor Swain, Ruffin, Badger, Devereux, and others.[16] Chief Justice Marshall had also been consulted about this matter and declared that he did not see the least impropriety in consequence of his judicial station in giving a written opinion, but from the fact that he was a resident of Virginia he thought doing so might be looked on as officious interference, so declined making a written statement. He told his questioners that if he were a member of the North Carolina legislature he would not hesitate to vote for any upright and conscientious man who was willing to take the ordinary oath. Marshall also asked who was to determine the truths of the Protestant religion.[17]

Another and more serious objection advanced by Gaston was the matter of debts; he owed $8,000 to the banks, which he felt by his ordinary pursuits could be paid off in two years. By accepting the proffered position he was giving up an income of $6,000 for $2,500. Devereux was told that if these pecuniary engagements were arranged so that Gaston could have four or five years to pay them, in yearly instead of quarterly installments, there would be no insuperable objections remaining.

To no other office was Gaston so attracted as this, but he feared that it would involve a departure from the state of independence in which he preferred to live. He disliked to have his conduct and opinions become a fit subject for everybody to criticize, and did not care to have every demagogue inquire whether the work he performed was worth the salary paid. He was, however, willing to undergo these petty annoyances if he was sure of being as useful to the state as his friends thought he would be, and gave them permission to place him in nomination if the financial arrangements were first made. His own personal inclinations were characteristically put aside as he told his friends:

> But I admit unequivocally that I have no right to consult this preference if it be at variance with my duty to my country. The hey-day of life is over and I am approaching to its close. I know that I am to stand before the judgement seat of an all knowing and just God to render an account of the deeds done in the body. With this assurance I should be a fool without excuse if the comparative comfort of the few years that remain to me could tempt me to decline any obligation which I have reason to believe He wills me to perform. It is His will that I should do all the good I can to my fellow men.

He hoped that he would make a good judge, but stated that the incessant practice in which I have been engaged, supporting and defending causes of all sorts, has I apprehend, rather given me dexterity in arguing a side than a correct judgment in finding out on which side the law is." However, the final decision in the matter was given to Swain, Badger, and Devereux. Devereux then arranged for a long-term loan and Ruffin was among those who signed as surety for the bond. The only apparent opposition to his election was made by Henry Seawell. That individual seemed to be extremely fearful that "the integrity of the Protestant religion would be seriously affected by Gaston's election to the bench," and inundated the West with letters stating the great anxiety of the Edenton circuit that he should be a candidate.[18] Thomas Polk, Badger, and Swain did what they could to obstruct Seawell's path. In the meantime Gaston went North to visit his daughter, Susan. When the House of Commons was convened a resolution offered to repeal the act creating the supreme court was rejected without debate by a vote of 102 to 23. On November 27, 1833, Gaston was elected to the vacancy created by the death of Chief Justice Henderson; 112 votes were cast for Gaston, 42 for Seawell, and 33 were blank. When the court met for the December term "Daniel pre-emptorily and promptly declined all claim to the distinction of Chief Justice," so the remaining two decided to settle the matter by lot, which fell upon Ruffin,[19] who thus became the third chief justice of the state.

Gaston's appointment met with practically universal acclamation throughout the state. William Hooper, great educator of his day, and president of the University of South Carolina, in a newspaper article on Gaston said, "The appointment of Mr. Gaston to the highest judicial office in the gift of his country, in spite of the verbal prohibition of the law, is one of the highest attestations of his pre-eminent merit." There were a few who labored to arouse prejudice because of his religion. Through a Virginia newspaper the insane Reverend Robert J. Breckenridge of Baltimore viciously attacked Gaston because of his religion, but was silenced by the facile pen of Bishop John England. Gaston himself had decided that such men as Breckenridge and other fanatical preachers who sought to arouse old prejudices against Catholicism were not worth the time wasted in replying. To sincere men he explained his actions; one such was the newspaper editor in Virginia who had allowed Breckenridge to use his paper to vent his spleen against Gaston. Another was William A. Graham, to whom Gaston related that on the subject of the disqualification a written opinion had been given him more than thirty years ago, when he first became a member of the legislature, by Samuel Johnston, "who of all men then living best knew and was best qualified to expound the Constitution."[20] In reply Graham stated that he had been entirely satisfied by Gaston's explanation contained in his letter to Devereux, and that his election had given a real stability to the court.[21] One of the most scholarly historians of the state declared that after Gaston's election opposition to the court disappeared, and that it was an important influence in preventing reversion to the old system.[22]

Gaston entered upon his duties in the winter term of 1833. He found them deeply interesting and far more arduous than he had anticipated, as there was a vast accumulation on the docket, which the new court hoped by renewed exertion materially to decrease. Always intensely scrupulous in his judicial duties, he never hesitated or scorned to seek the aid of other eminent lawyers. Before three weeks had elapsed he asked Chancellor Kent of New York, who was esteemed by the bench and bar of the country as one of the most learned of American jurists and after Marshall the ablest, for his opinion as to whether trustees were entitled to a commission on sales of property where the agreement of the parties made no allowance and no state law existed in the matter.[23] Although it had been a question on which the courts of the different states pronounced contradictory decisions, the experienced old jurist informed the new judge that he understood the rule denying compensation to trustees was now generally abolished. While replying to this question Kent took the occasion to express his astonishment that no provision was made for selecting a chief justice, saying, "It is curious that it be decided by lot. . . . I have not the honor of any kind of acquaintance with your associates and I don't doubt they are perfectly fit, but I only *know* that you are."[24] In the following June term another exchange of opinion concerning a case passed between them, Kent assuring Gaston that his opinion on the case in question was entirely correct.

Hopkinson was elated by the appointment of Gaston to the state's supreme court, but soon after this event expressed alarm over a rumor that the legislature of North Carolina was planning to vacate the court because of a judicial decision. Gaston relieved the Philadelphian's mind on this score, telling him that no such action had even been thought of, and gave him a rapid but comprehensive sketch of the court's position in the state:

> The Court which has a strong hold on the affection and respect of the better part of the community has indeed many enemies to encounter. Some of our circuit judges think unfavorably of it because it frequently reverses their decisions. The little lawyers carp at it when its determinations falsify their predictions and the radicals think it sheer aristocracy for three men to pronounce an Act of the General Assembly null because it violates the Constitution. But as yet our people have a deep rooted reverence for their institutions and especially for their judicial institutions; and any attempt to punish a judge because of an honest opinion would be regarded by them with horror. Much less would be tolerated any inquisition [sic] into the principles of his religious faith. The detestable spirit of demagogism which threatens the Union and every state of the Union with the direst calamities is not unknown among us and is I fear acquiring strength and obtaining a wider spread, under the name of Jacksonianism, every year. Whether it can be arrested or not, what harm it may make in North Carolina it is difficult to predict. But I think that it is among the last of the states which is to fall a victim to the destroyer.

At this time Gaston told Hopkinson that he would later send him a sketch of the views which induced him to adopt the conclusion that there was no constitutional disqualification of Catholics from taking and holding office in the state, while his deliberate determination to accept the office was regarded as a practical exposition of this part of the Constitution.[25] On several other occasions Gaston sought the guidance of Chancellor Kent, and on one case involving damages through the loss of services of a slave the latter told him, "Perhaps I have said a great deal too much, considering your far superior and more familiar information and knowledge on the subject of common law doctrines." At any rate Kent agreed with the view Gaston had taken in the law of the case.[26]

Because of North Carolina's position as a southern state of the Union, many if not a majority, and at least the most important, of Gaston's decisions concerned the life and happiness of the colored race, both slave and free. His views on slavery were well known in the state and had been publicly expressed shortly before his election to the supreme court in his courageous address at the University of North Carolina. This expression of views, as has been seen, was all the more intrepid because it had followed so closely the Nat Turner insurrection in Virginia and came at the time when the South, definitely on the defensive, was vociferously declaring slavery to be a positive good. In this address, given before many of the important men of the state and destined to reach all in the state and to be circulated extensively in other states, he emphatically declared:

> On you too, will devolve the duty which has been too long neglected but which cannot, with impunity, be neglected much longer of providing for the mitigation and, (is it too much to hope for in North Carolina) for the ultimate extirpation of the worst evil that afflicts the Southern part of our Confederacy. Full well do you know to what I refer, for on this subject there is with all of us a morbid sensitiveness which gives warning to even an approach to it. . . . Disguise the truth as we may and throw the blame where we will, it is slavery which, more than any other cause, keeps us back in

> the career of improvement. It stifles industry and suppresses enterprise; it is fatal to economy and prudence; it discourages skill, impairs our strength as a community, and poisons morals at the fountain head.

His public utterances were reinforced by private actions. Between 1821 and 1842 the priests stationed in New Bern baptized at least forty slaves of William Gaston; one entry in the records of the Catholic church there states that all the slaves of William Gaston were baptized.[27] In 1822 he had a slave who was permitted to keep a blacksmith shop in Kingston. Under the urgent importunity of this man "at great inconvenience" to himself he purchased the wife, who was for sale, as the blacksmith feared she would be separated from him. "Last Saturday," Gaston related to Susan, "she shot him." When Charles F. Mercer sent him a pamphlet concerning the newly formed Colonization Society, asking his influence to obtain a resolution from the North Carolina legislature approving it, Gaston informed him that he had long been a member of an auxiliary society for that object, and although he had not bestowed much reflection upon the subject it was of high interest to him.[28] He also freed at least one slave, placing the boy in charge of a priest "to receive moral and religious instructions, to be taught a useful trade, and, when qualified to make a fit use of his freedom. . . ."[29]

Gaston's judicial decisions followed in the same broad path of humanity, very often mitigating the hard lot of this people, although never conflicting with declared law. He never looked to the advancement of the white race but rather to the preservation of society; if a white man violated the law of society, even though it was a slave who suffered, the law must be enforced. In the ten years before his appointment to the supreme court, there was a marked uncertainty in regard to the protection of slaves from masters.[30] Gaston's most famous decision, in the case of State *vs.* Will, occurring in 1834, changed all this and became a landmark in a more liberal and humane attitude.

Will, the slave of James S. Battle, was indicted for the murder of Richard Baxter, an overseer, and condemned to death by Judge Donnell, but the judgment was appealed to the supreme court by the owner. According to the evidence, the drama leading to the tragedy had been swift. Baxter was in his own home, and as he was leaving his wife was heard to say, "I would not, my dear," but he took his shotgun down, called his foreman to follow with a whip, and mounting his horse rode toward the slaves, who were loading cotton on a wagon. Baxter ordered Will down from the wagon; the latter obeyed, at the same time taking his hat off in a humble manner, but after a minute of conversation, which no one heard, started to run from the scene. Will had not taken more than fifteen steps when Baxter fired the entire load into his back, and although it was enough to have caused death, the Negro kept running. He was headed off about five hundred yards away by the overseer and in the ensuing desperate struggle the slave inflicted a knife wound in Baxter's arm which resulted in his death.

Bartholemew F. Moore, the prisoner's counsel, in a powerful appeal demanded a more humane attitude toward the slave from the state. He maintained that Ruffin's decision five years before in the similar case of State *vs.* Mann, in which Ruffin had said that "the power of the master must be absolute to render the submission of the slave perfect," was not only abhorrent and startling to humanity but at variance with statute and decided cases, and that Judge Henderson had held otherwise, deciding it extended "to the services and labor of the slave and no farther." The well-known historian, John S. Bassett, said of this affair that "the slave was as fortunate in his judge as in his counsel. On the bench was William Gaston, as noted for his humanity as for his ability in his profession. . . . The task was performed clearly and emphatically."[31] Gaston delivered the opinion of the court, reversing the lower court's decision.

He declared that had the affair occurred between two freemen the homicide could not have been more than manslaughter; if between master and apprentice, the deed could not have been attributed to wickedness but to passion suddenly and violently excited, to a "brief fury" which deprived the mind of the calm exercise of its facilities, and which, although it did not excuse, did extenuate. Thereupon Gaston laid down what was to be the crux of his decision, appealing at the same time to the conscientious and to the conscience of the state when he said:

> Unconditional submission is the general duty of slaves. Unlimited power is, in general, the legal right of the master. However, there are exceptions. It is certain that the master has not the right to slay his slave, and I hold it to be equally certain that the slave has a right to defend himself against the unlawful attempt of his master to deprive him of life. There may be other exceptions, but in a matter so full of difficulties, where reason and humanity plead with almost irresistible force on one side, and a necessary policy, rigorous indeed but inseparable from slavery, urges on the other. . . . I fear to err, should I undertake to define them. There is no legal limitation to the master's power of punishment except that it shall not reach the life of his offending slave.

He furthermore stated that the act of the prisoner was not one of rebellion or resistance, so it afforded no justification for the barbarous action which followed his fleeing. It was instinctive to fly, human infirmity to struggle; terror or resentment, the strongest of human passions, had given the struggle its fatal issue. The act of the overseer was one of cruelty, and an illegal act of violence was not lawful even if committed in passion. In forcible language he continued:

> If the passions of the slave be excited into unlawful violence by the inhumanity of a master . . . is it a conclusion of law that such passions must spring from diabolical malice? Unless I see my way clear as a sun beam, I cannot see that this is the law of a civilized people and of a Christian land. I will not presume an arbitrary and inflexible rule so sanguinary in its character, and so repugnant to the spirit of those holy statutes which "rejoice the heart, enlighten the eye, and are true and righteous

altogether." The prisoner is a human being, degraded indeed by slavery, but yet having organs, dimensions, senses, affections, and passions like our own.[32]

Gaston spent much anxious time in preparing this case, as he felt it would be one of his most momentous decisions. Although the decision was sometimes assailed, and the owner of the slave criticized for daring to defend a mere slave, even the attorney general thought the law too harsh and desired its mitigation. Through Gaston the supreme court served notice to North Carolina that the slave had the right of being a human being even though a very degraded one. Those who decried the decision as one which would loosen the bonds of authority were mistaken for its results were beneficial as the cruel and thoughtless were checked and the cause of humanity advanced. "It was quoted and commented upon extensively throughout the Union. It fixed forever afterwards the rights of slaves . . . and made possible a more lenient policy toward slaves than existed in some other states," commented a prominent historian. In 1839, in the case of State *vs.* Hoover, the influence of this decision was seen when Ruffin delivering the opinion of the court stated that it was "murder when a master plainly contemplated a fatal termination to his cruelties," and that "the master's authority is not altogether unlimited." Ten years later in the cases of State *vs.* Caesar, Nash agreed with this interpretation of the law.[33] The final sequel of the personal factors involved contained an element of amusement not untinged with pathos. Battle sent Will to another plantation in Mississippi. His wife, later returning to North Carolina, said, "Will sho'ly had hard luck. He killed a white man in North Carolina and got off, and then was hung for killing a nigger in Mississippi."[34]

One of Gaston's first cases involved a free colored girl who had been bound out as an apprentice and absconding had been harbored by the defendant. Gaston pointed out in this case that the power of dissolving the indenture belonged to those who had formed it or to the court, and not to the apprentice, for during minority the latter might be seduced into an unfit service and lured away to vice and idleness and ruin. He criticized the existing laws on the subject and declared that defects in the indentures should be corrected, saying, "There is a numerous and helpless portion of the community subject to the operation of those laws which create an involuntary obligation of service, and it is of high importance that these laws should receive such a construction as will protect them from oppression and injury, while at the same time it secures the rights of their temporary masters."[35]

In another case concerning free men Gaston made a decision of the highest import to this section of the community when he declared them to be citizens of the state. In the case at hand the attorney general had insisted that the constitutional prohibitions regarding life, liberty, and cruel punishments need not enter into examination because the defendant, being a person of color, had never belonged to the political body and so was not a citizen. Gaston assailed this doctrine on several counts.

> The bills of rights said that all men had the right to worship; was this declaration to be understood as belonging solely to the citizens of North Carolina? According to the laws of the state all within it who were not slaves fell within two classes; free men or aliens. Slaves manumitted in the state became freemen, and, therefore, if born within North Carolina were citizens of North Carolina and all free persons born within the state were citizens of the state. Naturalization was the removal of the disability of alienage, while emancipation was the removal of the incapacity of slavery. The possession of political power was not essential to constitute a citizen, for if so then women, minors and persons who had not paid taxes were not citizens.[36]

A matter always arousing contention in the old South was the emancipation of slaves and concerning this practically every state had a code of law. In a case decided by Gaston in 1835 he held that manumission was the act of the owner. He stated that the power to perform this was restrained and regulated but could not be taken from the owner and conferred upon a judicial tribunal, for not even the legislature could emancipate a slave without the assent of the master.[37] In keeping with his humane protection of the rights of slaves he, in the case of State *vs.* Jarrott, decided that the insolence of a slave did not justify an excessive battery and that a knife and a fence rail were not lawful instruments to correct such insolence. Here, he pointed out that "habits of humility and obedience belonged to the conditions of slaves, and as the law would not permit one to resist or flee his passions ought to be tamed down to suit the condition, yet the law would be savage if it made no allowance for passion."[38]

Comparatively few cases involving federal law came before the supreme court. In one such Gaston ruled against a state law, stating under its authority to establish post offices Congress could require postmasters to devote their time and attention to the execution of their appropriate duties and by such an exemption to secure them against compulsory interruption in the performance of these duties. In this opinion he declared that there must be a proper respect for the constituted authorities of the general government and a due sense of the necessity of harmony between the institutions of the United States and the municipal regulations of the individual state.[39] He also maintained, in another decision, that because of the interests of the whole community the law imposed upon public carriers a responsibility far more rigorous than that which measured the liability of ordinary bailees for hire, so he could be excused from the nonperformance of this duty by nothing short of an act of God or of a public enemy.[40]

Generally speaking, courts of equity are established to detect latent frauds and concealments which the process of common law is not adapted to reach; to enforce the execution of such matters of trust and confidence as are binding in conscience, though not cognizable in a court of law, and other such affairs. Gaston's characteristic philosophy and charity found natural expression in the equity cases which came before the supreme court. The court, he said in one case, viewed with much jealousy absolute conveyances taken from embarrassed men after a negotiation for a loan of money, as it regarded such persons as in a state approaching moral duress, likely to be goaded on by distress into submission to whatever terms might be exacted. He stated, moreover, that even where the written contract clearly conformed to that on which the parties had agreed, equity would often relieve, because its terms were hard and grinding.[41] Another such decision held that the plaintiff, whose labor and money had been expended on improving property which the ancestor of the defendant had encouraged him to expect would become his own, must be compensated for the additional value which these improvements had given the property, for "it was against conscience that they should be enriched by gain thus acquired to his injury."[42] Gaston also thought that "credit, which is indispensable for the commerce of life, can scarcely be commanded in any country where a debtor has the power to jeopardize an existing debt by the gratuitous alienation of his effects," so a voluntary conveyance is necessarily and in law fraudulent when opposed to the claim of a creditor.

For the purposes of public improvement the legislature had passed an act which *seemed* to confer upon a court the power to render judgment for one individual or a company against another without notice. Gaston decided that "it would be seen on a little examination that the section would not stand a strict literal interpretation; that it must be helped by a reasonable construction to save it from absurdity." Although it may have been the purpose of the legislature to favor objectives of the company and facilitate its work, "we hold no more," said Gaston, "than that it must be exercised with a sacred regard to the principle which lies at the bottom of all justice and fairness, which ought never to be violated and which the legislature did not mean to violate, to pass on no man's rights until he has had the opportunity of being heard in their defense."[43] In a case seemingly too trivial to appear before a supreme court, he maintained that although ferocious dogs could be destroyed by any persons it would be monstrous to require exemption from all fault as a condition for their existence; that if such deflections from strict propriety as those enumerated be sufficient to give a dog a bad name and kill him, the entire race of those faithful and useful animals might be rightly extirpated.

Any view which might tend to look upon human life as cheap aroused the intense wrath of Gaston. Of this he said, "There is a recklessness – a wanton disregard of humanity and social duty – in taking or endeavoring to take the life of a fellow being in order to save oneself from a comparatively slight wrong – which is essentially wicked and which the law abhorred. You can only kill to save life or limb, or prevent a great crime, or to accomplish a necessary public duty." In this case he found that in case of a legal process that was civil in nature or, of a crime that was a misdemeanor only, an officer who, although he could not otherwise arrest or retake his prisoner, intentionally killed him was guilty of murder.[44]

In a long and passionate opinion Gaston dissented from his associates in the case of the State *vs.* Miller, which had as its issue the separation of the jury. He spent much anxious reflection in preparation of his decision, again and again reviewing the case of The People *vs.* Douglas for precedents. Because of his dissent from the majority opinion of Ruffin and Daniel he anxiously wrote Kent for his unbiased view of this dissent, saying that this circumstance made him doubt the correctness of his own opinion. The latter thanked him for allowing its perusal, remarking that it appeared to him to be "a piece of close, logical, forcible, analytical critical, and almost inescapable reasoning and justification of the principle of law and of the authorities applicable to the case."[45] The call for a mistrial had hinged upon the fact that one of the jurymen had been absent from the rest for a short period after all the evidence in the case was presented. The judge expressed the opinion that a fact was proved and the violation immaterial. Gaston held that in a criminal case and especially in one where life was at hazard the prisoner was to be considered as standing upon all his rights and waiving nothing on the score of irregularity, and that such separation was forbidden in all cases, because it tended to destroy the purity of jury trials. To his mind such an attempt to vest the judge "with the irresponsible and uncontrollable power to dispense with positive legal requirements intended to secure the upright administration of justice, and to declare when their nonobservance should and when it should not invalidate what was done in contempt of them, ought not to be under a government of laws. Trial by jury should be kept under the protection of the law and not left under the patronage of its ministers."[46] He maintained that one of the duties of judges was "to hand down the deposit of the law as they had received it without addition, diminution, or change; although it was a duty, the faithful performance of which was exceedingly difficult, they must refrain from all tempting novelties, listen to no suggestion of expediency, give in to no plausible theories, and submit to be deemed old fashioned and bigoted formalists, at a time when all around were running on in the supposed career of liberal improvement." It was thus, he felt, that a pause was created for thought amid the hurry of action, stability given to the public institutions and there was "that recurrence to fundamental principles which was essential for the preservation of law and order."[47] Warning them he cried, "If we must abandon law for discretion, let us cherish it with greater care on those important occasions in which as yet it has been preserved inviolate."[48]

Gaston always showed a remarkable respect for the dignity of the law, combining with this a deep humility, and a knowledge of human limitations, admitted only by those really great in soul and mind. Reading between the lines one is forced to notice this in many of his decisions, as in one in which he admitted that a certain opinion was his own and not that of the court, so he would be very willing to reconsider and discard his view should it prove erroneous. On another occasion he expressed regret that a case involving questions worthy of discussion had been submitted without discussion and manifested his willingness for a rehearing.

By inference he once rebuked the legislature but at the same time upheld its decree. In this case he said that it was the duty of the court to carry out the enactments of the legislature and that the court had no right to judge of their policy, so it would be a manifest departure from the province of judicial interpretation to treat as a fraud what the law sanctioned. He likewise felt it necessary to adhere steadily, insofar as possible, to the decisions of his predecessors, because carelessness in this respect could scarcely fail to involve them in error and throw the law in confusion. When interpretations were found to conflict, the latest must be presumed correct, although not so conclusively as to forbid examination. Concerning constitutions he warned that they were "not themes proposed for ingenious speculation, but fundamental laws ordained for practical purposes. Their meaning once ascertained by judicial interpretation and contented acquiescence they were laws in that meaning until the power that formed changed."[49]

His career on the bench of the supreme court was well described by his contemporary, John H. Wheeler: "The manner in which he discharged his important duties; his profound and varied literature; his extensive legal knowledge; his severe and patient research; his polished and clear compositions, render his opinions from this exalted tribunal, not only monuments of legal learning, but models of elegant literature." This is very true as a reading of almost any of his decisions will attest. His long and beautiful compositions of judicial literature were in vivid contrast to the short, abrupt citations of the mediocre Daniel. Judge William H. Battle thought his decision in State *vs.* Will and the dissenting opinion in State *vs.* Miller "one of the finest judicial arguments to be found in any country."

It has been said of Gaston that "belonging to a minority faith, he probably defended more minority causes than any man of his day."[50] This has been said with justice as any review of his career will reveal. His opinion in State vs. Manuel was cited in 1857 by Judge Benjamin R. Curtis of the United States Supreme Court in his dissent in the famous Dred Scott case, in which the majority opinion was that of Gaston's friend, Chief Justice Roger B. Taney. In his dissent Curtis said that Gaston's opinion had been declared sound law not only in North Carolina but also in other states which he enumerated. Kemp Battle, North Carolina jurist, once stated that Gaston did not have the reputation of Ruffin as regards law, but had a broad, statesmanlike view of legal principles and was much more a statesman than the latter.[51]

Gaston's greatest contributions to the judicial code of his state was the amelioration of the lot of slaves by warning his fellow countrymen that they possessed a human dignity, by protecting them from brutal conduct of irresponsible and cruel masters, and by granting to free colored people the right of citizenship. With broad, statesmanlike decisions he led the way to a policy of humanity and generosity to the humble and unfortunate. Of a deeply religious nature and training, his virtues and deeds shone forth not only in his daily life, but also in his legal philosophy, principles, and practice. Few judges of North Carolina made a greater impression upon the common people, none left behind such a deep memory as his name commands. A revelation of the state's regard for the jurist is seen in the supreme court building in Raleigh where his bust has been placed, and only two other jurists have been so honored. In the constitutional convention of 1835, of which he was a member, he again vainly attempted to aid "a minority cause" by seeking further to help the colored race when the convention decided to take away the suffrage from free Negroes.

## NOTES FOR CHAPTER EIGHT

1. *Ruffin Papers*, I, 455.
2. Raleigh *Register*, May 14, 21, 28, 1832.

3. *United States Catholic Miscellany,* Dec. 10, 1831.
4. Webster to Gaston, April 18, 1832, Gaston *MSS.*
5. Oliver H. Smith, *Early Indiana Trials and Sketches* (1858), pp. 21–22.
6. *Murphey Papers,* I, 380 (Murphey to Ruffin, Feb. 3, 1829).
7. *North Carolina Journal,* Dec. 19, 1832.
8. T. P. Devereux to Gaston, Dec. 19, 1832, Gaston *MSS.*
9. Gaston to Hannah, Dec. 31, 1832, Gaston *MSS.*
10. J. H. Bryan to E. Pettigrew, Jan. 2, 1833, Pettigrew *MSS.*, U.N.C.
11. Swain to Gaston, Aug. 15, 1833, Gaston *MSS.*
12. Ruffin to Gaston, Aug. 21, 1833, Gaston *MSS.*
13. T. P. Devereux to Gaston, Aug. 15, 21, 1833, Gaston *MSS.*
14. Ruffin to Gaston, May 23, 1832, Gaston *MSS.*
15. Gaston to Ruffin, Aug. 25, 1833, *Ruffin Papers,* II, 92.
16. Gaston to Devereux, Nov. 3, 1833, Swain *MSS.*, N.C.H.C.
17. Devereux to Gaston, Nov. 14, 1833, Gaston *MSS.*
18. Swain to Gaston, Nov. 8, 1833, Gaston *MSS.*
19. Hinton to Mangum, Dec. 30, 1833, Mangum *MSS.*, N.C.H.C. Gaston to Donaldson, Jan. 3, 1834, Gaston *MSS.*
20. Gaston to Graham, Nov. 12, 1834, Graham *MSS.*, N.C.H.C.
21. Graham to Gaston, Dec. 20, 1834, Gaston *MSS.*
22. W. K. Boyd, *History of North Carolina: The Federal Period,* p. 70.
23. Gaston to Kent, Jan. 24, 1834, Kent Papers, Library of Congress.
24. Kent to Gaston, Feb. 3, 1834, Gaston *MSS.*
25. Gaston to Hopkinson, Jan. 13, 1835, Hopkinson *MSS.*
26. Kent to Gaston, June 24, 1841, Gaston *MSS.*
27. Records of St. Paul Roman Catholic Church, New Bern, N. C. Edward Channing in his *History of the United States,* VI, 69, states that Gaston was one of the first southern statesmen to speak against slavery and that his popularity did not suffer in the least because of this. He was referring especially to the speech at the state university. Other references to Gaston and the Negro occur in V, 430; and VI, 194.
28. C. F. Mercer to Gaston, Jan. 7, 1828; Gaston to C. F. Mercer, Jan. 12, 1828, Gaston *MSS.*, N.C.H.C.
29. Record in the Georgetown University Archives, Sept. 1, 1824.
30. Bryce R. Holt, "The Supreme Court of North Carolina and Slavery," *Historical Papers of Trinity College Historical Society,* XVII, 1927, p. 72.
31. John S. Bassett, "The Case of State v. Will," *Historical Papers of Trinity College Historical Society,* II, 1898.
32. 18 North Carolina *Reports,* 121. Referred hereafter as N. C. *Reports.*
33. Holt, *op. cit.*, p. 24.
34. George S. Battle, "North Carolina v. Negro Will . . . A Cause

Celebre of Ante-Bellum Times," *Virginia Law Review,* VI, 1919–1920.

35. "Dowd v. Davis," 15 N.C. *Reports,* 61–70.
36. "State v. Manuel," 20 N.C. *Reports,* 385.
37. "Bryan v. Wadsworth," 18 N.C. *Reports,* 165.
38. 23 N.C. *Reports* 76.
39. "State v. N. L. Williams," 18 N.C. *Reports,* 378.
40. "Harrel & Co. v. Owen," 18 N.C. *Reports,* 276.
41. "Kimborough v. Smith," 17 N.C. *Reports,* 562.
42. "Albea v. Griffin," 22 N.C. *Reports,* 10.
43. "Wilmington & Raleigh R.R. Co. v. Baker," 20 N.C. *Reports,* 84.
44. "State v. Morgan," 25 N.C. *Reports,* 193.
45. Kent to Gaston, Oct. 7, ?, Gaston *MSS.*
46. 18 N.C. *Reports,* 541.
47. *Ibid.,* p. 531.
48. *Ibid.,* p. 536.
49. "State v. Manuel," 20 N.C. *Reports,* 385.
50. Holt, *op. cit.,* p. 22.
51. Kemp Battle, *An Address On The History Of The Supreme Court of North Carolina,* 1889, p. 59.

*No person who shall deny the being of God, or the truths of the Protestant religion . . . shall be capable of holding any office or place of trust or profit in the civil department within this state.*
— NORTH CAROLINA CONSTITUTION

*I love my country too sincerely to permit me to shut my eyes upon her defects or her wants. I wish to serve and disdain to flatter her. . . . Her signs are the reverse of those which were seen near the habitation of the lion in the fable. The tracks all proceed from, there are none coming to the state.* — WILLIAM GASTON

# CHAPTER NINE

## The Convention of 1835

THE state constitution of North Carolina was not in every respect a model for other states to follow, and although it had remained unchanged since 1776, a few years after that date it was the cause for the formation of two parties, whose bitter brawls were constantly disturbing the repose of the people from the mountains to the sea. Among its provisions the one which vested in each county the right to elect a senator and two commoners to the general assembly caused most of the trouble. The population of the eastern part being much more numerous than that of the rest of the state at that time, most of the counties were in that district. However, as the back counties began to fill up, their increased numbers made it inevitable that the West would demand a different basis of representation. As long as this was based on the county system the West could not obtain an increased number of representatives, and the East declined to agree to any plan which would destroy its control, so the state was divided into two sections, east and west of Raleigh. From 1776 to 1848 the legislature was one continual scene of struggle between the two.[1] As early as 1790 the West urged a reform, and at each successive annual assembly kept up the agitation, so that by 1818 this had become a real threat to the state. The West had twenty-eight counties and a majority of the population, while the East had thirty-four counties, most of the wealth, and controlled the assembly.

In the session of 1819–1820 the western members made a determined effort to gain their point and so debate on this question was almost the sole work done. The main argument of the eastern representatives was that the republican principles did not require that number alone should govern, and that one of the most important ends of government was the protection of property.[2] Gaston took this position, claiming that if numbers were to decide representation the West could gain only five more senators and eleven more commoners, but if wealth were also taken into consideration it would lose five members in the Senate and ten in the House, while if taxes levied were considered the West could secure but one more member for the House. His long and almost too ardent defense of the eastern position occupied the entire first sheet and part of the second of the local New Bern paper.[3]

Several times after this the West vigorously but vainly tried to effect their end. Finally, there was elected to the governorship in 1832 David L. Swain, one of the most remarkable men in the history of the state, who determined on this reform for the good of the state, and in his message of 1834 reviewing the history of the strife demanded appropriate action. Swain was most solicitous for the literary and conciliatory perfection of the message, so sent the most important paragraph to Gaston for his correction in its style and opinion on its sentiment, saying to him, "allow me to ask you to deal with it as from your own son . . . for your objections will be rejected with more hesitation than those of any other."[4] The East capitulated and a convention bill was passed in the assembly, providing that a popular vote should be taken on the question as to whether a convention should be called. The act defined the limits of the convention's power, practically assuring that the East would remain in authority; it allowed the convention to amend the constitution so as to reduce the number of the Senate to not less than thirty-four nor more than fifty, while the numbers assigned to the House were to be between ninety and one hundred and twenty, and among the other sections which could be amended were those concerning borough members, the election of the governor, and the religious disqualification. In the vote in calling the convention 27,000 out of 49,224 were cast in favor of the move, which was, according to Governor Swain, the largest vote cast in any election.

Gaston had advanced far in statesmanship since 1820, when he opposed the meeting of any convention, for he was now heartily in accord with Swain's wish to effect some compromise beneficial to the state. Early in the year there was a rumor that he would decline to attend the convention, which was indignantly denied by the editor of the local paper, who said, "In this county the prevailing desire is that Gaston be sent, and every friend of the state would be gratified by his selection. . . . When was he ever known to shrink from labor or shun responsibility when the interests of North Carolina required his service."[5] Craven County elected him as its representative to this convention and, in general, the ablest men of the state were sent by the counties. Among these were David L. Swain, Richard D. Spaight, John Branch, Charles Fisher, Weldon N. Edwards, James Wellborn, and Nathaniel Macon. Gaston's son Alexander, and a former law student, William B. Meares, were also there.

On June 4, 1835, the convention was called to order, and to the objections of Louis Wilson who expressed doubts that the legislature had the power to impose an oath on the members of the convention, Gaston replied that as yet no such body existed for according to the plain language of the legislative act there could be no convention until its members had taken the oath prescribed. As the people had ratified this act, the members should not depart from the spirit of the instructions on the very first day, as this might give rise to a question of the validity of subsequent actions. He thought it entirely irrelevant to inquire into the effect of the oath, for in ratifying the act the people had approved of it so it must be taken and each individual act according to the best dictates of his conscience.[6] After this hurdle was passed the next two days were spent in quarreling over such a minor political question as to who was to obtain the printing of the proceedings and other such matters. Committees were drawn up, Gaston serving on the one appointed to report a resolution for the manner in which it was expedient to take up business. Gaston heard it said that there had been too much discussion, but felt this was not so because "subjects of great magnitude were to be considered, so a free interchange of sentiments was profitable." When a certain question of one of the delegates aroused heated discussion, Gaston expostulated with the offending men, reminding them that without a spirit of courtesy and harmony it would be impossible to transact business, while nothing could have so great a tendency to destroy harmony as an attempt to withhold information. In his estimation there could not be too much information to those engaged in changing the fundamental institutions of the country. He concluded his plea on this score by saying:

> I voted for calling the convention. I was influenced by an ardent desire to quiet heart burnings, and was convinced of its expediency. This is no ordinary act of the legislature, but will be for the good or evil of North Carolina, for God knows how many generations. There cannot be too much information available.

The first constructive move in the real business of the convention was made by James S. Smith of Orange County, a westerner, who moved the abolition of borough representation.[7] Gaston was deeply affected by this question as New Bern was one of the borough towns entitled to representation in the House, so he spoke long and earnestly on the subject, asking the convention not to act on the proposition without discussion. He thought that the forefathers had some reason to give to a few of the incorporated towns a distinct right of representation, and observed that where portions of the community had certain interests there was always great danger lest their rights be overlooked if it were relatively weak in comparison to the rest of the state. Therefore, he felt that these should have a capable person to make their wants known and to see that they were treated fairly; representatives from a few of the towns guard the interest of all of them, and, although so few that their vote could have little influence on decisions, they could secure for these interests a fair hearing. Wondering how commercial concerns could be made intelligible to a body of country gentlemen except through the representatives of towns, he declared that for correct information in every art recourse must be to those who professed it. Stating that the town representatives had been among the most intelligent, liberal, and independent members of the legislature, he concluded, "There should be a precise equality of power in the formation of the government. Care must be taken that the deliberate will of the great body of the community should predominate, but care must also be taken that the voice of all be heard."[8]

To this Smith unkindly replied that the same members would probably be sent by the counties, but after James Wellborn came to his defense with a few remarks to the effect that seaports whose interests were distinct should have separate representation, Gaston again arose to trace the origin of the borough. In conclusion of this he stated that as North Carolina had no great commercial towns, their markets were in other states, the towns trying to build up commerce should not be disfranchised. He feared if representation were taken from them, lobbying would be resorted to, with the result that those whose consciences were in their pockets "might be convinced by arguments directed to the seat of their sensibility." Swain had not wished to take their privileges away from the towns, so spoke in support of Gaston, but after he had finished speaking Seawell popped up inanely to remark that he had not voted for this convention at all, because of conscientious scruples, and, if he had, his vote would have been in the negative. Following him Wilson attempted to prove the trade of New Bern no longer existed so that there was no need there for representation. Gaston admitted that the trade had diminished, but not in such a melancholy state as depicted by Wilson, for vessels in abundance came there from the West Indies. After so answering Wilson, Gaston turned to Seawell and gravely declared that one of his remarks, that concerning conscientious scruples, though probably not intended, seemed to be a reflection on him. The flustered Seawell disclaimed this intention and although he had to speak twice to do so, finally satisfied Gaston of his innocence of this intention. The latter may have remembered the letters written by Seawell to western members of the legislature concerning his religion at the time of his election to the supreme court. Although Gaston did not like Seawell, he was past the stage of allowing his emotions and temper to guide him, but Seawell must have felt he was a dangerous man to arouse. The West did not care too much about borough representation and did little discussing of this matter, but Gaston was pleading for another lost cause, as the votes cast upon the question ultimately and finally abolished such representation. The final count was seventy-three in favor of the abolition with but fifty opposed.

The next question confronting the convention was Negro suffrage, concerning which Gaston remarked that the inquiry was not whether the suffrage should be granted to free blacks but whether it should be taken away; the hardship lay in depriving them of something they had had for a long time. He concluded, "A person of that class, who possesses a freehold, is an honest man and perhaps a Christian, and I do think he should not be politically excommunicated and have an additional mark of degradation fixed upon him solely on account of his color."[9] However, he was speaking for another minority cause, although he almost won the convention to his way of thinking because the final vote to exclude Negroes from suffrage only passed by sixty-six to sixty-one. A later attempt by Gaston to introduce an amendment allowing free Negroes to vote who had a certain sum of money suffered defeat by a vote of 64 to 55.

At last, on June 16, the convention reached the real business for which it had been called, to set a new basis for representation. Several days were spent on this subject, and various proposals were made as to the best number of representatives. James Bryan told the assemblage that he had given serious attention to the calculation made by the distinguished justice of the supreme court which had assumed as its basis the numbers fifty and one hundred and twenty. "The prudent caution and remarkable correctiveness of that gentleman," continued Bryan, "in arriving at conclusions and satisfying his mind as to the truths of his results, before he gives to them the sanction and authority of his opinions and character, will weigh much with this house."[10] Bryan had discovered that this plan would give the West a majority of four in both Houses.

The judge always occupied the same seat, a little to the right, not far from the chair of the president. One who attended the convention said that he was courteous, but not familiar, and never indulged in pleasantry. Now, as he arose to speak on this, the attention of all was riveted upon him. He expressed the opinion that no other duty presented such difficulties as that of this reformation, for "who does not know that when any class of men is opposed by others as a class, whether it be a sect in religion or a party in politics, the vilest slanders and the most stupid falsehoods are mutually circulated and accredited? Right or wrong it became a maxim in party politics that no new county should be made in the West unless balanced by a new county in the East. With a great superiority of numbers on their side, the West were thus controlled and kept down, in this party warfare, by a minority of the people in the East. The question must be settled with justice to the West." He would regard as no ordinary calamity an omission to settle this question in such a manner so as to tranquilize the public mind. Gaston wished to settle the representation in the lower House by means of the federal representation and opposed a view which would exclude the counting of slaves in this scheme. He held that "although a slave is an article of property he is nevertheless a member of society and like other members of society, constitutes as a part of its strength or of its weakness. In apportioning representatives to population he cannot be overlooked for he is part of the population." Easterners expressed the fear lest with westerners in control of the assembly wild schemes of internal improvement would be put into effect, so in conclusion Gaston said:

> There is much in North Carolina to respect and love. In no land is justice administered with greater purity and in no state of the Union is there less of the violence and corruption of faction. In none is there a more orderly and kind and well disposed population. In none more republican simplicity and equality of conditions. It is emphatically the Southern land of steady habits. But I love my country too sincerely to permit me to shut my eyes upon her defects or her wants. I wish to serve and disdain to flatter her. . . . It is impossible not to regret that her resources remain as yet almost undeveloped. Who can see, without pain, the continued drain of emigration which is carrying away to more favored regions, her most enterprising and industrious citizens? Her signs are the reverse of those which were seen near the habitation of the lion in the fable. The tracks all proceed from, there are none coming to the state. Very much may be done for the improvement of her physical condition.
>
> If the only sure foundation of rational liberty be the virtue of the people, the best safeguard of that liberty is to be found in their intelligence. . . . Not a little has been done lately in the cause of education . . . but no efficient plans have yet been adopted for defusing information throughout the land, and bringing it home to the poor and humble. . . . Many an intellectual gem is permitted to remain buried in the caverns of obscurity and indigence. If righteousness exalt a nation, moral and religious culture should sustain and cherish it.[11]

As their beloved judge resumed his seat the audience on the floor and in the galleries broke out in deafening applause, which continued for some time. The portrait he drew of his state, said one of the papers, "seemed to affect the great and crowded assemblage, and his friends unanimously declared this one of the ablest and most noble intellectual efforts that was ever witnessed. . . . "[12] Another paper declared that this able and conciliatory speech arrested the spirit of procrastination in the state on this topic.[13] At any rate, federal representation became the basis for representation in the House.

The next amendment to be considered was whether the meeting of the assembly should be held annually or biennially. After several speakers had advocated one or the other, Gaston gave his view in favor of biennial meetings. It was true that a power increased in magnitude when it was delegated for a longer time; and so he was in favor of frequent elections, but only frequent enough to secure responsibility and not too frequent for the public convenience. He ridiculed the idea some had of the necessity for watching the Federal Congress, reviewing and discussing their measures under consideration, and declared that the proper duties of the assembly were within the state. Gaston then spoke at some length on the relation of the general government to the state, declaring that not the power of that government should be dreaded but rather its vast patronage and influence. His last words on this were in a tone of satire as he laconically observed that "If the Assembly met only every two years there would be saved much of the mischief of rash public and foolish private Acts, and of that time now miserably expended in getting up such trash. Biennial meetings would give the country one year of repose from electioneering strife and its tricks. From year's-end to year's-end the people are now so teased with importunate solicitations for their favor that they have no time to reflect on the merits of their numerous lovers."[14] His desire for biennial elections was shared by eighty-five to the opposition of but thirty-five.

From June 26 to July 2 the time of the convention was given to the question which provoked the most heated discussion, the most animated statement and response, the most loathsome forms of bigotry, the lowest depth of ignorance, and the highest flights of oratory of any other subject to come before this body, that of amending the thirty-second article of the constitution. "No person who shall deny the being of God, or the truths of the Protestant religion . . . shall be capable of holding any office or place of trust or profit in the civil department within this state." This article was called up for consideration to amend by Weldon B. Edwards, and when Smith of Orange County tried to lay it on the table, Spaight opposed his move, while Gaston after some discussion gave notice that it would be useless to try to stifle discussion of it. Edwards then returning to the fray scornfully said, "Liberty of conscience is a natural right, inviolable and inalienable, but the provisions of this article are not consistent with the Bill of Rights because legal religion and political liberty are wholly incompatible. Whenever a government shall presume to say that a citizen, however exalted his merit or distinguished his abilities, shall not, if he entertain particular religious opinions, participate in the affairs of the country – that government is far behind the age in which we live . . . and this is a foul stain on our character."[15] He was followed by James W. Bryan of New Bern who took the same stand, asking what were the tenets of the Protestant religion and what tribunal was to determine its orthodox character.[16] Bryan "respectfully asked" which of the various denominations was to be regarded as the correct one, and told his hearers that ages before Protestantism was conceived of, this venerable and apostolic Church had dispensed the light of divine truth to the world, and that it was founded upon the prophets and apostles, with Christ Himself as the cornerstone. He claimed that he was an Episcopalian, and in a long and able address described the faith of the Catholic Church, and pointed out several current erroneous and ignorant beliefs on that religion, concluding by naming several famous Catholics who had risked their lives in the Revolutionary War. Gaston told John H. Bryan of his brother's act, with the remark that it had gained great applause, and was excellent for its matter and admirable for its manner.[17] Carson of Burke County approached the subject with a puzzled manner, maintaining that he had anticipated no difference of opinion about this, as he thought the age forbade it. Hearing some rumors that certain delegates were claiming to have been instructed how to vote, he sarcastically asked if their command had come from God. He warned that if the article were retained he would not only vote against ratification of all the amendments but would also denounce the entire work.[18]

These men were followed by those in favor of retaining the article. Jesse Cooper of Martin County justified their cause by stating that "the good old Constitution had been standing for fifty years," and as this article was a dead letter, there was no use in repealing it, although they should guard against anything calculated to embarrass their liberties. Perhaps with even a sly glance in Gaston's direction and a chuckle hard to suppress, he magnanimously declared that no doubt there were some honest Catholics, and when he found one he would protect him, but in this process the hundred dishonest ones could not be let in. Their fathers, according to Cooper, knew what a Roman Catholic was, and so were afraid lest if this article was not included they might have a harder struggle than the one they had just finished. He was afraid that if this article was removed the people would say that the convention wished to bring oppression down on them and seize their liberties. He was followed by Wellborn who opposed striking out any more words than necessary, breathlessly explaining that he had been talking this over with Cooper who had told him that he had been told by another person that this person had heard a Catholic say that it made no difference to him whether he swore on a New Testament or a spelling book.[19] Smith again appeared upon the scene, excitably exploding that he "wished it kept as Sleeping Thunder, to be called up when necessary to defeat some deep-laid scheme of ambition."[20]

This wily, whimsical, and wholesome desire was not encouraged by Swain who disliked to keep this Sleeping Thunder laying around for fear it might fall into the hands of men who would abuse it "by dealing damnation around the land, on all they deemed their foe." Branch, too, was adverse to having his slumbers threatened, wishing to destroy the whole article. After him the "venerable Macon," in no uncertain terms, condemned such intolerance. Macon felt that no one could tell to what spirit of conscription it might lead, and asked if the son of a father who had been inhumanly murdered by the Tories was unworthy of a seat in their legislature. He then told an episode about Charles Carroll which had occurred when that individual signed the Declaration of Independence, and referred in glowing terms to Bishop John Carroll. Many others spoke, either for or against the article, among whom was Kenneth Rayner, who in a long and able speech professed a belief that the principle of religious liberty "reaching its acme, was now about to take a retrograde movement."

On June 30 it was rumored about town that on this day Gaston would speak on the subject. He had been ready for this day at least three weeks before, and, after careful and long preparation, sent his speech to Bishop John England for comment. The bishop thought it could not be more theologically precise and further remarked:

> The distinction between allegiance and religious attachment, obedience and respect, is most felicious, and expressed precisely what I had long desired to embody in a document for this country. I would suggest an amendment in the expression of the distinction between papal and episcopal power. That power is not only executive, it is also judicial and in some degree legislative. . . . [21]

At an early hour in the morning citizens began to crowd the galleries and there was such a vast concourse that room was made for them even on the floor. One of the correspondents covering the event heard from all around frequent allusions made to Gaston, and as the latter entered the hall "a breathless silence pervaded the vast assembly and hundreds of eyes threw their eager gaze upon his expressive countenance."[22] Another writer noted that the hall was crowded with ladies, and the galleries were a dense and living mass of beauty and fashion.

The judge rose slowly and "with great deliberation, amid breathless silence" began to speak, and as usual with him, the first few sentences were spoken haltingly as he seemed nervous and embarrassed, but after a few sentences the words flowed on and on with a rush.[23] He began with the confession that after his arrival at a mature age he had deliberately embraced, from conviction, the faith that had early been instilled into his mind by his mother. He felt that as the clause was part of the written fundamental law of the land it should be expounded according to the well-established rules of legal interpretation. Therefore, unless it contained a clear disqualification it must be considered as leaving unimpaired the right of the citizen to hold, and the country to confer, office. There could be no restriction upon the people's choice of whom they wished to serve unless it was unequivocally imposed by themselves, but the language of this clause was most unclear. Gaston then described the process of reasoning through which he had gone to arrive at the conclusion that he had not been prohibited from holding his present office.

After asking the entire convention whether it wished purposely to leave the Constitution unintelligible, he turned the full force of his invective upon the delegates from Orange County, demanding proof that they had been instructed to vote against amending this article. If such were the case he felt that an interchange of opinion, consultation, and discussion was useless. Sarcastically he said:

> Dead is it? Then it is fit for cleanly riddance. Asleep is it? After experience of the manner in which the delegates from

> Orange are disposed to execute pledges given in behalf of their people . . . we must be excused if we are not over hasty in relying on this unauthorized guaranty.

Indignantly he declared that to be disqualified for office would be an indignity he could not be made to feel, even though the consciousness that it was unmerited might enable him to treat it with calm scorn. He maintained that the union of church and state allowed rulers to enlarge their dominion by extending it over the minds of their subjects, and put at their disposal the high places of the church, as well as enlisting in their services its ministers and teachers; also it made kings and princes and magistrates the head of God's spiritual kingdom rendering it a sacrilege and treason to resist their sway. He asked that either this appendage of an established church be blotted out or else that a church be set up as the church of the state, for with the exception of New Jersey and North Carolina every other state and most of the countries of Europe had perfect religious liberty. The judge then launched into a description of his faith, objecting to the term allegiance to characterize the connection existing between the Catholic citizens and the pope, emphatically stating that he owed no allegiance to any man or set of men on earth, save only to the state of North Carolina and, insofar as the state had parted with her sovereignty, to the United States. Speaking of the pope's authority he alleged that it was but spiritual and enforced only by spiritual censures, and as for the much abused penance, "nothing so effectually as this compels self-examination, keeps down pride of heart, checks progress in crime, or restrains irregular appetite and passion; Voltaire had claimed that the wit of men could never devise a happier security for human morals." Answering the charge that the Catholic Church was unfavorable to freedom, Gaston called attention to the fact that the oldest and purest democracy on earth was the little Catholic republic of Saint Marino, not a day's journey from Rome.

To the assertions that the West would not ratify the amendments if this article was touched, Gaston caustically replied, "If the West reject because of this, then the evil complained of has not been as sore as they would have us believe or else such is the bitterness of their sectarian hate, as to render it utterly unsafe to trust them with the political power of the State."[24]

For two days Gaston had riveted their attention. On the first day, after three hours, it was seen that he was tired, so someone moved to adjourn until the next day, but "on account of some manifestation of opposition because of the rapt attention" he continued until it was noted that exhaustion had almost completely claimed him. The reporter from the New Bern paper wrote his editor that when the celebrated justice had turned the great versatility of his talents, with the force and energy of his powers upon the delegates of Orange County, it had appeared that this torrent of sarcasm, wit, and humor would bear down everything before it and in common destruction overwhelm the county of Orange. "I looked around in vain for the instructed," the amused correspondent said, "and began to fear that the Pope, in the shape of the Old Boy Himself, had spirited them away for abusing the Catholics . . . never was defeat more effectual." Gaston had given, according to this observer, a succinct history of the Catholic religion in this country, beautiful sketches of distinguished men and characteristic anecdotes. "We shall never hear its like again," concluded he.[25]

The convention had been watched with interest throughout the United States, and, especially was the debate over the thirty-second article noted and remarked upon. The Norfolk *Beacon* described how "the venerable Macon and the eloquent Gaston have fought shoulder to shoulder."[26] The Raleigh *Register* reported that Gaston's speech "was decidedly the greatest effort, which has ever been our good fortune to hear, and surpassed the most elevated anticipation of an audience long sensible to that gentleman's great and merited fame. It will hereafter be ranked among the first specimens of popular oratory that our country has ever produced and be read with delight as long as talents and learning are admired. But the rich and finely modulated intonations of his voice must be lost to all who did not witness. . . . "[27] This reference in the *Register* was copied in the New York *Register* and *Diary* and the *Catholic Miscellany;* indeed practically all of the papers in the country which spoke of the convention acquired their information from the Raleigh paper. Many of them copied from it the entire debates of the body. There came high praise also from Chancellor Kent, who "highly approved of its logic and admired its whole texture, taste, candor, and eloquence." The New Yorker enthusiastically exclaimed, "You have placed the Catholic faith in a strong point of view. You have demonstrated the folly and absurdity of instructions, and the narrow and persecuting spirit that would retain the clause in question which I think with you disgraceful to the state and age."[28]

The next day discussion was resumed by others. Burges S. Gaither of Burke County expressed his sorrow that such a strong prejudice should prevail in his section, but thought this would entirely vanish when people read Gaston's able exposition of the doctrines of his religion. However, even now John Joiner wished to keep their "sleeping thunder to be used when wanted," as he believed it was intended to prevent Roman Catholics from being admitted to office. Thereupon, the Edwards amendment to expunge all tests from the constitution was put to a vote, but was negatived 87 to 36, Branch, Swain, Spaight of Craven, Macon, Rayner, Roulac, Judge Daniel, and Gaston being for it. Two more amendments met the same fate, then one was introduced which simply substituted the word "Christian" for "Protestant." Governor Branch then expressed his disfavor with the proposal, growling that "some people were so ignorant or so blinded by prejudice as to believe Catholics were not Christians, and anyway why should not the same boon be granted to Jews." Judge Toomer wished not to touch the article, as he felt it was no bar to Catholics, but paid a singular tribute to Gaston as he said:

A distinguished member of this Convention publicly professing

> and openly avowing the doctrines of the Catholic Church has been recently appointed by the Assembly to one of the highest judicial stations in the state. Profoundly learned in the law, and eminently skilled in the solution of constitutional questions; of irreproachable character and fastidiously scrupulous in matters of conscience; of retired habits; not seeking but declining office, he accepted the appointment in obedience to the public will. . . . The executive signed it . . . the Supreme Court accepted him . . . and the appointment was hailed by the people with acclamation. . . .

Morehead spoke in the same vein, saying that Gaston was admitted to his seat without a single whisper of objection from any quarter, but on the contrary, with the general approbation of the whole country. The vote was then taken on this substitution, and passed with seventy-four in favor and fifty-one in opposition. Morehead and Seawell voted even against this clause, as did Governor Branch upon principle, because he was totally opposed to all such tests.

Among other questions yet to be considered was that of giving the election of the governor to the people, and taking away from the legislature the power to grant divorces. Gaston was not in favor of the former because the governor's only political power lay in granting pardons, and all required of him was that he be a gentleman in character and manners, so there was nothing rendering it necessary that he should owe his appointment to the people. As for the latter, he felt it ridiculous that a legislature should act in this capacity, as it could not ascertain the circumstances of cases, and if this "solemn contract entered into between man and wife, the sacredness of which Heaven is invoked to witness" why could it not also investigate contracts for the sale of land? He thought the best interests of society demanded that the marriage tie should be indissoluble but by death. The judge told a story of how a couple was divorced by the legislature, but had been unaware of the fact, because the deed was done by a friend who felt sure they both desired it. He wondered how some good men would feel, in looking over the proceedings of the legislature, to find that they were divorced from their wives without even the knowledge of what was going on. After other business was taken care of Gaston reported from the committee appointed to draw up the amendments proposed, which were voted on by the convention and passed 87 to 20. He then offered a resolution "returning acknowledgements to the venerable president for his manner of presiding over the body," and on his motion the convention adjourned *sine die*, July 11, 1835.

The results of the convention had been a compromise, so the West really did not win a great victory, although in the House, which was to consist of one hundred and twenty men, the county unit of representation was abolished for the federal system; the Senate's number was fixed at fifty. Although the western men were not greatly disturbed by the borough representation, and took little part in the discussion over the "free Negro vote," both were abolished. The assembly was forbidden to grant divorces and pass private laws, the election of the governor was given to the people, while his term was increased to two years. The general assembly thereafter was to meet biennially, and the word "Christian" was substituted for the word "Protestant" in the thirty-second article.

Among other amusing sequels to the convention which may have occurred, was one related by Bishop England to Gaston. It seemed the former had been returning to Fayetteville, and found that two delegates from Anson County were in the stage with him. In the ensuing discussion he discovered that Joseph White had voted for the alteration of the religious clause while William Morris had voted against it. Morris told the bishop of an incident of the convention, during which Judge Seawell quoted a passage from what he claimed was the notes of a Catholic Bible, to show the Catholic belief that St. Peter had the same power as God, and Gaston had demanded the book from him, but Seawell had remained silent. A few days later

Morris was at dinner with Seawell, who told him that he had sent Gaston a copy of the book. The bishop then asked Morris if he believed that Seawell had done so, and was answered unhesitantly in the negative. However, Morris had not believed it was his business at the time to say this to Seawell.[29]

Before ratification by the people had been secured, Gaston expressed confidentially his views on the different amendments to a friend. He thought the West would not rest until the existing constitution was changed, so warned his confidant that the question was between this amended document and what would be imposed if it were rejected. He felt that the system of representation was more liberal to the East than it would be in the future, while "but for the solicitude of the western delegates in the last assembly to call a convention and the prudent advantage taken of it by liberal and enlightened members of the East it would have been impossible to make Federal numbers the basis of representation in the Commons." Gaston observed that there was much dissatisfaction in the large interior and mountain counties and attributed it to the influence of "the man who represents us in Congress, who endeavored to make the western delegates in the convention dissatisfied with it by declaring that it was unjust to the West, which should be represented in the House by proportion to their free population exclusively." Expressing regret for the loss of borough representation because it would keep a few valuable men out, he told his friend that the counties around New Bern were jealous of her franchise. He admitted that if the constitution could have been amended without the clause giving the election of the governor to the people he would have voted against this section "as a man who loves good order and deprecates the virulence of faction." On the issue of the free Negro he confessed there might be delicacy and difficulty, but at the same time thought himself correct in his stand. He thought that the public liberty was materially secured by the provisions to the judiciary, and could not commend too highly the restrictions placed on private legislation. Concerning the thirty-second article he was most dissatisfied, saying:

> It ought to have guaranteed the most unlimited freedom of opinion just as long as they did not disturb the peace of a city by their conduct. . . . The meanest of all two-legged creatures, time-serving, popularity hunting politicians found that here was a fund of ignorance and prejudice which might be made to operate to their immediate advantage . . . frightened those who would have done better but for cowardice, and nothing more could be affected than the paltry change proposed.

In his opinion it was to the best interest of North Carolina that the people should ratify their work, and he professed to be confirmed in this by the "most prudent and sagacious men of the country."[30] Gaston had probably done more than any other single man of the convention, speaking the oftenest and longest, and serving on many, if not most, of the committees.

The people, after heated controversy, charges, countercharges, and amid the fulmination of both sides, finally ratified these amendments by a majority of 5165 votes. Craven County rejected them by 270 to 131. Of the 48,377 votes cast, 26,771 were for ratification as against 21,606.[31] Every county in the West voted for it, while every county in the East, except one, voted against it.

## NOTES FOR CHAPTER NINE

1. Wagstaff, "State Rights and Political Parties in North Carolina," *Johns Hopkins Historical Studies*, XXIV, 61.
2. *Ibid.*, p. 62.
3. *Carolina Sentinel*, Jan. 22, 1820.
4. Governor D. L. Swain to Gaston, Oct. 9, 1834, Gaston *MSS*.
5. New Bern *Spectator*, Jan. 23, 1835.
6. *Proceedings and Debates of the Convention of North Carolina Called to Amend the Constitution* . . ., 1835, p. 4. Cited hereafter as *Proceedings and Debates*.
7. *Ibid.*, p. 32.

8. *Ibid.*, p. 35.
9. *Ibid.*, p. 79.
10. *Ibid.*, p. 104.
11. *Ibid.*, pp. 126–145.
12. *National Gazette,* July 11, 1835.
13. New Bern *Spectator,* June 12, 1835.
14. *Proceedings and Debates,* p. 176.
15. *Ibid.*, pp. 215–218.
16. *Ibid.*, pp. 221–229.
17. Gaston to John H. Bryan, June 29, 1835, Gaston *MSS.*
18. *Proceedings and Debates,* p. 241.
19. *Ibid.*, p. 243.
20. *Ibid.*, p. 244.
21. Bishop England to Gaston, June 6, 1835. *American Catholic Historical Society Records,* XIX, 155. Referred to hereafter as *ACHS Records.*
22. New Bern *Spectator,* July 10, 1835.
23. J. H. Wheeler, *op. cit.*, II, 116.
24. *Proceedings and Debates,* pp. 265–303.
25. New Bern *Spectator,* July 10, 1835.
26. *Literary and Catholic Sentinel,* Aug. 1, 1835.
27. Raleigh *Register,* July 7, 1835.
28. Kent to Gaston, Nov. 26, 1835, Gaston *MSS.*
29. Bishop England to Gaston, July 22, 1835, *ACHS Records,* XIX, 158.
30. Gaston to [Barth. ?] Moore, Aug. 16, 1835, Manly *MSS.*, U.N.C.
31. *Proceedings and Debates,* p. 425.

*I am solicitous for others of the Church who cannot have the same facilities and who long for an opportunity for practicing the duties of their religion.* — WILLIAM GASTON

*You cannot believe how much I think of you. . . .*
— BISHOP SIMON BRUTÉ

CHAPTER TEN

# Southern Catholic

THE name of Gaston is inextricably bound with the Roman Catholic Church in the state of North Carolina and especially so in New Bern. The earliest known Catholics to be located there were the English merchants, Gerard and Joseph Sharpe, who in 1774 lived in New Bern. In this same year these two brothers were visited by their sister, Margaret, who married Alexander Gaston the following year, but in the meanwhile the two Sharpes had died, leaving no children. There was no priest there at the time, and it is not known what official presided at the marriage of Alexander and Margaret.

The first priest to visit New Bern, and probably the entire state, was Patrick Cleary, an Irishman, who had been a canon of the church of Funehal, and came to the town around 1784 to claim the property of his dead brother. Mrs. Gaston arranged one of the rooms of her house for a chapel where he celebrated Mass. Three or four other Catholics attended, among whom was John Devereux. Father Cleary baptized a few children and performed other religious duties, but was in no position to give instructions, as he spoke English with difficulty. He had not intended to remain long at this place, but the litigation over the property was so involved and extended over such a long period that the poor man was fated never again to leave New

Bern, for he died some time in 1790 and was buried in the cemetery of Christ's Church. So far as is known he was the first priest to be buried in the state, and at least up to 1825 it is believed he was the only one. For some time after his death the few Catholics there were without the ministrations of a priest, but Mrs. Gaston instructed her children in the Catholic religion and taught them their prayers.

When her son became a student of Georgetown College he soon came into contact with Bishop John Carroll, the founder of the college, and told him of the situation in North Carolina. The bishop wished to send a priest into the state, but said he had none for the purpose.[1] When William Gaston was forced to leave the college his mother advised the president of the situation, and at the same time asked him to inform the bishop that if the latter would send a missionary into the state she would take care of part of the expenses involved.[2] However, nothing of the sort could be done by Bishop Carroll, who simply did not have the priests.

In 1798 another Irish clergyman, a certain Father Burke, came to New Bern from Norfolk, remaining but a short time. Some years later Father Gallagher came there to witness the wedding of William to Hannah McClure. In July of 1807 and June of 1808 Father Michael Lacy of Norfolk spent a few days in the town, attending to the spiritual needs of the few Catholics. Late in 1811, Margaret, William's mother, who had done more for the Church than any other person in the state, died and was buried in Cedar Grove Cemetery.

Bishop Carroll had not forgotten the few Catholics of North Carolina and told Gaston that he hoped to have a priest there soon. In replying to the Bishop's letter of consolation over the death of his mother, he informed him that he intended to visit the North that summer to choose a new home, which might be in Baltimore. Of this decision, he said, "Tender and strong are the ties which bind me to my native state, but considerations of a paramount nature require of me to break them. I have a family of lovely and promising children, and I am above all things solicitous that they be reared in some place where a regular and stated observance of all the ordinances of the Church may keep alive and reimpress on their minds a sense of religious duty."[3] However, that summer war broke out with England, Gaston entered politics actively, and was soon representing his state in Congress; the following year his wife died and the children went to his sister.

The bishop was not able to find a priest for the state, so for several more years the people had no religious ministration. Again from Norfolk, in 1819 and 1820, New Bern was visited briefly by the Reverend Nicholas Kearney. The latter year he remained a fortnight, preached several times, baptized a number of children and received three converts into the Church.[4] After Father Kearney's first visit Gaston wrote to Bishop Maréchal, asking that a priest be sent to Washington, North Carolina. He told the bishop that there the priest's expenses would be paid by "Mr. Hanrahan and Mr. Leroy, who will also furnish board, servants and horses. I will do the same at New Bern and he can stay at my house. I am solicitous for others of the Church who cannot have the same facilities and who long for an opportunity for practising the duties of their religion."[5] Gaston had already placed his children in Catholic boarding-houses in the North, so they were taken care of, as his third wife had died in this same year. Although Bishop Maréchal could not grant his request, it was not long before the state received the attention it wished, in the person of dynamic John England, bishop of Charleston, South Carolina.

John England was born in 1786 at Cork, Ireland, and was ordained a priest in 1809. Later he became the president of a college there and has been accounted by some as most responsible, after O'Connell, for raising the agitation which finally resulted in Catholic Emancipation for England. He was consecrated the first bishop of Charleston on September 21, 1820, and refused to take the customary oath of allegiance to England, announcing his intention to become an American citizen. He arrived in Charleston December 30, 1820, to find that his diocese covered the states of South Carolina, North Carolina, and Georgia.

Ten days after his arrival in the new diocese he appealed to Gaston for aid as he had been unable to find anyone who could give him information on North Carolina, but knew it was in a dreadful situation, and because of the statements made to him of Gaston's zeal for religion, knew the latter would respond.[6] The following May he informed Gaston of his approaching arrival in New Bern, and asked him to make proper arrangements for his preaching.[7] May 24, 1821, the first bishop to visit New Bern was welcomed at the Gaston home. Here, in the large ballroom in the front of the house, the bishop celebrated Mass. He remained in town until June 4, administering the sacraments and at night preaching in the courthouse, "always to a very large and respectable congregation." Before leaving the bishop appointed five of the principal Catholics to conduct services every Sunday at the little chapel in Gaston's home. The need of a church was discussed, and a treasury was created to receive funds for the building; Gaston contributed $700, John Devereux $500, Peter Brughman $400, Francis Lamott $200, and Benjamin Good $200. Later a lot, 106 feet by 199 feet, was purchased from Richard L. Mason for $1,500.[8] The bishop returned for a short visit the following November.

His first appointment for the state, the Reverend Anthony O'Hannon, came there in May of 1822, but remained scarcely two weeks because of poor health. The following year the bishop came back and at this time preached in the Presbyterian Church, which was placed at his disposal. By this time Bishop England had become a popular man in New Bern, not only because of his friendship with William Gaston, but also through his own radiant personality. During his visit there in February of 1824 he published a constitution for the Church in North Carolina, "with some few amendments suggested by the Honorable

William Gaston."[9] St. Paul the Apostle was named patron of the diocese. Gaston and Benjamin Good were appointed church wardens, and these two with Peter Brughman and Francis Lamott were made vestrymen.[10] By summer a priest, Father Francis O'Donoghue, was appointed to the state. He was followed in 1833 by Father Peter Whelan; in 1834 by Father R. S. Baker; in 1835 by Father John Fielding; in 1839 by Father Andrew Doyle; and in 1841 by Father Edward Quigley. In 1832 Bishop England estimated there were 500 Catholics in North Carolina. He had difficulty in getting priests to remain in New Bern, for, as they told him, they received nothing there in support except what Gaston and Manly contributed. In 1838 there were two priests in the eastern section of the state, but difficulty was experienced in raising funds for their subsistence. Gaston wrote to the Catholics of Washington, North Carolina, asking them to help provide for their traveling expenses. He told them that the Catholics of New Bern had already adopted such a plan. "It will be disgraceful to us if we cannot in this way insure $500 to $600 for the two. $100 will be contributed from here and I will answer for $100 or $150, if needed. . . ."[11]

In June, 1839, a resolution was passed to build a church, and on October 28, 1839, at a meeting in Gaston's office a plan for a wooden church to cost $4,000 was submitted by William H. Burgmin. It was found there was a balance of $500 remaining in the treasury; Gaston then pledged $500, Mathias Manly $500, and Bishop England $500 toward the new church. One of the town's residents, a Dr. Hays, who was a Protestant, had been interested in the church's struggle and left in his will an estate valued at $1,100 to them. A contract was drawn between Gaston and Hardy Lanes to build the church for $3,784.34, and work was started on it in 1840. England told Gaston that "we will do nothing without you, we will do everything with you." The following year it was finished, but was not blessed until 1844 by England's successor, Bishop Reynolds.

Bishop England was a man of extraordinary ability, courage,

and accomplishments. In 1822 he founded the first distinctively Catholic newspaper, the *United States Catholic Miscellany*, and also found time to write a new edition of the missal in English. In 1823 eastern Florida was added to his diocese. Four times he went to Europe to collect funds for his impoverished diocese. Chancellor Kent felt that he had revived classical learning in South Carolina. He was asked to speak before Congress in 1826, which was the first time a Catholic priest was so honored. After this event he talked to President Adams who expressed great surprise that Gaston was a Catholic church warden.[12]

England found in Gaston a firm friend and helpful coadjutor. The latter gave him letters to various friends in other parts of the state, so that the bishop found his way paved before him.[13] He told Gaston that "no person knows here that I write to you, otherwise I suppose you should have treble postage to pay for all the affection this would contain." When in Raleigh he stayed with the Taylors. After establishing the *Miscellany* he was constantly writing Gaston for aid in the venture, asking for both funds and new subscribers. He also asked him to "translate some select edifying passage from some of those good books of which you are so fond . . . or . . . in the shape of a letter or of a paragraph or of a dissertation . . . you could greatly relieve my editorial labors." He told him that he wished a candid opinion upon the paper and what improvement was necessary. Gaston's answer must have been frank, for later England hoped that he was better pleased with it than before.[14] In 1826 England needed $1,000 for the printing office, and again turned to his friend in North Carolina, remarking, "I do not know whether you ought to be asked to add to your former loan under a better prospect of repayment, but if you could, any aid would be highly useful."[15]

Gaston's legal advice was often sought by Bishop England. When the latter sought to do something about the scandalous proceedings at St. Mary's in Philadelphia he informed Gaston of it. Gaston was indirectly and in a minor way drawn into the affair. One of the participants, the Reverend Hannon, went to Charleston, and on a missionary tour, arrived in New Bern, where he sought the advice of Gaston. Before leaving Philadelphia Father Hannon was assured that he would not be involved further, but heard, while in South Carolina, that legal proceedings had not been dropped, and that if he did not return his surety would be forfeited. Gaston was suspicious of the news, for he felt that the object in view to get Hannon back in Philadelphia was "to enable one of the contending factions to get a triumph over the other." Gaston advised him to take no step until he could ascertain the true state of affairs, and in order to do this wrote to Joseph Hopkinson for the desired information.[16] Seven years later in the Harrold Case England again sought his advice.[17] As early as 1823 the bishop asked him if he could not procure a change in the thirty-second article of the constitution.

Without Gaston the priests who came to New Bern could not have been supported nor could the church have been built. Bishop England baptized Gaston's grandchildren and his son-in-law, Manly, confirmed the latter and Gaston's daughters, and married Susan, and often expressed to Gaston his love for him and his children. The two remained firm friends until England's death in April, 1842.

Another bishop whose love for Gaston was as strong as that of Bishop England was the first bishop of Vincennes, Simon Bruté de Rémur. Father Bruté had been introduced to Gaston by Father Grassi at Georgetown when the North Carolinian was in Congress. Between 1821 and 1836 Bruté wrote at least one hundred and forty letters to Gaston. The two exchanged views on literature, art, and culture. Bruté's letters were replete with spiritual matters, and he often asked Gaston's help in preparation of some dissertation.

Bruté was born March 20, 1779, at Rennes, France.[18] He entered the medical profession, receiving in 1802 the first prize in an examination over 1100 other students. Napoleon was eager to obtain the services of Dr. Bruté and in April of 1803 appointed him physician to the First Dispensary in Paris. Bruté refused the appointment as he had determined to enter the priesthood. In June, 1808, he was ordained priest and again Napoleon sought to honor him but the distinction offered by the emperor was declined.[19] For the next two years he taught in the seminary of St. Sulpice, and then decided to go to America as a missionary. He was sent to teach at the Catholic college of Mt. St. Mary's near Emmitsburg, Maryland, of which he finally became president. In 1834 he was named first bishop of the diocese of Vincennes, which covered almost the entire northwest territory.

While at Emmitsburg Bruté had occasion often to see Gaston's children and kept the father informed concerning them. His letters were always filled with his expressions of affection for his friend. He wished to see Gaston become bishop of North Carolina, and often spoke to him of his desire.[20] When rumors reached him that Gaston might become vice-president he was disturbed saying, "I find no courage to wish that happiness to you but to this country I wish it."[21] When Gaston's nephew, John Louis Taylor, took his degree at Emmitsburg, Bruté asked Gaston to preside at the commencement, but his duties on the supreme court prevented the judge even from attending the exercises. He had been greatly interested in his nephew's progress, as he had financed his education at the college.

Bruté discussed the policies of the *Catholic Miscellany* only with Gaston to whom he confessed, "It made me bleed along pages of the *Miscellany*, when all that candor . . . why will he write before passion is cooled . . . why no friend, no consul with whom to read over."[22] Bruté felt that Bishop England's espousal of the Irish cause in his paper was unwise. After he became bishop of Vincennes he told Gaston that he was reduced to begging openly; that when the latter wrote him "he should pay the postage and ballast your letter with a note of $10 . . . for I am as poor as Job."[23] In 1839 this ardent French bishop passed to his reward.

Gaston was always a pious Catholic; his religion influenced his daily actions and perhaps sometimes his decisions upon the bench. His children were often edified to see their father, walking up and down under the grape arbor in the back yard reading his prayers from a missal or some other prayer book. It can truthfully be said that he was the greatest Catholic of North Carolina, for the state has never produced another to equal him.

## NOTES FOR CHAPTER TEN

1. Gaston to his mother, Nov. 24, 1792, Gaston *MSS*.
2. Reverend F. Neal to Margaret Gaston, Oct. 18, 1793, Gaston *MSS*.
3. Gaston to Archbishop Carroll, Jan. 30, 1812, B.C.A. 3Y3.
4. *United States Catholic Miscellany,* March 17, 1824.
5. Gaston to Bishop Maréchal, Aug. 20, 1819. B.C.A. 17C1.
6. Bishop England to Gaston, Jan. 9, 1821, Gaston *MSS*.
7. Bishop England to Gaston, May 17, 1821, *ACHS Records,* XVIII, 367.
8. Records of St. Paul's Church.
9. *Carolina Sentinel,* March 6, 1824.
10. Records of St. Paul's Church, Feb. 15, 1824.
11. Gaston to Benj. Laverrder, Jan. 22, 1838, Raleigh Diocesan Archives, Bishop's Home.
12. England to Gaston, Jan. 29, 1826, *ACHS Records,* XIX, 104.
13. England to Gaston, June 13, 20, 1821, *ACHS Records,* XVIII, 371, 374.
14. England to Gaston, Oct. 13, 1824, *ACHS Records,* XIX, 101.
15. England to Gaston, Feb. 21, 1826, *ACHS Records,* XIX, 106.
16. Gaston to Joseph Hopkinson, June 12, 1822, Hopkinson *MSS*.
17. England to Gaston, Nov. 7, 1829. *ACHS Records,* XIX, 140–143. The letters of Gaston to England were turned over to the diocese of Charleston by the family, as they involved many ecclesiastical questions. These were accidentally destroyed in a disastrous fire.
18. M. S. Godecker, *Simon Bruté de Rémur,* p. 3.
19. *Ibid.,* p. 37.
20. Bruté to Gaston, Dec. 7, 1828, Bruté *MSS*., Notre Dame University Archives.
21. Bruté to Gaston, July 27, 1832, Bruté *MSS*.
22. Bruté to Gaston, Aug. 14, —— Bruté *MSS*.

23. Bruté to Gaston, Jan. 10, 1835, Bruté *MSS*.

The letters of Bruté to Gaston are rich in information for the student of Bruté. They are long, written sometimes in French, sometimes in English, with lengthy passages in Latin, or a combination of the three. These letters have not been used heretofore. I have been unable to find any of Gaston's letters to Bruté.

*To administer justice in the last resort with a steady hand and an upright purpose appears to me to be among the highest of civil functions . . . how can I better serve my country.* — WILLIAM GASTON

*The legislature will take pleasure in electing you to any vacancy agreeable to you . . . and by your election the old North State would be given much more weight and standing abroad.* — RICHARD HINES

# CHAPTER ELEVEN

# Sage of the Old North State

CHIEF JUSTICE JOHN MARSHALL, after almost thirty-five years spent in the service of this country, died on July 6, 1835, and immediately conjecture was rife over the country as to his successor. In North Carolina there was but one name mentioned, that of Gaston. Friends of these two judges claimed that Marshall had often stated that he would retire if he were sure the North Carolinian would be appointed to the vacancy. The New York *Courier* of July 22, 1835, in discussing the vacancy recommended Gaston, but thought that "he was too pure a patriot and too good a man and possessed too much fitness for the station to be thought of for a moment at the White House. . . ."[1]

Editors throughout his own state strongly urged that he be given the place. An editorial from the New Bern *Spectator* is typical of the rest. It said: "If Jackson be really desirous to secure the appointment of a man of profound ability and uncompromising integrity . . . nineteen-twentieth of all parties would be pleased with William Gaston. . . . There is we presume no individual in the Union, who would have been sooner selected by Marshall."[2] This same editorial appeared in the Elizabeth

City *Star*, the *Georgia Courier*, and the *National Gazette* of Washington; all copying it from the Raleigh *Register*. Susan informed her father that Webster had told her "you are the *only* one who should succeed Judge Marshall." Later, she wrote, "The very few who are worthy to succeed him are the last Jackson would appoint. Mr. Edward Livingston (whose place adjoins ours on the river) is talked of, and I hear and learn that there is some talk of Chancellor Kent."[3] However, this talk was generally wishful thinking, for everyone knew that the president would make a political appointment. Some time previously Jackson had nominated Roger B. Taney to a vacancy on the court, but the Senate had not confirmed the appointment. Taney had served Jackson well, writing a powerful message for the president on the Bank of the United States, and as secretary of the treasury had done Jackson's will during the historical fight over that bank. Jackson was anxious to reward him for his loyalty, and to wipe out the injury of the rejection, so sent in his name to the Senate for the chief justiceship. To his satisfaction Taney was confirmed; with the appointment another of Gaston's friends sat upon the bench.

There is little doubt that Gaston would have been pleased with this appointment, and, if offered, would have accepted the position. He was more than satisfied with his position on the bench of North Carolina, for he refused other offers. As early as 1830 he had been "strongly pressed at the legislature to permit his name to be held up for the appointment to a senatorship," and although confessing to his daughter that he was far from insensible to its attraction, rejoiced that personal duties forbade him to yield to its allurements, feeling that he owed it to his family to pursue the business of his profession.[4] His appointment had been assured by the legislature.

To this Susan replied, "Do think of yourself, for your name alone would be an inheritance to your children."[5] In 1834 there was a vacancy in the supreme court and the papers of the state urged his appointment, but the Raleigh *Register* pointed out that it was not within his judicial district, so he was not eligible.[6] Governor Swain informed him that he was the choice for this post by newspapers "here and out of the state."[7]

One of the most active and most useful years of Gaston's life was that of 1835. The winter term of the court kept him well occupied in the first months; in the spring he was forced to spend much of his time at the plantation; during the summer he was exhausted by his efforts in the constitutional convention; after this activity he was again employed in the business of the court for the summer term, and as soon as this was finished he started preparing his address to be delivered at Princeton in the fall. Several times before, he had been asked by this university to speak at commencement, and as he was visiting Susan that fall, accepted the invitation for that year.

As the Presbyterian church, where the ceremony usually took place, was burned down, his address was given "under a tent in the rear of the old college edifice." The graduating class, numbering fifty-three, was the second largest in the history of the school. Several master of arts degrees were also awarded, and, upon Gaston, Nicholas Biddle and a few others, there was conferred an honorary doctor of laws.[8] Among those present during his address of two hours that afternoon of September 29 were the governor of New Jersey, Chancellor Kent, Biddle, his daughter Susan and her husband.

After advising the graduating students concerning their course in life, Gaston attacked some of the prevalent evils of the day, especially the spirit of lawlessness, lynch law, and mob rule, which pervaded the west and southwest, of which he said:

> When from one end to the other of the country, we behold lawless associations asserting the prerogative of vindictive justice, legislating for what they fancy to be crimes . . . by such rules of evidence as best suit their rage . . . there is cause for dread that a spirit is rife in the land which must be put down. Rebellion against the law is in the nature of treason. Law deserves our obedience; it alone can reconcile

> the jarring interest of all, and blend into one harmonious union the discordant materials of which society is composed. . . . Even in a family, much must be wisely overlooked.

In attacking the spirit of bigotry, he said:

> We have witnessed it in a city surrendered for days and nights to outrage and arson; in helpless people of color hunted from their dwellings like beasts of prey from their caverns. . . . Every instance of successful revolt against the state's collective will impairs its beneficial sway, until finally the state itself sinks into political servitude.

Speaking against this mob spirit he pointed out that every individual of which it was composed would refuse to submit his rights to the judgment of such a body, and maintained that the law would rather that many guilty should escape with impunity than one innocent being suffer wrongly.

During this time the press was most violent and vindictive. The editors, Gaston exclaimed, seemed to wish to attract to themselves popular favor by overwhelming their adversaries with hatred; their detractions he likened to assassination, to stabbing an enemy in the back. He felt that one should be slow to charge opponents with wicked acts, as one could not know when he was likely to commit a rash mistake. Feeling that the character of the nation was deeply involved in the character of her public men, he asked that, in the name of justice and decency, they not be assailed with charges of corrupt purposes. He thought that other countries could not think much of our institutions if distinguished men, known only as our leaders, were indiscriminately held up to scorn. He concluded:

> If our country cease to be the land of law, order and freedom, our name will cease to be reverenced. The light of American freedom now shines as a beacon to many afar off; a star of hope to the affrightened, of gladness to the benevolent and of encouragement to the oppressed. But extinguished, it will

> be remembered as a delusive meteor which rose full of promise . . . and then left the world in deeper darkness than before. Our country will remain . . . if the soul of national freedom be kept alive.[9]

Commenting on the affair, the *National Gazette* remarked that a more seasonable and wholesome gift could not have been made to the scholars of America, and that it revealed profound research and a discipline of ancient learning. "From a Southern statesman," the paper continued, "the withering denunciation of lynch-law came with a ten-fold potency."[10] The *National Intelligencer* felt that this address should be sent into every American household.[11] Other papers, invariably mentioned that it had been thirty-nine years since the great Southerner had left his university. This address and the one delivered before the University of North Carolina may well be read by college graduates of today with much profit.

The society wished to publish the address, so Gaston asked Dr. Beasley to go over it for him, but this the latter refused to do, because his only objection to it had been the conclusion, which was a stanza of poetry. When the speech was published this did not appear. Beasley also felt that Gaston should be more cautious in speaking about the late violations of law, especially in the West, as it would give his enemies a point to seize on, and although what he had said was sound doctrine, he should try to render it less offensive.[12] However, this Gaston refused to do, as he felt that the atrocities mentioned should be fearlessly characterized, while he himself had no popular purpose to gratify.[13] In other words, he was no politician who had to watch every word uttered lest it offend one or another.

From here Gaston went to his daughter's home on the Hudson, and while there spent some time with Chancellor Kent. One evening the two were discussing Martin Van Buren, sometimes known as "The Red Fox." Kent thought him to be "a man of very superior and positive ability, who in practicing law before me for twenty years, always seized the strong points of his own case and the weak points of his adversary, which is proof of ability in any man." Gaston regarded him as "distinguished by that quality which estimated the value of men according to their uses to himself." "He regards men," said Gaston, "as I do those snuffers, valuable when needed, but after being used, of no further value, until wanted again."[14]

While in New York Gaston purchased a library for the supreme court of North Carolina at a cost of $1,361.75.[15] From New York he traveled on to Philadelphia, to Washington, and then back home. There he spent much of his leisure time on the plantation, experimenting with buckwheat as a good green crop to enrich the land. At the close of this year he was honored by two more colleges; the Philodemis society of Georgetown made him an honorary member as did the Phi Beta Kappa Society of Yale University, and the next year this latter society elected him the orator for the commencement exercises. In 1836 the two literary societies of the University of Alabama and that of the Rutgers College made him an honorary member; these were followed in the next few years by those of the University of Georgia, St. Mary's College of Baltimore, Caldwell Institute, and Davidson College of North Carolina. In 1837 Georgetown again asked him to give the address at graduation, as did Ohio's Miami University in 1840 and several other colleges at various times. These invitations he invariably had to refuse, generally because of his duties on the bench. In 1839 the University of New York conferred an honorary doctor of laws upon him.[16] In this same year he refused another invitation to speak at the state university, tendered to him by his old friend, David Swain, who was now its president. Gaston also obtained some satisfaction from a letter of George Bancroft, the historian, who wrote to thank him for mentioning his work in connection with his speech at the convention on toleration.[17]

A visit to Susan with his two youngest daughters became a yearly event for him. On these occasions he would visit in other parts of the country, going to Boston and Philadelphia, and at least once to Niagara Falls. In these latter years of his life the judge was not so hard pressed by business, although the two terms of the supreme court demanded incessant attention at the time, for he was very scrupulous about this work. During a case, with a gold mine said to be worth millions at issue, the three justices spent many an hour in careful consideration of the facts, but Gaston told his daughter, Eliza, that "I feel deeply the responsibility of being one of three to determine on a matter of such magnitude. But I think I see very clearly that the difficulty in the cause bears no proportion to the value of the subject in controversy."[18]

His advice was often sought by legislators both in the state assembly and the national Congress. Hugh Waddell and William A. Graham asked him what he thought should be done with the surplus revenue which the United States had allotted to North Carolina, which of the great public works was entitled to primary attention, and whether it would be practical to establish a system of common schools. They also wished his opinion on the necessity of amendments to the revenue system.[19] Bryan also asked his advice in legislative matters, having become perplexed over the distinction between public and private acts. He told Gaston that unless he forbade it, his name would be offered for the senatorship to the United States Congress in the assembly, and that he was certain to receive the place, but Gaston absolutely refused the proffer.[20]

During court sessions in Raleigh he stayed with the James F. Taylors. Mrs. Taylor was the widow of the former attorney general and adopted daughter of Gaston's sister, Jane, and John L. Taylor. This home was always full of children, and on winter evenings if there was no company the children would usually gather around him for a story from *Arabian Nights* or sometimes a song. On clear and starry nights all would troop outside and the judge would point out the different stars and constellations to them. He loved the society of the young, and they loved him; to most of their entertainments he received invitations, which he always accepted, if only for a few minutes, and he never missed the weddings of his younger friends. These probably reminded him of his sad losses, for at times he had spells of depression and would be seen by some to sigh deeply and become very motionless. When the session of the court was over he returned to New Bern, where his two youngest daughters and he would ride about the plantation and take long walks together.

In April of 1837 another grief was thrust upon the family, as Eliza, the wife of Alexander, mother of two young boys, Hugh and William, and a daughter, Susan, passed away at the age of twenty-nine. Two years later Alexander married again, his bride this time being Sarah Murphy, who completely won the old judge's heart.

From close friends and strangers alike came long letters, often with requests for money. Webster, at the zenith of his power and fame, wrote "of the things which would augment my happiness, one is, that I should hear from you oftener and another is that I might see you sometimes. . . . As it is, to hear of you, as I do, and as much as I do, is no small gratification to the feelings of an old and true friend."[21] Robert Walsh, a prominent literary figure and editor of the *National Gazette* asked him for a list of his publications and stations in life; Walsh was going to Europe and wished to publish while there sketches of the most "eminent men among the living writers of America." From South Carolina B. F. Perry wrote to ask aid in drawing up a new judiciary system for the state as the old system had been abolished during the Nullification movement, and he wished to adopt some system that would be permanent. Commenting on the system of North Carolina, he asked if it worked entirely and whether Gaston approved of it.[22] Even President Swain asked urgently for his help in settling a domestic crisis arising within the College.[23] By 1836 Gaston was completely out of debt, and was shipping cotton regularly to Donaldson.

The last political scenes in which he was to take even a remote interest was the Whig triumph in 1840. Gaston was disappointed at the nomination of General William Henry Harrison by the national Whig convention confessing that he did not feel the same interest in the election as he would have had Clay been nominated, although he felt the prospects of the Whig success was as great. He told Donaldson that Harrison "was a gentleman born and bred, with old fashioned notions of honor," but his opinion of Calhoun, for whose political rectitude he had lost all respect, was less cordial. Of him he said, "Sometimes I think he has a bee in his bonnet. I would not be surprised if there were symptoms of mental alienation which often attend an intellect of the highest order. His fancying himself as perpetually stationary when all the world is changing around him . . . is like that. Since I have known him, he has oscillated like a pendulum from one extreme to the other."[24] By April he had little doubt of a Whig victory, because of the accounts he had heard of the "awakening of the people in other states." Again he expressed preference for Clay as president, but admitted that the chances were much better with Harrison.[25] The national Whig convention had not adopted a platform, so wide latitude was left to the state conventions which met later. That of North Carolina met in Raleigh on October 5 amid scenes of wild excitement. Here, for the first time in public, was played Judge Gaston's *The Old North State*, which later became, and is now, the state song.[26] The following November the Whigs elected Harrison to the presidency, and made John Tyler vice-president. The preceding August in the state elections North Carolina had also elected a Whig governor by about an 8000 majority, and the party obtained a majority of six in the Senate and thirty-two in the House.

Although very desirous of a Whig victory Gaston had taken no active part in the campaign. In September he had been asked by a committee of Whigs from Alabama to attend a rally there, but to this invitation he replied:

There is a deeply rooted sentiment with the people of "the

> good old North State" that their judges ought to keep aloof from political contention. The unaffected respect that I feel for all those habitual opinions which give a character to the states and which cannot be uprooted without injury to its fundamental institutions . . . makes this inaction . . . of high public expediency. . . . There should be in a community a class of citizens qualified with their mild influence . . . to check excesses.[27]

With the Whigs in control of the state Gaston became the choice of the legislature for the United States Senate. Richard Hines told him that he had traveled much in the eastern and middle part of the state and found that it was the wish of Whigs both in and out of the legislature that he be one of the senators. "No doubt," said Hines, "the legislature will take pleasure in electing you to any vacancy agreeable to you . . . and by your election the old North State would be given much more weight and standing abroad."[28] John G. Bynum wrote him in the same vein, saying that he could best begin his political life by taking part in "such an elevation."[29] Thomas L. Clingman was another to urge Gaston to accept the post, telling the latter he found much doubt in the legislature about his willingness to accept, and that his devotion to the interest and honor of North Carolina was known to all, so there would be no opposition from any member to the appointment.[30] However, to all such importunities Gaston turned a deaf ear, declining, as he told Hines, because with his present condition he was perfectly satisfied; it suited his domestic habits and gave the repose and intellectual activity his "old age" desired.[31] To Bynum he gave a more studied reply:

> My duties now are as important to the public welfare as any. . . . To give a wholesome exposition of the laws, to settle the fluctuations and reconcile the seemingly conflicting analogies of judicial decisions; to administer justice in the last resort with a steady hand and an upright purpose, appears to me to be among the highest of civil functions. And so long as God spares

me health and understanding to perform these faithfully, how can I better serve my country?[32]

Gaston's refusal left the Whigs in some confusion, as they were at a loss for an acceptable candidate. Some felt that Swain's prospects and claim to the place would be strong, "if Judge Gaston did not run." Swain was assured by a friend that he would be supported by most of the western Whigs, by Bynum, Clingman, and Hoke. This same man felt that everyone realized the election of Badger would be unpopular in the state and dangerous to the Whigs.[33] Among the prospects were Mangum, Bryan, Governor Owen, Shepherd, Graham, and Williams. Paul Cameron claimed that Mangum was the first choice of all, and that "Judge Gaston has but to say that he would go into service and no one would stand in his way." He also told Ruffin that with Gaston and Mangum out of the way Graham would probably be elected.[34] The legislature did nothing until this question was solved, and Cameron's predictions proved correct, for W. P. Mangum and William A. Graham were sent to the Senate.

After these two senators arrived in Washington Graham wrote Gaston that the congressional delegation of North Carolina intended to call to President Harrison's attention that few of their citizens had ever held high federal offices and that one was due the state. Should the president then offer them either the secretary of state or the mission to England or France, they would then recommend Gaston. However, if the office of attorney general were offered, Badger would be named.[35] To this Gaston replied at once, asking that no such nomination be made, as he had a sincere desire to keep aloof from political life for the rest of his days.[36] Webster received the post of secretary of state, and Badger that of attorney general. Gaston had hoped that Webster would remain in the Senate. When Susan learned of his rejection of the senatorship she was at first disappointed, but later admitted that her father's decisions "were ever right." Gaston comforted her with the assurance of his own satisfaction, saying:

> To administer justice in the last resort, to expound and apply the laws for the advancement of right and the suppression of wrong is an ennobling and indeed a holy office, and the exercise of its functions while it raises my mind above the mists of earth-borne cares and passions, always seems to impart fresh vigor to my understanding, and a better temper to my whole soul.[37]

Two months after taking office Harrison died, and the Virginian, John Tyler, took his place for the full term. Tyler immediately vetoed a bank bill passed by the Whig Congress, and soon earned their active dislike by other vetoes until he was read out of the party. Gaston did not know the new president personally, but had always had a high opinion of his honesty of purpose. When the first veto occurred he advised Graham that if "honest men did not aid the president he would seek it elsewhere," and that the proceedings in Congress should be marked with decorum. He felt that all the party objects would be sacrificed unless allowances were made for an isolated case, and that the party could not but believe but that the president would have wished to act with it; he hoped that no further attempt would be made at that session to create a bank.[38]

That same year Father James Ryder, president of Georgetown University, asked Gaston to deliver the oration at the celebration of the landing of the fathers in Maryland.[39] This invitation was also refused by Gaston on the plea that the honor should be given a citizen of Maryland and that his voice was not what it had been. "I feel and acknowledge the claim which the college of Georgetown has upon me, its eldest pupil, to join in carrying into execution the celebration which to the honor of that institution it has been the first to propose," he replied. He told the president that he was proud, as a Catholic, of the heroism of the noble band, which adhering inflexibly to its sacred faith, had preferred exile, privation, danger, and death to a hyprocritical conformity, and that as an American citizen, he would never cease to be grateful for the glorious precedent which they were the first to establish, by which it was shown that an undoubting conviction of the truths of one's own religion was compatible with a regard for the rights of conscience in others. With that accustomed desire to remain free of public affairs he concluded, "As the close of life approaches – calmly and gently as I thank God it does come on – I feel a constantly increasing desire, and believe that there is an increasing fitness, that I may be allowed to spend the remainder of my days in the discharge of accustomed duties . . . remote from public glare, and exempt from the ambition of display."[40]

With such a feeling, Gaston would have become panic-stricken had the plan of a certain Georgian been carried through, or even had he only read the letter of T. Pollock Burgwin to J. M. Berrien and N. P. Tallmadge he would have been flustered. As the next campaign approached, it was expected by all that Henry Clay would become the candidate for president. Burgwin was concerned with the choice of a fit associate for Clay, and claimed that with two such names as Clay and Gaston there could be no defeat. He maintained that Gaston had every requisite necessary, "an ardent devotion for his country, with a patriotism not marred by a sectional line, prejudice or feeling; although sixty years of age never once had the breath of slander dimmed either in public or private life his purity of character." Burgwin told them that "as a statesman, orator, and jurist, he was pronounced by Chief Justice Marshall to have no superior in this country."[41] There is little doubt but that Clay, now reconciled with Gaston, would have welcomed this move. However, Gaston was now concerned with the supreme court, and affairs of his family. In September of 1842 Eliza asked his consent to marry George Graham, and two months later Gaston was writing from Baltimore to Mrs. Graham. She had been married by Archbishop Eccleston on November 14 in Washington, D. C.

Family matters were constantly demanding his attention. Alexander's debts were a source of worry, so he worked out a solution to them by giving his son in advance his share of the inheritance and by asking the creditors to give the former more time.[42] Feeling that his grandson, William's, education was being neglected, he offered to finance it by sending him to Emmitsburg, Raleigh, or to the New Bern Academy. He now had but one daughter, Kate, remaining with him, as the rest of the children were married.

In the summer following Eliza's marriage Gaston was involved in a serious accident, which made the use of crutches necessary for some time, and delayed his appearance at the summer term of the court. At a banquet held in Raleigh, in honor of the fiftieth anniversary of the Raleigh Guards, a toast, fated to be the last paid to him, was characteristic of North Carolina's regard. It ran: "In the councils of the country the eloquent and fearless defender of your rights – in the judiciary of the state the able and upright expounder of your laws."[43] The sands of life were rapidly running out, and a premonition of its nearness seemed apparent. In December he made his will, leaving to Alexander's children, Susan, William, and Hugh, one third of all his land in North Carolina and Tennessee and one third of that on the south side of the Trent River; two thirds of the land on the Trent to Susan Jane Donaldson and to his granddaughter, Hannah Manly, with the exception of the tract inherited from his father on Brice's Creek between the Hotston and Bullen branches, the tract purchased from Nathaniel Smith, two tracts in Tennessee purchased from A. D. Murphey, and a couple others which he left to Catherine Jane Gaston and Eliza Graham. To his sister he left $100 a year for the rest of her life; to his nephew, John Louis Taylor, he left $500; to the Roman Catholic Church in New Bern he left $100 a year for five years.[44]

A few days before the Christmas of 1843, in what seems to have been the last letter written Susan, he exclaimed, "I fear that the whole family will never meet again in this world, but it is my humble supplication to Almighty God that we will be found together, not one cast away or left behind, in our home beyond the grave. . . ."[45] At this time Gaston's six feet of height was but little marred by a scholarly stoop and he was a little stout, with a florid complexion, and his dark hair, above the calm blue eyes, was abundantly streaked with gray. He had reached a stage where shabby clothes meant nothing; his sister often gave them away in order to force him to buy new apparel.[46]

On the morning of January 23, 1844, Gaston, after a cold shower which he took every morning, came in early to the Taylor home for breakfast. It was a fine, sunny day, and he was in the best of spirits, entertaining the rest during the meal with a recitation, from memory, of a long poem called, "The Vanity of Human Wishes." After breakfast he spent another half hour with them, and then left for his office until the supreme court convened, where a divorce case was being heard. During this trial he took notes, but at two o'clock he became faint and sick at the stomach, so he retired from the bench and started for home but had to step into the governor's office where he rested upon a couch until a carriage was obtained. He was then taken to his office, his sister and Dr. Haywood were called, but it was three hours before he could be brought back from the unconscious state into which he had sunk. By this time his office was overflowing with friends, among whom were Chief Justice Ruffin, Governor Morehead, Attorney General Whitaker, Dr. Haywood, and Charles Manly. After recovering he was never more brilliant in conversation, poetry, Greek, and Latin flowing from his lips, amid other joking and laughter. When Ruffin proposed applying a hot mustard plaster he murmured in protest, " 'Tis astonishing, Ruffin, with how much fortitude you bear my troubles."

Finally, in a moment of silence, he began to tell of a party which he had attended at Washington some years before. It seemed that there Tobias Walker had avowed himself a freethinker in religion. "From that day I always looked on that man with distrust," said Gaston. "I do not say that a Free-Thinker may not be an honorable man; that he may not from high motive scorn to do a mean act; but I dare not trust him." With solemn earnestness the judge sat up, and looking at those about him, emphatically declared, "A belief in an over-ruling Divinity, who shapes our ends, whose eye is upon us, and who will reward us according to our deeds, is necessary. We must believe there is a God – All wise and All mighty." With the last word he sank back with a groan, and never uttered another word, for within five minutes death had claimed him. The merry voices in the office were now stilled, as eyes were dimmed with tears and flushed laughing countenances became white with pain. They found it hard to realize that this magnetic and beloved personality was no more, remembering that in the morning he had been on the bench. The only relative at hand was his sister, for the rest of the family was scattered. All North Carolina was profoundly shocked by the suddenness of his passing. At eight o'clock that night his death was announced to the astonished people of Raleigh, few of whom even knew of his illness. He was buried in Raleigh, but later his remains were taken to New Bern for burial in old Cedar Grove Cemetery, by the graves of his parents and daughter.

Announcing his death in the chambers of the supreme court, the attorney general declared that "his eulogy is on the lips of the whole country; the force of his example will perpetuate his praise." Among other remarks in this address Whitaker said that the evening before his death, Gaston had mentioned that death had no terrors to him, and that the years he had numbered were but so many steps in the completion of the journey assigned him by his Master. The members of the bar adopted a resolution to wear crepe for thirty days and to attend his funeral in a body. This resolution mentioned his "undeviating pursuit of right which only an ardent and animating religious faith can bestow and adequately sustain," and proclaimed that he had left behind a rare and happy memory, dear alike to his brethren, friends, and country. In reply the chief justice exclaimed, "His loss will be deeply felt and deplored by the whole country. In our opinion, his worth as a minister of justice and expounder of the laws is inestimable."[47]

His fellow citizens of New Bern met at the courthouse to pay their tribute to his memory. Judge John R. Donnell delivered an address during which he said, "His fame as a distinguished statesman and profound jurist belongs to his country – she will cherish it among her brightest jewels, and the pen of the historian will hand it down to the latest posterity. . . . We believe that he never did an intentional wrong. . . . We will cherish his memory and teach our children to emulate his example, and to impress upon their children's children, to the latest generation . . . that our town was the birth place and home of GASTON."[48] The day his body arrived all business was suspended in the town, bells tolled, and flags were at half-mast. Here everyone wore crepe for thirty days, and the Negroes of the town, in a meeting of their own, resolved upon the same procedure, besides voting to place a picture of the judge in every one of their homes.

Every newspaper in the state expressed a deep grief at their loss, and the highest admiration for his character and career. The Raleigh *Register* stated that "for forty years he has been the ornament of his profession, the idol of his friends, and the admiration of all who knew him." After describing his qualities the editor, in a high flight of literary language, concluded, "He has gone down from among us like the sun at sea, leaving the brightness of his noontide splendor to be equalled only by the milder radiance which shall linger and play like a halo of beauty around his memory."[49] Another Raleigh paper proclaimed him as the favorite son of North Carolina, who would be assigned in the ranks of the most illustrious men of the age, to whose labors the state was indebted for the proudest monuments of wisdom in its legislation. "He imparted to the standard of morality and religion, of public virtue, a tone and sentiment, elevated, just and pure," said the editor.[50] All papers praised his pure and spotless integrity. The *Tarboro Press,* stopping the presses to announce his death, remarked, "His political career, and his eminent judicial services, are portions of the history of the state; his fame, the common property of the country, will be cherished as a jewel of rare lustre and inestimable value."[51]

Papers in other parts of the country had much the same things to say, and almost every editor commented about his manner of death. The *National Intelligencer* speaking of the "painful intelligence brought by the Southern mails," stated that he was widely known in other states as an eminent statesman and one of the purest and most upright of men, as well as a profound and accomplished jurist.[52] The *National Gazette* of the same city spoke of him in like manner. The New York *Freeman's Journal,* noticing that death had been busy in high places, declared that "few men in our country had secured to a greater extent the esteem of all classes of his fellow-citizens." The New York *American* stated that like Emmett, he had fallen in the harness, so now "a shining light of the American Bar is extinguished."[53] The *Catholic Miscellany* announced that the Carroll Institute was making arrangements for an eulogium to be delivered by an eminent member of the Philadelphia Bar.[54]

Among private individuals there were like expressions. From Washington, Representative Kenneth Rayner reported that the news had oppressed all there greatly. "The Sensation, which the news of his death produced here," wrote Rayner, "went to show how high was his reputation for talents and for virtue even in the most distant parts of the country. The exclamation made by almost everyone was – his death is a public loss, he was one of the great men of the nation, etc. – so the loss of such a man, severely felt at any time, in this period when private virtue is so rare among the great, is a public calamity."[55] Paul Cameron thought it was a grievous dispensation to all of North Carolina. Ruffin's son stated that "like him I would live, like him I would die," when he reported to his father that both societies of the university had resolved to wear crepe for a month, and that classes had been suspended there by Governor Swain on reception of the news. Plans were made for addresses concerning him at various places; Governor Swain was asked to write a sketch of his life for a new state historical magazine, which on his refusal was performed by Judge Battle. Poems were written about him for publication here and there. Eleanor M. Jones wrote one of several stanzas, one of which was:

> Favored son of Carolina
> Carolina loves thy name
> And her mothers tell their children
> In thy footsteps liveth fame.

Cardinal Gibbons, in a sermon on the mission of parents, alluded to him saying, "There is no man whose name is more tenderly enshrined in the hearts of the people of North Carolina . . . his name is a household word in every town and hamlet."[56] When Henry Clay arrived in Raleigh the following summer he paid a moving tribute to Gaston, and remarked that he had once differed with Gaston, but found out afterward that he was right.[57] Several years before Nicholas Biddle had told Gaston, "I am so accustomed, like the rest of your countrymen, to consider what you say as decisive that . . . "

It was felt by all that the "complexion of the next legislature would be a new subject of interest" because of the appointment of a new justice. Some thought that Badger should be the man, but Frederick Nash was finally selected. Later, Gaston's son-in-law, Manly, also sat on the supreme court bench.

The quotation of Biddle's given above is expressive of the high regard for Gaston felt by the entire country. It is difficult to estimate his place in our history, but it is certainly no task to form an opinion of his place in the history of the state of North Carolina. His many public services, culminating in the ten years on the bench of her supreme court, places him in the first rank of her statesmen. His decisions in the court concerning the status of slaves earn for him the right to be considered a great humanitarian; many of his other decisions attest his right to be known as a great jurist; while his great speech and fight in regard to the disqualifying clause of the state constitution place him among the foremost of those great men to whom we owe our religious liberty. His many speeches and addresses, with his decisions delivered in the supreme court, will always put him among our literary lights, for these examples of pure and perfect English, of right thought and sound reasoning, deserve to be studied by every student of the language.

Gaston can be proclaimed to be one of the foremost Catholics of his time, if not the greatest Catholic of the South, for he lived up to his faith as few laymen have, and gave an example admired by those most prejudiced. Even Thomas Grimke of South Carolina, although thought to be spotless by his contemporaries, could not be compared in his private life with the pure virtue and fine sense of propriety of Gaston's. As for his influence in the history of the country, perhaps the archivist of the United States, Dr. Robert D. W. Connor, has best summed it up when he said, "Probably no other American who had so brief a public career ever enjoyed among his contemporaries such an extraordinary wide and favorable reputation for statesmanship and legal learning, although two-thirds of adult life was spent in the practice of a country lawyer."[58] His daughter thought that his name was a great inheritance, and Edward Everett expressed the same feeling, on resting his hand upon the marble tombstone, which was simply inscribed WILLIAM GASTON. It was enough.

## NOTES FOR CHAPTER ELEVEN

1. Quoted in Charles Warren, *The Supreme Court in United States History*, II, 8 *n* (Rev. ed.).
2. New Bern *Spectator*, July 21, 1835.
3. Susan to Gaston, Aug. 17, 1835, Gaston *MSS.*
4. Gaston to Susan, Feb. 20, 1830, Gaston *MSS.*
5. Susan to Gaston, April 29, 1830, Gaston *MSS.*

6. Raleigh *Register*, Sept. 9, 1834.

7. Swain to Gaston, Sept. 19, 1834, Gaston *MSS.*

8. The *National Gazette*, Oct. 6, 1835.

9. *An Address Delivered Before the American Whig and Clisophic Societies of the College of New Jersey.*

10. October 6, 1835.

11. October 6, 1835.

12. Dr. Beasley to Gaston, Oct. 5, 1835, Gaston *MSS.*

13. Gaston to Beasley, Oct. 12, 1835, Gaston *MSS.*

14. R. B. Creecy, "A Night Spent With William Gaston," *University of North Carolina Magazine, VIII,* No. 3, Oct., 1858.

15. Coon, *Public Education in North Carolina,* p. 728.

16. *MSS.*, July 17, 1839, Gaston *MSS.*

17. George Bancroft to Gaston, Oct. 9, 1837, Gaston *MSS.*

18. Gaston to Eliza, Jan. 24, 1836, Gaston *MSS.*

19. Hugh Waddell and Will A. Graham to Gaston, Nov. 2, 1836, Gaston *MSS.*

20. J. W. Bryan to Gaston, Dec. 3, 1836, Gaston *MSS.*

21. Webster to Gaston, April 22, 1836, Gaston *MSS.*

22. A. F. Perry to Gaston, July 19, 1836, Gaston *MSS.*

23. Gaston to Swain, June 28, 1839, Swain *MSS.*, N.C.H.C.

24. Gaston to Donaldson, Jan. 30, 1840, Gaston *MSS.*

25. Gaston to Donaldson, April 13, 1840, Gaston *MSS.*

26. There are several versions of the reason and place of its writing, as well as of the tune to which it was written. It seems to have been written to a foreign tune; some say that he was attracted by the music of Swiss bell ringers passing through the town. The Raleigh *Register* of October 13, 1840, says, "Some foreign minstrels had a concert in the city and one of their airs was so beautiful as to attract universal attention and produced a desire among the ladies for words to it. In a playful moment Judge Gaston sought to gratify them." It was supposed to have been first published at this convention, but Eliza told her father on July 2, 1840, that they had heard it played in New Bern the night before, and that "twenty voices joined in the chorus. It rang through our drawing-room and might have been heard at a great distance." In 1842 a letter to Gaston (seemingly from Tennessee) from an admirer stated that it had "become a great rallying song in the West for North Carolina's sons." However, Gaston must not be blamed too much for it, because many other leading literary figures of the time also, and often, indulged in attempts to write fine poetry. All through life Gaston was asked to write epitaphs for tombstones and generally complied with such requests. Many a stone in North Carolina bears an inscription from his pen.

27. Gaston to Whigs of Alabama, Sept. 29, 1840, Gaston *MSS.*
28. Richard Hines to Gaston, Sept. 26, 1840, Gaston *MSS.*
29. John G. Bynum to Gaston, Oct. 21, 1840, Gaston *MSS.*
30. T. L. Clingman, Nov. 13, 1840, Gaston *MSS.*
31. Gaston to Hines, Sept. 30, 1840, Gaston *MSS.*
32. Gaston to Bynum, Oct. 31, 1840, Gaston *MSS.*
33. N. W. Woodfin to Swain, Nov. 8, 1840, Swain *MSS.*, N.C.H.C.
34. Paul C. Cameron to Ruffin, Nov. 18, 1840, *Ruffin Papers,* II, 188.
35. Will A. Graham to Gaston, Dec. 16, 1840, Gaston *MSS.*
36. Gaston to Graham, Dec. 27, 1840, Gaston *MSS.*
37. Gaston to Susan, Dec. 22, 1843, Gaston *MSS.*
38. Gaston to Graham, Aug. 19, 1841, Graham *MSS.*, N.C.H.C.
39. Rev. James Ryder to Gaston, Nov. 16, 1841, Gaston *MSS.*
40. Gaston to Ryder, Nov. 24, 1841, Georgetown University Archives.
41. March 24, 1842. Letter in possession of Mrs. Rosa Berrien Burroughs. Reprinted in Savannah *Morning News,* July 22, 1934. Library of Congress.
42. Gaston to Michael Hoke, Feb. 28, 1843. Chief Justice Hoke *MSS.*, U.N.C.
43. Raleigh *Register,* Aug. 22, 1843.
44. Craven County Will Book, D, p. 93.
45. Gaston to Susan, Dec. 22, 1843.
46. Reminiscences of Miss L. N. Taylor, who was just past twenty at Gaston's death. Gaston *MSS.*
47. 26 N. C. *Reports,* 1 ff.
48. *Circular,* New Bern, Jan. 29, 1844.
49. Raleigh *Register,* Jan. 26, 1844.
50. *Democratic Signal,* Jan. 26, 1844.
51. *Tarboro Press,* Jan. 27, 1844.
52. *National Intelligencer,* Jan. 29, 1844.
53. New York *Freeman's Journal,* Feb. 3, 1844.
54. *U. S. Catholic Miscellany,* Feb. 24, 1844. Notice of his death is in the Feb. 14 issue.
55. Kenneth Rayner to Ruffin, Jan. 29, 1844. *Ruffin Papers,* II, 220.
56. Cardinal James Gibbons, Discourses and Sermons on Various Subjects, p. 61, Georgetown University Archives.
57. Raleigh *Register,* June 25, 1844, contains this.
58. R. D. W. Connor, "William Gaston: A Southern Federalist of the Old School and His Yankee Friends," *Proceedings of the American Antiquarian Society,* XLIII, 1933.

# Bibliography


## I. Manuscript Sources

*Private Papers*

Baltimore Cathedral Archives. Miscellaneous Collections.
Berrien, John M. Library of Congress.
Bryan, John H. North Carolina Historical Commission. Raleigh.
Biddle, William. Duke University. Durham.
Bruté, Bishop Simon. University of Notre Dame. Notre Dame, Indiana.
Cameron, Duncan. University of North Carolina. Chapel Hill.
Carroll, Archbishop John. Baltimore Cathedral Archives.
Clay, Henry. Library of Congress.
Galloway, Maxcy, Markoe Collection. Library of Congress.
Gaston, William. University of North Carolina.
——— North Carolina Historical Commission.
——— Letter Book, May 1818–May 1836. University of North Carolina.
——— Miscellaneous *MSS*. New York City Public Library.
Georgetown University Archives. Miscellaneous *MSS*. Washington, D. C.
Graham, William A. North Carolina Historical Commission.
Hoke, Chief Justice Michael. University of North Carolina.
Hopkinson, Joseph. Pennsylvania State Historical Society. Philadelphia.
Kent, James. Library of Congress.
King, Rufus. New York Historical Society.
Mangum, Willie P. Duke University; North Carolina Historical Commission.
Manly, Matthias. University of North Carolina.
Nicholson, Joseph H. Library of Congress.
Pettigrew, E. University of North Carolina.
Raleigh Diocesan Archives. Bishop's Home. Raleigh.
Stanly, Hawks Papers. New York Historical Society.
Swain, David L. North Carolina Historical Commission.
Swift, Joseph T. University of North Carolina.
Wheeler, John H. Library of Congress.

## II. Printed Sources: Documents and Writings of Contemporaries

*a) Documents*

Annals of Congress. Debates and Proceedings. Thirteenth Congress, First Session, May 24, 1813, to Fourteenth Congress, Second Session.
Gaston, William. Circular to the Freemen of the Counties of Wayne,

Greene, Lenoir, Jones, Craven and Carteret Counties. New Bern, September 19, 1808.
——— Circular to the Freemen of Wayne....New Bern, 1810.
——— Circular to the Freemen of Wayne....of the 4th Congressional District. New Bern, March 15, 1813.
——— Circular to the Freemen of Wayne....Washington, April 19, 1814.
——— Circular to the Freemen of Wayne....Washington, March 1, 1815.
——— Circular to the Freemen of Wayne....New Bern, June 12, 1815.
——— Speech of the Honorable William Gaston of North Carolina on the bill to authorize a loan of twenty-five millions of dollars. Delivered in the House of Representatives of the United States. February, 1814. Washington, Printed at the Office of the Sen. (Also: Printed by R. Allison, Georgetown.)
——— Speech....on the militia....in the United States Congress. Georgetown, 1816.
——— Speech....on the Embargo.... Georgetown, 1816.
——— Speech....in support of the proposition of Mr. Stanford's to expunge from the rules of the House of Representatives the Previous Question. Georgetown, 1816.
——— Address on the Administration Convention.... Raleigh.... December 20, 1827. Raleigh, 1827.
——— Address Delivered before the American Whig and Cliosophic Societies of the College of New Jersey, September 29, 1835. 2 ed. Princeton, 1835.
——— Speech of the Honorable Judge Gaston Delivered in the recent State Convention of North Carolina. Baltimore, 1835.
North Carolina. Craven County. Deed Books. II, XII, XIII, XV, XIX, XX, XXI, XXXVI, XXXVII, XXXVIII, XXXIX.
——— Craven County. Will Book D.
——— Colonial Records 1662–1776, 11 volumes and State Records, 15 volumes. Raleigh, 1886–——.
——— House of Commons. Debate on the Bill Directing a Prosecution against the Several Banks of the State.... From December 29, 1828 to January 6, 1829. Raleigh, 1829.
——— House of Commons. Journal. 1807, 1808, 1828, 1830.
——— Senate. Journal. 1800, 1812, 1818, 1819.
——— Journal of Internal Improvement Convention.... At Raleigh, July 4, 1833, With Address of Committee.... Raleigh, 1833.
——— Journal of the Convention Called....to Amend the Constitution....4th June, 1835. Raleigh, 1835.
——— Proceedings and Debates of the Convention of North Carolina Called to Amend the Constitution of the State....June 4, 1835. Raleigh, 1836.
——— Law Reports.
Haywood, John. Reports in the Superior Courts....and Federal Courts. 1799–1806.

Martin, F. X. Martin's Reports of the Superior Court 1799–1802. New Bern, 1802.

Supreme Court Reports. Cases Argued and Determined in the Supreme Court of North Carolina 1833–1844. Volumes I–XXVI. Raleigh, 1836–1844.

Pasquotank Superior Court, March, 1807. Den on demise of William B. Shepherd and Wife *vs.* J. Relfe. Argument by Wm. Gaston.

Carteret Superior Court, Sept., 1811. Trial of Edward Tinker, Mariner, for Murder of Youth called Edward.... New Bern, 1811.

——— New Bern. Circular. Jan. 29, 1844. (On the death of William Gaston.)

——— New Bern. Christ's Church. Register of Baptisms, Burials, Marriages.

——— New Bern. St. Paul's Roman Catholic Church. Records.

A Republican. Remarks on Mr. Gaston's Speech to the Freemen of Wayne.... Oct. 21, 1808. New Bern, 1808.

*b) Writings of Contemporaries*

Adams, John Quincy. Memoirs. Edited by C. F. Adams. 12 volumes. Philadelphia, 1874–1877.

Bigelow, Abijah. "Letters of .... to his wife, 1810–1815." *Proceedings of the American Antiquarian Society,* n.s., XL (Worcester, Mass., 1930), 305–406.

England, John. *Works of Rt. Rev. John England.* Edited by S. G. Messmer. 7 volumes. Cleveland, 1908.

——— "Correspondence of John England with Hon. William Gaston, 1821–1840." *American Catholic Historical Society Records.* Volumes XVIII, XIX. (Philadelphia, 1907–1908).

Jackson, Andrew. *Correspondence of Andrew Jackson.* 6 volumes. Washington, 1928.

Jones, Hamilton C. "Letter from .... the Elder." *North Carolina University Magazine,* Volume XXIII, April, 1893.

Murphey, Archibald D. *The Papers of Archibald D. Murphey.* Edited by W. H. Hoyt. 2 volumes. Raleigh, 1914.

Ruffin, Thomas. *Papers of Thomas Ruffin.* Edited by James G. de Roulhac Hamilton. 4 volumes. Raleigh, 1918.

Webster, Daniel. *Letters* .... Edited by Claude H. Van Tyne. New York, 1902.

——— *Writings and Speeches* .... National Edition. 18 volumes. Boston, 1903.

Yancey, Bartlett. "Letters to ...." Edited by J. G. de R. Hamilton & H. G. Wagstaff. *James Sprunt Historical Publications.* Volume X, no. 2 (Chapel Hill, 1911).

III. General: Books and Magazines

Adams, Henry. *History of the United States During the Administration*

*of Thomas Jefferson and James Madison.* 2 ed. 4 volumes. New York, 1930.
Bassett, John S. "The Case of State *vs.* Will." *Historical Papers of Trinity College Historical Society.* Volume II, 1898.
Battle, George. "North Carolina *vs.* Negro Will, a slave of James S. Battle: A Cause Celebre of Ante-Bellum Times." *Virginia Law Review.* Volume VI, 1919–1920 (University, Virginia, 1920).
Battle, Kemp. "Life and Character of William Gaston." *North Carolina University Magazine.* Volume I, April, 1844.
——— *An Address on the History of the Supreme Court of North Carolina.* Raleigh, 1889.
Battle, William A. "Judge Gaston as a Literary Man." *North Carolina University Magazine.* Volume X, December, 1860.
Beveridge, Albert J. *Life of John Marshall.* 4 volumes. Boston, 1919.
Boyd, William K. "Currency and Banking in North Carolina, 1790–1836." *Historical Papers of Trinity College Historical Society.* Volume X, 1910.
——— "Federal Politics in North Carolina, 1824–1836." *South Atlantic Quarterly.* Volume XVIII, January–April, 1919.
Connor, Henry G. "The Convention of 1835." *North Carolina Booklet.* Volume VIII, no. 2, October, 1908.
——— "The Granville Estate and North Carolina." *University of Pennsylvania Law Review.* Volume LXII, no. 9, 1914.
Connor, Robert D. W. "William Gaston: A Southern Federalist of the Old South and His Yankee Friends." *Proceedings of the American Antiquarian Society.* Volume XLIII, 1933 (Worcester, 1934).
Coon, Charles. Ed. *Public Education in North Carolina: A Documentary History, 1790–1840.* 2 volumes. Raleigh, 1908.
Creecy, R. B. "A Night Spent with William Gaston." *North Carolina University Magazine.* Volume VIII, no. 3, October, 1858.
——— *Grandfather's Tales of North Carolina History.* Raleigh, 1901.
Ellet, Elizabeth. *The Women of the American Revolution.* 2 volumes. Philadelphia, 1900.
Fisher, Josephine. "Francis James Jackson and Newspaper Propaganda in the United States, 1809–1810." *Maryland Historical Review.* Volume XXX, June, 1935.
Fuess, Claude M. *Daniel Webster.* 2 volumes. Boston, 1930.
Garland, Hugh A. *Life of John Randolph of Roanoke.* 2 volumes in 1. New York, 1853.
Gilpatrick, Delbert H. *Jeffersonian Democracy in North Carolina, 1789–1816.* New York, 1931.
Guilday, Peter. *Life and Times of John England.* 2 volumes. New York, 1927.
Hamilton, J. G. de R. "Party Politics in North Carolina, 1835–1860." *James Sprunt Historical Publications.* Volume XV, no. 1, 2, 1916.
Hannon, W. B. "William Gaston." *Journal of the American Irish Historical Society.* Volume X, 1911. New York, 1911.

Holt, Bryce R. "The Supreme Court of North Carolina and Slavery." *Historical Papers of Trinity College Historical Society.* Volume XVII, 1927.

Ingersoll, Charles J. *Historical Sketch of the Second War Between the United States and Great Britain.* Philadelphia, 1845.

Johnson, Guion G. *Ante-Bellum North Carolina: A Social History.* Chapel Hill, 1937.

M'Laughlin, J. F. "William Gaston: The First Student of Georgetown College." *American Catholic Historical Society Records.* Volume VI, 1895 (Philadelphia, 1895).

MacLean, John. *History of the College of New Jersey.* Philadelphia, 1877.

McSweeney, Edward F. *The Gastons.* Boston, 1926.

Manly, Matthias E. "Memoir of Honorable William Gaston." *North Carolina University Magazine.* Volume X, no. 4, November, 1860.

Martin, Francois X. *History of North Carolina.* 2 volumes. New Orleans, 1829.

Moore, John W. *History of North Carolina.* 2 volumes. Raleigh, 1880.

*The National Portrait Gallery of Distinguished Americans.* 3 volumes. Philadelphia, 1835.

Newsome, Albert R. "The Presidential Election of 1824 in North Carolina." *James Sprunt Historical Studies.* Volume XXIII, no. 1 (Chapel Hill, 1939).

Norton, Clarence C. "The Democratic Party in Ante-Bellum North Carolina, 1835–1861." *James Sprunt Historical Studies.* Volume XXI, nos. 1–2 (Chapel Hill, 1930).

Pratt, Julius W. *Expansionists of 1812.* New York, 1925.

Purcell, Richard J. "Judge William Gaston: Georgetown University's First Student," *Georgetown Law Journal,* May, 1939, pp. 839–883.

Sears, Louis M. *Jefferson and the Embargo.* Durham, 1927.

Seaton, Josephine. *William Winston Seaton . . .* Boston, 1871.

Shea, John G. *History of Georgetown University.* Washington, 1891.

Swain, David L. *Early Times in Raleigh.* Compiled by R. S. Tucker. Raleigh, 1867.

Swisher, Carl B. *Roger B. Taney.* New York, 1935.

Ticknor, George. *Life, Letters, and Journal of . . .* Edited by George Hillard and Anna T. Eliot. 2 volumes. Boston, 1876.

Wagstaff, Henry McGilbert. "Federalism in North Carolina." *The James Sprunt Historical Publications.* Volume IX, no. 2. Chapel Hill, 1910.

——— "State Rights and Political Parties in North Carolina." *Johns Hopkins University Studies.* Series XXIV, nos. 1–8. Baltimore, 1906.

Warren, Charles. *The Supreme Court in the United States History.* 2 volumes. Rev. ed. Boston, 1937.

Weaver, Charles C. "Internal Improvements in North Carolina." *Johns Hopkins University Studies in Historical and Political Science.* Volume XXI, nos. 3–4. Baltimore, 1903.

Wheeler, John H. *Historical Sketches of North Carolina, 1584–1851.* 2 volumes. Philadelphia, 1851.

IV. Newspapers (Unless stated otherwise of North Carolina)

*Carolina Sentinel*
*Carolina Watchman*
*Catawba Journal*
*Democratic Signal*
*New Bern Gazette*
New Bern *Spectator*
*North Carolina Free Press*
*North Carolina Journal*
*North Carolina Mercury and Salisbury Advertiser*
*North Carolina Tarboro Press*
*Raleigh Minerva*
*Raleigh News and Observer*
Raleigh *Register*
*Raleigh Star*
*Western Carolinian*
*Literary and Catholic Sentinel* (Boston)
*National Gazette* (Washington)
*National Intelligencer* (Washington)
*New York Freeman's Journal*
*The Metropolitan* (Baltimore)
*The United States Catholic Miscellany* (Charleston, S. C.)

# Index